VIBRATIONS AND FORMS

FINDINGS
FROM
PSYCHEDELIC ADVENTURES

SECOND EDITION

RALPH H. ABRAHAM

Vibrations and Forms: Findings from Psychedelic Adventures.
Copyright 2021 by Ralph H. Abraham. All rights reserved.

No part of this book may be used or reproduced in any manner without written permission from the publisher except in critical articles and reviews.

For information contact:
Epigraph Publishing Service
22 East Market Street, Suite 304
Rhinebeck, New York 12572
www.epigraphPS.com

Book Design by Deb Shayne

ISBN: 978-1-951937-96-6
Library of Congress Control Number: 2021902165

Bulk purchase discounts for educational or promotional purposes are available. Contact the publisher for more information.

Dedicated to my Indian teachers:

    S. D. Batish
    Neem Karoli Baba
    Debabrata SenSharma

Front cover image: This is the original color image from a video of a computer simulation of vibration in a morphic field. The grayscale version occurs in chapters 16, 20, and 22.

Back cover image: This is the original color image from a video of an analog (Macroscope) simulation of vibration in a morphic field. The grayscale version occurs in chapter 6.

CONTENTS

Prologue	7
Acknowledgments	13

PART 0. BACKGROUND

1. Mathematics and the Psychedelic Revolution	19
2. Entheogens in the Himalayan Foothills	39
3. Chaos Math, Brain Science, and Mind Philosophy	53

PART 1: PHYSICAL MODELS, 1972-1982

4. Psychotronic Vibrations	61
5. Vibrations and the Realization of Form	69
6. The Function of Mathematics in the Evolution of the Noosphere	93

PART 2: SPIRITUAL MODELS, 1982-2005

7. Dynamic Models for Thought	117
8. Vibrations in Math, Music, and Mysticism	145
9. Mechanics of Resonance	153
10. Visual Music Instruments and Chaos	173
11. Cathedral Dreams, Concert	187
12. Cathedral Dreams, Review	197
13. MIMI and the Illuminati	201
14. The Electronic Rose Window	217
15. Vibrations, Part 1: Communication	225
16. Vibrations, Part 2: Simulations Results	235
17. Vibrational Resonance	243
18. A Two-Worlds Model for Consciousness	259
19. Vibrations and Forms	269

6   Vibrations and Forms

PART 3. ATOMIC MODELS, 2005-2011
20. A Digital Solution to the Mind/Body Problem   395
21. Consciousness and the New Math   317
22. The Emergence of Spacetime from the Akasha   327

PART 4. APPLICATIONS, 2011-2018
23. Shamanism and Noh   357
24. Mathematical Perception   371
25. Hip Santa Cruz and the Chaos Revolution   387
26. Theosophy and the Arts   399
27. Vibrations and Spiritual Communication   411

   Epilogue   441
   References, Ralph Abraham   445
   References, Others   451
   Index   469

Prologue

This book is a collection of writings, from 1973 to 2018, on a vibrational theory of mind. Here, mind includes higher mind, or cosmic consciousness. The word vibrations is a material metaphor applied to an immaterial realm. This way of thinking is sometimes called emanationism. The material metaphor is derived from cymatics, a branch of acoustic physics dealing with the emergence of form from sonic vibrations forced upon a fluid.

Background

My mathematical career began in 1958 at the University of Michigan. My interests progressed through related areas of pure math, as I wandered from Ann Arbor to Berkeley, Columbia, and Princeton, where in 1967 I had an epiphany during my first LSD experience.

This epiphany, typical of the LSD experience, awoke me to the existence of realities beyond ordinary perception. This created my sympathy with the emerging Hip Subculture, and attracted me to Santa Cruz, where the Hip revolution was taking off. So LSD triggered my move from Princeton University to UC Santa Cruz in 1968, where I settled down.

This epiphany not only moved me physically from the East Coast to the West Coast of America, but also swerved my career from pure math to applied and computational math. Besides my main line of research on Chaos Theory, I developed a sideline of vibration theory and models of consciousness. This thread accounts for about 20 percent of all my writings since 1967. This book is a collection of my

8 Vibrations and Forms

writings on this sidetrack, from 1973 to the present.

Occurring in the 1960s, my epiphany was empowered by psychedelics and the emerging hip culture. Here is a condensed chronology of my five-year psychedelic period, from the first trip in November, 1967, through November, 1972.

1967-68, LSD, discovery of higher mind
1968-69, DMT, visual vibrations as signs, ideas
1972, February, visited Hans Jenny, cymatics
1972, June - August, Nainital, with Neem Karoli
1972, September - November, Nainital, with Ray
1972, December, Kathmandu with Ray
1973, January, returned to Santa Cruz
1973, Wrote psychotronic vibrations [Ms#14][1]

Psychedelic Inspiration

My fascination with vibrations was occasioned by the actual experience of higher mind, that is, cosmic conscience, under the effect of psychedelics — especially LSD 1967-68, and DMT, 1968-70.

My experience, impossible to describe in words, was no doubt conditioned by my mathematical training, in which the perception of higher dimensional geometries has been developed. Psychedelic perception revealed a vibrating visualization, somewhat like an abstract animation or light show.

This experience was then intellectualized through my experiences of ancient philosophy in India in 1972. My sidetrack of writings on this began in 1973, and is ongoing. Little by little, I am trying to evolve my understanding of the cosmic mind, as revealed in hundreds of trips in my five-year psychedelic odyssey.

My intellectual journey through this landscape is evolutionary. I follow the long tradition of mystical literature, and now write amid the growing modern field of psychedelic information theory.[2]

This journey is not continuous. It has four major periods:
1. Psychedelic period: 1967-1973
2. Physicalist period: 1974-1982
3. Spiritualist period: 1982-2005
4. Atomic period: 2005-2020

This progression will be clarified in the following chapters.

Each phase begins with a bifurcation, or crucial trigger:
1. LSD, November, 1967
2. Meeting Terence McKenna, August 1972[3]
3. Meeting Rupert Sheldrake, 1982[4]
4. Meeting Sisir Roy, 2005

My emphasis upon triggers is conditioned by my work in chaos theory, in which major changes of state, called bifurcations, are initiated by very small external forces.

On Methods

My analytical method is different from most, in two ways.

(1) I freely use mathematical concepts, especially those of chaos theory. Nevertheless, I hope to be understandable to anyone with a little patience.

(2) The literature on this topic falls into two categories: physicalist and spiritualist.

The physicalist view of reality denies the existence of spirit. soul, higher mind, and so on. The spiritualist view, on the other hand, not only acknowledges the existence of spirit, but also awards it a superior importance in things. Since 1982, I belong to this latter group.

Plan of this Book

Gregory Bateson's seminal book, *Steps to an Ecology of Mind*, appeared in 1971. In the Introduction, titled, *The Science of Mind and Order*, he wrote:

> The title of this book of collected essays and lectures is intended precisely to define the contents. The essays, spread over thirty-five years, combine to propose a new way of thinking about *ideas* and about those aggregates of ideas which I call "minds." This way of thinking I call the "ecology of mind," or the ecology of ideas. It is a science which does not yet exist as an organized body of theory or knowledge.

In this spirit, I have collected here all of my writings on akashic vibrations. Part I brings forward the three articles that chronicle my odyssey from 1967 to 1973. The remainder of the book presents all my papers on vibration in chronological order. These are divided into three Parts: The mechanistic or physical period, 1972-1982, the spiritual period, 1982-2005, and the atomic period, 2005-2020, in which the akasha is discretized.

Notes

1   The Ms numbers refer to my personal bibliography at the end of the book.
2   See (Kent, 2010) for an introduction to this field.
3   See (McKenna, 1993) for the definitive account of his adventures just prior to our meeting.
4   See (Sheldrake, 2009) for a recent account of his theory of the morphic field.

12 Vibrations and Forms

Acknowledgments

This thread is not smoothly continuous. There have been four major periods:
1. Psychedelic period: 1967-1973
2. Physical period: 1974-1982
3. Spiritual period: 1982-2005
4. Atomic period: 2005-2020

So many friends have helped me through these. Here I express my gratitude to some of these helpers. (An * denotes passed away.)

1. Psychedelic period: 1967-1972

Re everything:
    Paul Lee, Ray Gwyn Smith, Fred Abraham
    Harry Burnham*
Re math:
    Steve Smale, Chris Zeeman*, René Thom*
    Tim Poston*, Gottfried Mayer-Kress*
Re Eagle math project, Summer, 1968:
    Ellis Cooper, Ernie Fickas
Re my first LSD trip, November 1967:
    Tim Leary*, Richard Albert*, Ralph Metzner*
    Karl Morgenstern, Bob Solomon*, Jose Arguelles*
In my first years at UCSC, 1968-1971:
    Paul Lee, Harry Noller, Emelia Hazelip*
In Amsterdam, September 1972:
    Simon Vinkenoog*, Bill Levy*, Jack Moore*
    Thatcher Clarke, Paul Kramerson, Kit Galloway
Re cymatics, January 1972:
    Hans Jenny*

Re India, June, 1972:
    Ram Dass*, Neem Karoli Baba*

2. Physicalist period: 1972-1982

Re consciousness, August 1972:
    Douglas Hansen, Terence McKenna*
    Ray Gwyn Smith
In Geneva 1972-73:
    Stan*, Louise*, and Dutch White*
Re complex systems, 1973:
    Erich Jantsch*
Building the macroscope, 1974:
    Lauren Brennen, Steve Furnald, Paul Kramerson
    video people and electronics and machine room
From 1980 on:
    Alan Garfinkel, Nina Graboi*, Timothy Poston*
    Frederick Abraham, Walter Freeman*
    William Hoffman, Dan Sunday

3. Spiritual period: 1982-2005

Re morphic fields, 1982:
    Rupert Sheldrake
Re the Trialogues, 1985:
    Nancy Kaye Lunney, Esalen Institute
    Andra Akers*
Re the Cathedral concert, 1992:
    William Irwin Thompson*, James Lovelock
    Robert Schwartz
Re consciousness, March, 2000:
    Prasun Kumar Roy, Professor,
        Indian Institute of Technology,

Benares Hindu University (IIT/BHU)
Einstein Institute, Visva-Bharati University,
Shantiniketan, INDIA

4. Atomic period: 2005-2018

Re consciousness, 2005:
    Sisir Roy, Professor,
        Indian Statistical Institute (ISI), Kolkata
    Swami Prabhananda, Secretary,
        Ramakrishna Mission Institute of Cuture (RMIC)
    Debabrata SenSharma*, Professor, RMIC
Re the akashic field, 2007:
    Ervin Laszlo, General Evolution Research Group (GERG)

Finally, I am grateful to Dr. Paul A. Lee for suggestions and corrections on the manuscript, and especially to Debby Shayne for technical support and thorough proofreading of the entire text.

16 Vibrations and Forms

PART 0
BACKGROUND

18 Vibrations and Forms

Chapter 1
Mathematics and the Psychedelic Revolution

Abstract

Recollections of the impact of the psychedelic revolution on the history of mathematics and my personal story.

Publication

Ms #124, written 2008. Published in *MAPS Bulletin*, 18:1, Spring 2008: Special Edition: Technology and Psychedelics; pp. 8-10.

Contents

Introduction
Math in the 1960s
Vibrations and forms
Conclusion
Notes

Mathematics and the Psychedelic Revolution

Introduction

In 1972 I met Terence McKenna and became close friends, and ten years later we were joined by Rupert Sheldrake in a special triadic bond. We developed a habit of conversing on common interests in a style that evolved into a form we called a *trialogue*, and eventually we performed public trialogues. These occurred sporadically from 1989 until 1996. The Esalen Institute was very hospitable and helped us organize and record these trialogue events, which led to our two volumes of published trialogues. In a typical trialogue, one of us would lead off with a trigger monologue of fifteen minutes or so.

My conversation starter for one of our trialogues in 1996 was the basis of the following section, on my supposed revolutionary role in the psychedelic history of mathematics in the 1960s, and the origin of chaos theory. The next section, based on an invited lecture in Calcutta in 2006, describes the change in my own mathematical history wrought by the psychedelic revolution of the 1960s.

Math in the 1960s

One day I was sitting in my office with my secretary, Nina, when there was a knock on the door. Nina said, "This is a friend of a friend of mine, who wants to interview you." I was very busy with the telephone and the correspondence, so he came inside and I answered his questions without thinking. After a month or so, when a photographer arrived, I began to realize that I had given an interview for *Gentleman's Quarterly* (*GQ*) magazine. I called my children and asked them what was GQ magazine. They live in Southern California and know about such things. I was in Italy when the magazine finally arrived on the stands. I had been proud, in spite of my style of dress, that I had been the first one in our circle of family and friends to actually be photographed for GQ. But I was shocked in Florence to open the first page of the magazine, and see my picture occupying a large part of the first page, with the table of contents, with the heading: "Abraham sells drugs to mathematicians." There were some other insulting things in the interview, that as far as I can remember, was largely fiction. I didn't mention it to anybody when I came back to California, and was very pleased that nobody mentioned it. Nobody had noticed. There were one or two phone calls, and I realized that nobody, after all, reads GQ. If they do look at the pictures, they overlooked mine. I was safe after all at this dangerous pass.

Suddenly, my peace was disturbed once again by 100 phone calls in a single day asking what did I think of the article about me in the *San Francisco Examiner*, or the *San Jose Mercury News*, and so on. All the embers in the fire left by GQ had flamed up again in the pen of a journalist. A woman who writes a computer column for the *San Francisco Examiner* had received in her mail box a copy of the *Gentleman's Quarterly* article, in which Timothy Leary was quoted as saying, "The Japanese go to Burma for teak, and they go to California for novelty and creativity. Everybody knows that California has this resource thanks to psychedelics." Then the article quoted me as the supplier for the scientific renaissance in the 1960s. This columnist didn't believe what was asserted by Timothy Leary and others in the *GQ* article, that the computer revolution and the computer graphic innovations of California had been built upon a psychedelic foundation. She set out to prove this story false. She went to Siggraph, the largest gathering of computer graphic professionals in the world, where, annually, somewhere in the United States 30,000 people who are vitally involved in the computer revolution gather. She thought she would set this heresy to rest by conducting a sample survey, beginning her interviews at the airport the minute she stepped off the plane. By the time she got back to her desk in San Francisco she'd talked to 180 important professionals of the computer graphic field, all of whom answered yes to the question, "Do you take psychedelics, and is this important in your work?" Her column, finally syndicated in a number of newspapers again, unfortunately, or kindly, remembered me.

Shortly after this second incident in my story, I was in Hollyhock, the Esalen of the far north, on Cortes Island in British Columbia, with Rupert and other friends, and I had a kind of psychotic break in the night. I couldn't sleep and was consumed with a paranoid fantasy about this outage and what it would mean in my future career, the police at my door and so on. I knew that my fears had blown up unnecessarily, but I needed someone to talk to. The person I knew best there was Rupert. And he was very busy in counsel with various friends, but eventually I took Rupert aside and confided to him this secret, and all my fears. His response, within a day or two, was to repeat the story to everybody in Canada, assuring me that it's good to be outed. I tried thinking positively about this episode, but when I came home I still felt nervous about it and said "no" to many interviews from ABC News, and the United Nations, and other people who called to check out this significant story. I did not then rise to the occasion, and so I've decided today, by popular request, to tell the truth.

It all began in 1967 when I was a professor of mathematics at Princeton, and one of my students turned me on to LSD. That led to my moving to California a year later, where I was given a bottle of DMT in 1969. A friend verified that it was pure DMT, and I smoked up a large quantity of it.

That resulted in a kind of secret resolve, which swerved

my career toward a search for the connections between mathematics and the experience of the logos, or what Terence calls "the transcendent other." This is a hyperdimensional space full of meaning and wisdom and beauty, which feels more real than ordinary reality, and to which we have returned many times over the years, for instruction and pleasure. In the course of the next 20 years there were various steps I took to explore the connection between mathematics and the logos. About the time that chaos theory was discovered by the scientific community, and the chaos revolution began in 1978, I apprenticed myself to a neurophysiologist and tried to construct brain models made out of the basic objects of chaos theory. I built a vibrating fluid machine to visualize vibrations in transparent media, because I felt, on the basis of direct experience, that the Hindu metaphor of vibrations was important and valuable. I felt that we could learn more about consciousness, communication, resonance, and the emergence of form and pattern in the physical, biological, social and intellectual worlds, through actually watching vibrations in transparent media ordinarily invisible, and making them visible. I was inspired by Hans Jenny,[1] an amateur scientist in Switzerland, a follower of Rudolf Steiner, who had built an ingenious gadget for rendering patterns in transparent fluids visible.

About this time we discovered computer graphics in Santa Cruz, when the first affordable computer graphic terminals had appeared on the market. I started a project of teaching mathematics with computer graphics, and eventually tried to simulate the mathematical models for neurophysiology and for vibrating fluids in computer programs with computer graphic displays. In this way evolved a new class of mathematical models called CDs, cellular dynamata. They are an especially appropriate mathematical object for modeling and trying to understand the brain, the mind, the visionary experience and so on. At the same time other mathematicians, some of whom may have been recipients of my gifts in the 1960s, began their own experiments with computer graphics in different places, and began to make films.

Eventually, we were able to construct machines in Santa Cruz which could simulate these mathematical models I call CDs at a reasonable speed, first slowly, and then faster and faster. And in 1989, I had a fantastic experience at the NASA Goddard Space Flight Center in Maryland, where I was given access to, at that time, the world's fastest supercomputer, the MPP, Massively Parallel Processor. My CD model for the visual cortex had been programmed into this machine by the only person able to program it, and I was invited to come and view the result. Looking at the color screen of this supercomputer was like looking through the window at the future, and seeing an excellent memory of a DMT vision, not only proceeding apace on the screen, but also going about 100 times faster than a human experience. Under the control of knobs which I could turn at the terminal, we immediately recorded a video, which lasts for 10 minutes. It was in 1989 that I took my first look through this window.

To sum up my story, there is first of all, a 20-year evolution from my first DMT vision in 1969, to my experience with the Massively Parallel Processor vision in 1989. Following this 20-year evolution, and the recording of the video, came the story with GQ and the interviews at Siggraph in the San Francisco Examiner that essentially pose the question, "Have psychedelics had an influence in the evolution of science, mathematics, the computer revolution, computer graphics, and so on?" Another event, in 1990, followed the publication of a paper in the *International Journal of Bifurcations and Chaos*, when an interesting article appeared in the *Monthly Notices* of the American Mathematical Society, the largest union of research mathematicians in the world. The article totally redefined mathematics, dropping numbers and geometrical spaces as relics of history, and adopting a new definition of mathematics as the study of space/time patterns. Mathematics has been reborn, and this rebirth is an outcome of both the computer revolution and the psychedelic revolution which took place concurrently, concomitantly, cooperatively, in the 1960s. Redefining this material as an art medium, I gave a concert, played in real time with a genuine supercomputer, in October, 1992, in the Cathedral of Saint John the Divine, the largest Gothic cathedral in the world, in New York City.

Vibrations and forms

My main goal in this section is to give an idea, especially a visual idea, of my experiments with vibrations and forms in consciousness, over the past thirty years. The visual representations, computer graphic animations, may be best understood in the context of my personal experiences in actual consciousness exploration during the years 1967 to 1972 which motivated the work, and the philosophical frames, or maps of consciousness, in which I am trying to understand my experiences. These maps are based jointly on my own experiences, and on philosophies of Greek, Jewish, and Indian origin. I must thank Dr. Paul Lee for his tutelage on the Platonic and Neoplatonic philosophies of the Greek tradition, and Dr. SenSharma for his explanations of the Kashmiri Shaivite or Trika philosophy and other features of the Indian tradition.

My story begins in 1967, when I was a professor of mathematics at Princeton University. This is a wonderful university, especially for mathematics, and I was privileged to have colleagues and undergraduate and graduate students, whom I remember fondly to this day. Also, the 1960s was the time of student political unrest, and concomitantly, the time of the Beatles, and the Hip Subculture, or "sex, drugs, and rock and roll", as they used to say. My wonderful students were involved in these popular movements, and through them, I also became involved.

In 1967, the three notorious and defrocked psychology professors of Harvard University — Timothy Leary, Richard Alpert (later aka Baba Ram Dass), and Ralph Metzner — were barnstorming about the USA plumping the powers of LSD as an agent of spiritual growth. Leary, under the influence of Vedanta and Gayatri Devi of Los Angeles, used to affect Indian dress, and hold forth on Eastern philosophies. I heard their performance in the Lower East Side of New York City, and decided to try LSD and see for myself. In November, one of my undergraduate students helped me onto the path, and my first experience was an epiphany indeed.

Through this epiphany, I became fascinated with the exploration of consciousness, as we called this path, and continued the work in irregular episodes as I followed my career to the University of California at Santa Cruz in 1968, and subsequently to Amsterdam, to Paris, and to Nainital in the Himalayan foothills. In 1973, I returned to Santa Cruz, and migrated from personal explorations back to academic research on consciousness, chaos theory, and other concerns. My walkabout of five years was over, but was to have a lasting effect on all aspects of my life. I had had hundreds of meditations of the sort practiced in Yoga Nidra, that is, lying prone through the night, in the so-called fourth state of consciousness, and amplified by small doses (eg, 25 mg) of LSD.[2] Like Yoga Nidra meditation, the LSD experience provides a trip to the fourth state lasting typically about eight hours, during which sleep is held at bay. These sessions were usually done alone, but sometimes in teams of from two up to a dozen or so others, flying, so we thought, in group formation like a flock of birds. Marijuana use was ubiquitous during this period, but in my experience it made no important contribution to my research and, generally, I avoided it.

At one time, around 1969, we used large doses of DMT, and this period was crucially important to the whole evolution of my mathematical understanding of consciousness, based on geometry, topology, nonlinear dynamics, and the theory of vibrating waves. For in these experiments, although lasting only a few minutes, the reciprocal processes of vibrations producing forms and forms producing vibrations were clearly perceived in abstract visual fields.

Our perspective during this time and later, was gnostic. That is, we rejected teachers and teachings, and sought to discover cosmology for ourselves. Throughout this period, most of us in the Hip Subculture were apprenticing ourselves to teachers of ancient traditions from East, Mideast, and the West, sharing our experiences, traveling to faraway lands to find teachings, and so on. Teachers travelled through California, and we circled the globe in search of them. Personally I experienced yoga, martial arts (judo and aikido), prehistoric moon rituals, musical meditations, fasting and strict diets (eg, macrobiotics), and Native American ceremonies. This was the background of my interest in vibrations and forms in the field of consciousness.

My walkabout was blessed with two special learning experiences, one in Paris at the beginning of the year, the other in the Himalayan foothills, in the Summer and Fall. This was the final year of my walkabout, following which I returned to ordinary reality and my post at the University of California at Santa Cruz, an arduous process taking about a year. I began 1972 as a visiting professor at the University of Amsterdam, teaching catastrophe theory. At the same time, I had a visiting position at the Institut des Hautes Etudes Scientifiques (IHES) at Bures-sur-Yvette outside Paris. I used to commute weekly on the train, which I loved. At this time, IHES was newly formed, and had only two permanent professors, David Ruelle and René Thom, both of whom were superb. Thom was one of the great mathematicians of the 20th century, and had received the Fields Medal at the International Congress of Mathematicians in 1956 for his work in differential topology. I had met him in 1960 in Berkeley, where we began working together on the foundations of catastrophe theory. During 1966, I had written my first books, *Foundations of Mechanics*, *Transversal Mappings and Flows*, and *Linear and Multilinear Algebra*, while René had written his foundational work on catastrophe theory, *Structural Stability and Morphogenesis*, which I arranged to have published by my publisher, Bill Benjamin.

Early in 1972, René and I were both stymied in our work and were browsing the borderlines of science looking for clues. I had been reading Kurt Lewin on topological psychology, and on arriving at IHES one day, I asked René what he was working on. He pulled a book from his desk and began showing me photo after photo of familiar forms from nature: spiral galaxies, cell mitosis, sand dunes, and so on. These forms, he said, had been photographed in vibrating water. The book was *Kymatik*, by Hans Jenny, a medical doctor from Dornach, a suburb of Basel, Switzerland. I was thunderstruck to see images from my meditations on the pages of a book, especially in support of the vibration metaphor of the Pythagoreans.

I immediately called Jenny in Dornach, and he agreed

to meet me. I took the train to Basel, and was met at the station by Jenny's son-in-law, Christian Stutten, who drove me to Dornach. Along the way I learned that Dornach was the world headquarters of the Anthroposophy movement founded by Rudolf Steiner, the esoteric Christian follower of Madame Blavatsky's *Secret Doctrine*, around 1900. Jenny was a follower of Steiner, and lived in Dornach along with many other Anthropops. Jenny greeted me in his home, showed me part of his lab, and an animated film of some experiments in progress. I collected his papers and books and went home to Paris and Amsterdam, inspired.

As the winter progressed, I thought much about morphogenesis and the mathematics of coupled systems of vibrating membranes and fluids, while continuing to teach catastrophe theory in Amsterdam, and giving many lectures on these subjects at universities all over Europe. Also, my chemically assisted meditations continued, and in them, I pursued the vibration metaphor in conceptual space, and simultaneously, in experiential space.

These experiences were dominated by rapidly vibrating patterns of brightly colored abstract forms, somewhat like the video art and rock concert light shows of the 1960s. The scintillating light caustics projected by the bright sun on the bottom of a swimming pool also give an intimation of the visual aspect of these meditations. An excellent computer simulation has been achieved by Scott Draves in his art works called *Electric Sheep*, and may be seen on his website.[3]

Suddenly, the spring semester in Amsterdam was over, grades were recorded, and I had a small savings account. It occurred to me to pay India a brief visit before school began again in the Fall of 1972. Here I was influenced by the ambiance of Amsterdam culture, in which I met so many people who had just returned from, or were about to go

Mathematics and the Psychedelic Revolution 31

again to, India. One young man just returned told me how he organized his explorations of the Himalaya: just sit in a tea shop until somebody offers you an experience, then accept it, he said. Just go with the flow. This was my plan. One day at the Kosmos, a psychedelic and meditation hall run by the Dutch government (bless it), I looked up and saw my old friend Baba Ram Dass. The former Richard Alpert, he was among the Harvard trio of professors who had encouraged my decision to experiment with LSD in 1967. Then he had lived briefly in my house in Santa Cruz, California. He had stayed for a time in Nainital, near the western border of Nepal in the Himalayan foothills, where he became attached to a guru called Neem Karoli Baba. I told Baba Ram Dass about my plan to visit India and he gave me instructions for connecting with Neem Karoli Baba. Find your way to Nainital, he said, then hang out at this particular hotel, and if I was supposed to meet Neem Karoli Baba, somebody would approach me and take me to the ashram outside Kainchi, a small village.

And so, late in June, 1972, it came to pass. I went to the ashram with a group of western devotees in a taxi. But on arrival I felt a bit disappointed by the amplified music and carnival atmosphere. I saw the devotees sitting in darshan formation in front of Neem Karoli Baba on his tucket, all in silence. Something seemed to be going on but I was blind to it. Someone would give him prasad, a fruit for example, and he would immediately toss it to someone else. I went back to the hotel in Nainital determined to go on with whomever next approached me.

This process took no time at all. Once back at the hotel, I met a young barefoot Canadian dressed in a simple smock. He introduced himself as Shambu. As I had been on the road for a long while with a highly evolved travel kit that fit into a small shoulder bag, I was greatly impressed by his kit, which required not even a bag. Shambu explained that he had been living in a cave in the jungle for several months with two other saddhus. There were three small caves by a stream in the jungle, two miles from the nearest town. One of the saddhus had just left, and the village had dispatched Shambu to find a replacement. Apparently the villagers felt their prosperity was only possible with all three caves occupied by appropriate persons engaged in full-time spiritual practice. Smoking ganja apparently counted as spiritual practice, worship of Shiva it seems. Shambu was sure that he had been guided to me as I was the chosen person.

Shambu put me on a bus with the usual sort of instruction: ride the bus to the end of the line at Almora, from there I would be guided somehow. This was monsoon season, and there had been heavy rain. After a short while the bus was firmly halted by a major road washout. Everyone climbed out of the bus. Looking down the slope, I was surprised to see Neem Karoli Baba's ashram for the second time. What a coincidence! Then someone came out to say I should come in at once, as Neem Karoli Baba was asking for me. Was this really happening, or was there some mistake? Neem Karoli Baba gave me a bag of breakfast cereal. He said I was going to need it in the jungle. Two young Indian devotees were told to guide me on a trek through the jungle around the washout, and put me on a bus for Almora on the other side. By this time I was losing my Western mind, and all this seemed more like paranormal phenomena than conspiracy theory.

It was midnight when, finally, the second bus arrived in Almora. The village was dark, but moonlight through a clearing in the clouds showed the shops in silhouette. A man descended from the bus after me. He had a bearer with a long box balanced on his head. I asked him where he was going, hoping for a clue for my next steps. He said that he was a student of Jim Corbett, the famous hunter of maneating tigers. I had just read Corbett's book, *Maneaters of the Kumoan*. Actually, we were now in the Kumoan Hills. The man said the long package was his rifle. There was a maneating panther on the loose nearby, and he was about to spend the night in a tree overlooking a fresh human kill, hoping to shoot the panther. This was his job, he had been sent by the government. I decided not to follow him into the jungle.

I followed some other people who descended from the bus. They seemed to know where they were going, on a footpath into the jungle. One by one they vanished into side paths, and then I was walking alone into the dark unknown, following this single-track footpath. I could not stop to sleep, for fear of the panther. As long as the path continued, and looked like it was used by humans, I would continue, until I found where it went. Another village or whatever. Seemed like a plan, for an hour or so, until there was a fork in the path. In the dark I could see no indication which way to go. Just then I was startled by a rustle very close by. I could see only grey on grey in the darkness. Then a voice said in clear English, "Good evening saheb, I am from the Wisdom Garden School. I have been waiting for you. You are to go this way". Then he pointed to the left fork, and vanished. So on I went, until I heard voices. Following the sound, I came upon a group of Western hippies in a house, who offered me a place to sleep. Apparently this was the Kasa Devi Ridge, where the German Lama Govinda had established himself some years ago, after going totally native in the Himalaya. In the morning they showed me the way to a village nearby, which was Dinapani, my destination. The headman interviewed me in his chai shop, approved me for cave service, and asked his young son to guide me into the jungle to the cave.

Indeed, there were three caves and two jungle babas, who were muni, that is, they did not speak. Not out loud at least. But voices in my head made me welcome, and spelled out the rules. I must keep a fire going in my cave every night, or a panther would come to claim the space. I must go to the stream every morning to wash, and worship Shiva in an underwater grotto that has been used for centuries and has a polished lingam. The dhuni (small ritual fire) must be kept going. Food would be brought by villagers every morning on their way into the forest to tap turpentine trees.

All went well for a week or so. I thought of writing my mother to say I had found a place where I should stay for a few months to further my education, but I could not manage to write. Every night I practiced my yoga nidra, and explored further the vibrational realms. There seemed to be instruction regarding the use of 'tools of light" for self-defense and self-maintenance. I practiced, according to these instructions, during the day, while sitting meditation by the dhuni after my bath with Shiva and the daily meal of dhalbhat (rice and lentils), gor (raw sugar), and the mandatory chillum (straight pipe) of hashish.

Then the trouble began. I had some unwelcome orders during the night, perceived as disembodied speech in my head. I was to leave this place immediately. I resisted. Then the orders were repeated with physical discomforts, which would go away as soon as I agreed to leave in the morning. But in the morning I changed my mind. And so on, in a cycle.

Until one day, around my 36th birthday, July 4, while the other two yogis were away on mysterious missions and I was hard at work meditating by the dhuni, I saw a person approaching, far down the jungle path. This figure got larger and larger, and eventually resolved into a vision from hell, a wild man with a spear, clothed primarily in ashes. He sat down by the fire and accepted a toke from my fully loaded chillum. My paranoia subsided, as apparently he meant no harm. After an hour or so staring into the distance, he turned to me and spoke in unaccented American, "Don't you understand, you are supposed to leave here. I am going to get up and leave now, and you are to follow me". Which he did. And I did, after collecting my small bag from the cave. After a walk of a mile or so down a path I had not seen before, he said, "I am going this way, you go that way", and disappeared around a bend. I followed the indicated jungle path, I am not sure how far, and it led directly to Neem Karoli Baba's ashram. Again, the old fellow was apparently expecting me, bellowing, "Where is that professor from California? Bring him here." And so, reluctantly, began my relationship with Neem Karoli Baba.

I was set up with a house, a library of Sanskrit classics in English translation, and a few devotees for company — including one with Sanskrit skills, Kedarnath, his partner, Uma, and their baby, Ganesh, born during one of our meditations. I was informed by Neem Karoli Baba that I had a mission to relate my meditation experiences to the Sanskrit classics, and transmit the understanding somehow to my colleagues in the USA. These sources included the Vedas, a few Upanishads, works by Sri Auribindo, and the *Yoga Vasishta*, a primary text for the Trika philosophy of Kashmiri Shaivism.

I became known at Veda Vyaasa. I remained in this setup for six months, most of the time with Ray Gwyn Smith, now my wife, who had arrived from California in the meanwhile. The night meditations amplified by microdoses of LSD continued, as I had brought a supply with me from Holland right from the start. *Yoga Vasishta* was a great inspiration and support for my ideas of vibrations and maps of consciousness.

Neem Karoli Baba and the entire satsang departed for warmer climes to the south, after the thermometer in Nainital dropped below freezing in October. Ray and I departed in December for a Himalayan trek in Nepal, where I donated my library to a local university. We walked about 400 miles and returned to California early in 1973. And thus ended my miracle year, 1972, and also the five year period of one-point focus on spiritual exploration. After returning to Santa Cruz and my job as math professor at UCSC, I reinterpreted the mission given me by Neem Karoli Baba as a program of academic research on vibrations and forms in mathematical models, and in physical fluids as well.

What I learned about cosmos and consciousness during this final year of the five-year project cannot be said in words. perhaps mathematics will be helpful. I imagined this as my task intended by Neem Karoli Baba. But I had to go on alone, as both Neem Karoli Baba, and Hans Jenny died at this time.

Conclusion

There is no doubt that the psychedelic revolution in the 1960s had a profound effect on the history of computers and computer graphics, and of mathematics, especially the birth of postmodern maths such as chaos theory and fractal geometry. This I witnessed personally. The effect on my own history, viewed now in four decades of retrospect, was a catastrophic shift from abstract pure math to a more experimental and applied study of vibrations and forms, which continues to this day.

Notes

1. (Jenny, 1967)
2. (Saraswati, 1998)
3. (www.draves.com)

Chapter 2
Entheogens in the Himalayan Foothills

Abstract

Reporting a miraculous week of entheogens and sadhus at a temple in the montane jungle of the Himalayan foothills in 1972.

Publication

Ms #148, written November 3, 2015. Early version published in *One Toke to God: the Entheogenic Spirituality of Cannabis*, Mark J. Estrin, ed., 2017: ch 17, pp. 127-133.

Contents

Introduction
Dinapani
The Cave
Back at the Ashram and the Aftermath
Conclusion: Cannabis as Entheogen

Introduction

In the Fall of 1968 I arrived in Santa Cruz, California to begin a tenured position as Associate Professor of Mathematics at the University of California Santa Cruz (UCSC). My first three years there were dominated by two opposite programs: political actions regarding academic freedom and civil rights at UCSC, and the Hip cultural (and psychedelic) revolution in downtown Santa Cruz. During this time I lived in a twenty-four room Victorian mansion with an extended family. As hippies, we were very involved with spiritual and mystical ideas and literature, such as the books of Gurdjieff, *Meetings with Remarkable Men* and *In Search of the Miraculous*. We hosted many short term visitors with similar interests, such as Baba Ram Dass. I then found it convenient to go on extended leave for two and a half years. During the 1971/72 academic year I was living in Amsterdam, teaching catastrophe theory in the university. As the school year came

Figure 1. Nainital, 1972.

to a close, I decided to go to India for the Summer of 1972, despite the monsoon season, to seek out gurus and ashrams. I happened across Ram Dass in the basement of the Kosmos (a center for spiritual seekers), who gave me instructions for finding his guru, Neem Karoli Baba, in India. I was to find my way to the Evelyn Hotel in Nainital, and await a contact. Nainital is a Himalayan resort town surrounding a small lake, at an altitude of 6,500 feet, somewhat like Lake Tahoe in California. It is part of the Kumaon region of Uttar Pradesh (present day Uttarakhand), a region of montane jungle, famous for man-eating tigers.

Thus, the evening of Tuesday, June 20 found me in Old Delhi, at the train station, seeking transportation to Nainital. A third class train departing at 4 am would get me to Moradabad for four and a half Rupees (about 50 US cents). A distance of 100 miles, it took 9 hours, and immersed me in Indian culture for the first time: medieval desert villages, animals, families, local food, all seen through the open window of a tightly packed third class train. After a bus for a few miles to Haldwani in the Nainital district bordering the Kumaon hills, a collective taxi 20 miles to Nainital village, and a short hike, I arrived at the Evelyn Hotel around 9 pm. From Delhi it had taken 17 hours and about $2. Thus, on Wednesday, June 21, I arrived at the hotel, seeking a guru called Neem Karoli Baba, awaiting a miracle. Soon I was contacted by some of his devotees, and it was arranged that I could visit the temple the next day. Early in the morning on Thursday, June 22, I went with a group by taxi the 25 miles to his secluded ashram and temple in Kainchi.

Here I remained for most of the second half of 1972, as the story is told in *Love Everyone*.[1] The first two weeks were full of miracles. I disappeared from the ashram scene for a stay in the jungle near Dinapani, a village near Almora, 40 miles from Nainital, then returned to Kainchi. After returning, Neem Karoli set me on a study project on the Sanskrit literature on vibrations in cosmic consciousness, a theory of the interconnections of the several planes of individual and collective mind, which has occupied me ever since, resulting in some twenty papers and a book. Here I write the story for the first time of the week from Thursday, June 22, through Friday, June 30, inclusive, based on my aging hand-written journal of that time. I am grateful to Dr. Paul A. Lee and Anjani O'Connell for generous assistance with this manuscript.

Dinapani

Following my first day at the Kainchi ashram, June 22, I felt that I should move on. The scene of the devotees and devotions made me uncomfortable. I did not understand at first that some kind of telepathic conversation connected the people seated in a circle around Neem Karoli. I yearned for something more solitary, some direct inspiration along the lines of my readings and psychedelic trips in Santa Cruz.

After returning from that first day in Kainchi to the Evelyn Hotel, a jungle yogi approached me. He was drinking tea, dressed in a simple, clay-stained robe. A 23-year old Canadian called Sambhu, he had been living in a cave in the jungle near Almora for two years but had to leave it. The villagers living nearby supported him and three other jungle babas as it was believed they brought prosperity to the village, which consisted of just a few houses and two tea shops. He said that I had been chosen to replace him, and gave me instructions for traveling to his cave. I was to take the bus to Almora, then walk 3 miles through the jungle to Dinapani, and seek out the head man, Prem Singh, at his tea house. Following Sambhu's instructions, I transformed myself into a jungle yogi look-alike. I gave away all my possessions, bought a brown robe, a blanket, and a small shoulder bag for my journal, pen, sewing kit, tooth brush, and LSD stash, ready to set off on the bus to Almora.

The monsoon was raging, roads were flooded, and there were many mudslides. Every day I would go the the bus terminal, only to find out that there was no bus, the road was closed. Finally, on Sunday, June 25, I got a bus in Nainital for Almora, but after a short ride it halted as there had been a new mudslide. We all stepped off the bus, and I was amazed to see that we were at the entrance to Neem Karoli's temple. I went inside, and Neem Karoli asked Jai, one of the devotees, to guide me to Almora. He gave me a large plastic bag of cracked wheat gruel for my trip.

Jai took me on a hike through the jungle circumnavigating the mudslide, and we boarded a bus to Almora on the other side. Due to the delay, I arrived in Almora late, around 7 pm. Several people left the bus there. One, carrying a long rifle, said he was a disciple of Jim Corbett, the author of *Man-Eaters of Kumaon*. A local person had been killed by a tiger, and this man had been called to sit in a tree over the corpse hoping to shoot the tiger.

In the light of a full moon, I followed two men along a path into the jungle. Soon they disappeared into a side path, and I carried straight on, hoping for good luck. I could not stop to rest for fear of the man-eating tiger. Eventually the path branched, and I hesitated, trying to decide which way to go. At once, a man popped out from behind a tree. Telling me that he was from the Wisdom Garden School, he said *This way sahib. This way to Dinapani.* Following his pointing hand, I walked on.

Around 10 pm I heard very soft voices. Following the

sound, I found three English freaks in a tea house. They took me home for the night. On the porch of their large stone house, I mused on the concert of birdsong and crickets, and the occurrence of synchronicity in their symphony and in all that had happened to me since leaving Amsterdam. I slept well on the porch in my new blanket.

In the morning, Monday, June 26, I walked on a short way and arrived at the village of Dinapani. The local people seemed to be expecting me, and took me to Prem Singh's tea shop. He asked me some penetrating questions about my motivation, then directed his son Aram to guide me to my cave. After a two mile walk he left me at the side of a small river.

The Cave

Soon I was approached by Cornelio, a scantily dressed jungle yogi who seemed to be expecting me. Sambhu had told me there were four caves and a small temple under construction at this location, known as Ganga Sagar Mandir. The other yogis, Cornelio, Alessandro, and Len, were muni, that is, practicing non-speaking yogis. Cornelio silently led me to a very small open cave. I spread my blanket, and fell asleep.

In the morning, Tuesday, June 27, I awoke to voices that seemed to sound inside my head. There was nobody nearby. I was told that food had arrived, and I should come to the duni, a small stone fire pit and platform near the river. Two men from the village had brought food. I learned that each morning they brought food and charas (hashish). Our job was to eat, smoke, and perform puja to Siva every day. In fact, smoking charas was considered there as a form of Siva worship. Under the full moon this night, Cornelio, Alessandro, and I dropped acid by the fire. I awoke the next morning with my bare legs covered by leeches.

Every day began with a wash in the river including clothing, a cup of tea in the cave before sunrise, then to the temple around 9 am. Puja included swimming in the river, in which there was an underwater lingam, a sacred object of Siva. I kept the fire going and smoked hash in my chillum, while the yogis marched about in the jungle performing puja. From the duni I could see that they moved in perfect synchrony, although they could not see each other. I had never smoked much cannabis, but in these few days I inhaled enough for a lifetime. Three days passed in this pattern, June 27, 28, and 29.

Meanwhile I was receiving instructions experientially in mathematical models of consciousness. The central ideas were of vibrations and resonance between parallel levels. Years later I learned that these ideas had been studied extensively in a branch of medieval Sanskrit philosophy called Kashmiri Shaivism, and I devoted a book to this philosophy, written jointly with quantum theorist Sisir Roy.

My personal course in miracles soon came to an end. Voices in my head every night demanded that I leave my cave and return to Kainchi. There were also some physical discomforts. Only when I promised to leave next morning would the voices and pains stop, and I could sleep. But in the morning I would change my mind, and the cycle would repeat.

But on Friday, June 30, while my two companions were away and I was working at my job with my fire and chillum, I saw a small figure in the distance. As it came closer, I saw it was a fierce looking jungle yogi in rags and dreads, carrying a brass bucket. This turned out to be Durga Chaitanya, from California, whom I had met in Nainital. Silently he sat next to me at the duni, sharing the chillum. After some time he turned to me and explained he had been sent on a journey by Neem Karoli, and had a message for me. I was to return to Kainchi. He said he was going to leave at once, and I was to follow him. Which I did. With my little bag and my blanket, we strode off into the jungle. Eventually the path branched, he pointed to the right, and turned to the left. After some hours, I found myself in a village, where I could catch a bus to Nainital. I arrived home around 3 pm.

Back at the Ashram and the Aftermath

On Saturday, July 1, I returned to the ashram. Neem Karoli was calling for the professor from California. He then gave me some texts on vibrations and consciousness. These included the Bhagavad Gita, the Mahabaratha, the four Vedas, and Yoga Vasistha. I was given the name Vasishta, and later renamed Veda Vyasa.

For the next five months I studied these texts, and tried to conform the mystical writings with my own transcendental experiences. With the aid of Kedarnath and (so it seemed) instructions from Neem Karoli delivered in my dreams, I retranslated some of the Sanskrit proper nouns. One of these terms, *akasha*, I interpreted as an immaterial field connecting all of the 36 tattvas (levels) of the Kashmiri model of cosmic consciousness.

Returning to California in 1973, I continued these studies, and my proper mathematical research turned into new directions. In 1974 I created a fluid dynamics lab to study chaotic vibrations, including an instrument for the visualization of vibrations in transparent fluids called the macroscope.

It was not until 2005 when I returned to India on a Fulbright grant and stopped at the Ramakrisna Mission in Kolkata that I discovered the Sanskrit literature of Kashmiri

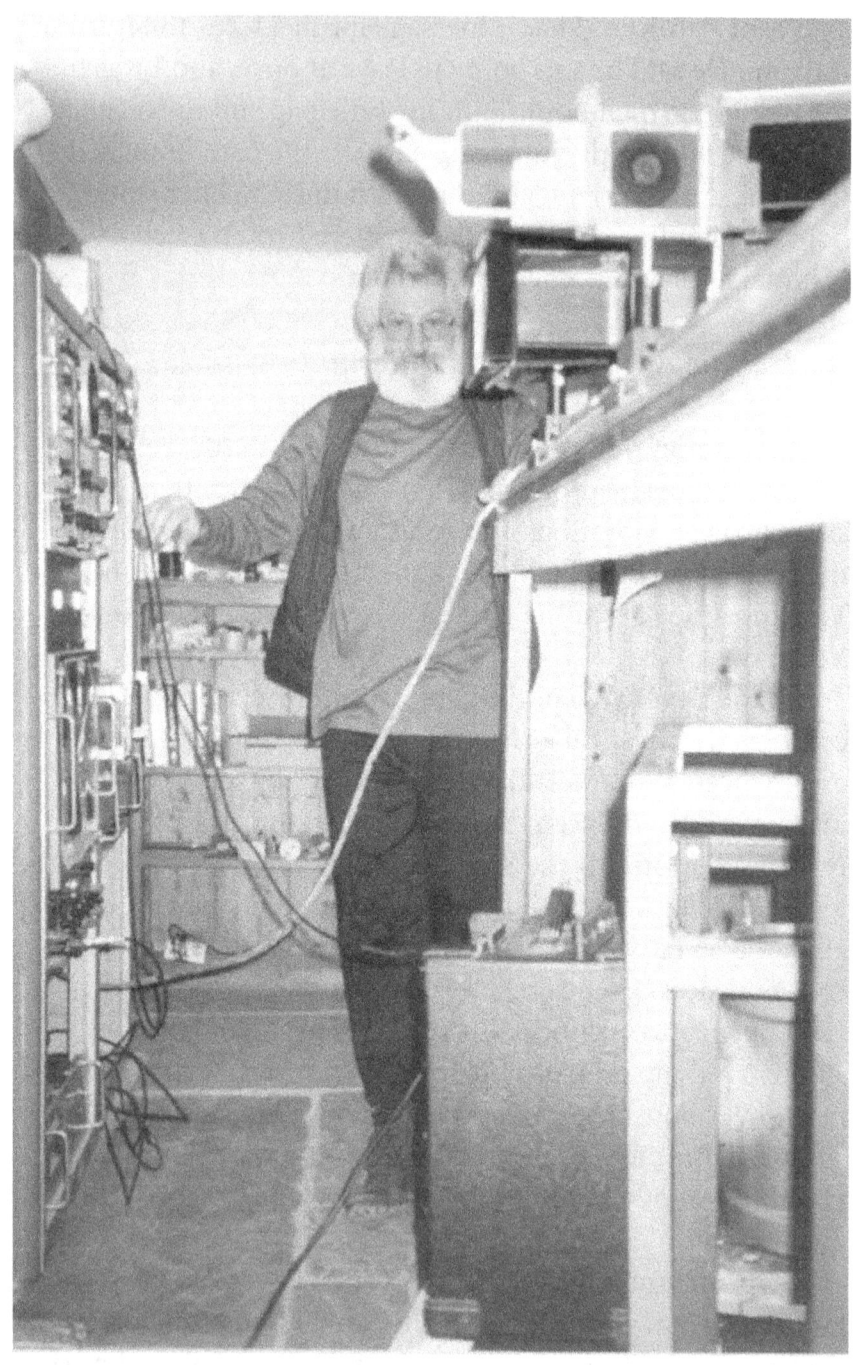

Figure 2. Santa Cruz, 1974. Macroscope Lab at UCSC.

Figure 3. Santa Cruz, 1975. Visual Math Lab at UCSC.

Shivaism on *spanda* (vibrations) and models of consciousness. Amazingly, my Siva puja (hashish smoking) in a cave in 1972 had given me a precognition of my study of Shaivism in 2006, and a book on the akashic vibrations in 2010.

Neem Karoli had brilliantly prescribed the information that I needed for a new direction in my mathematical work. And also, he correctly predicted that I would propagate these ideas, higher consciousness and vibrations according to the yogis, in the West.

Conclusion: Cannabis as Entheogen

In the Himalayan foothills, jungle babas harvest charas in the wild. They rub cannabis plants with their palms, and roll the oil into a ball called a guli. Sadhus sometimes wear these gulis in their hair. A bit of the charas is pulled from the guli and put into a ritual pipe, called a chillum. Inhaling the smoke may be preceded by an invocation, such as Ba Boom, Siva, Boom Shankar. To this day, smoking the chillum is regarded in India as puja to Siva. It is possible that Gordon Wasson was wrong, and Soma is actually cannabis.[2] In any case, properly used, it is an effective entheogen in my experience.

My casual smoking of cannabis in California had never provided me with a spiritual experience, as I had discovered with LSD. But given the set and setting of a Siva temple in the Himalayas, steeped for centuries in the ritual use of the chillum with local charas, cannabis is indeed entheogenic. In these sacred sessions, the spiritual wisdom of the ages descends down the great chain of being from the akasha to us.

Notes

1   (Markus, 2015; pp. 204-205)
2   An exhaustive case for this thesis, comparable in scope to that of Gordon Wasson, is presented in (Bennett, 2010).

Chapter 3
Chaos Math, Brain Science, and Mind Philosophy

Abstract

Since 1960 at least, I have been sharing chaos thinking with my brother Fred and, reciprocally, learning about brain research from him. This is a brief reminiscence of those early years.

Dedicated to Walter Freeman (1927–2016)

Publication

Ms #152, written in January, 2017. Published in *Intentional neurodynamics in transition: The dynamical legacy of Walter Jackson Freeman*, special issue of *Chaos and Complexity Letters*, 11(1), 179-182 (2017). F. D. Abraham, ed.

Contents

Introduction
Chaos Math, the Early Years
Brain Science, Primitive Thoughts
Mind Philosophy, Some Experiments and Fantasies
Conclusion

Introduction

After my freshman year in engineering at the University of Vermont, I moved to the University of Michigan for a developmental trajectory from electrical engineering to experimental particle physics, applied math, then finally pure math. In 1960, with a fresh PhD, I moved to Berkeley for my first job. The math department there had just expanded into a major international center. I met and began joint work with Steve Smale and a large and changing group on dynamical systems theory. Meanwhile, Fred had finished his PhD at Illinois and moved to UCLA in 1962.

Chaos Math, the Early Years

During my first year in Berkeley, 1960-61, my group included Steve Smale, Moe Hirsh, Mauricio Peixoto, Bob Williams, René Thom, Chris Zeeman, and other mathematicians of note, some of whom became main figures in chaos theory and catastrophe theory as the 1960s unrolled. The next year, 1961-62. Steve moved to Columbia university, and the following year I followed him there to facilitate our joint work. After that year, in 1963, he returned to Berkeley, while I remained at Columbia, and then moved to Princeton in 1964. These were golden years for mathematics, while the world around us suffered the Bay of Pigs, the Cuban Missile Crisis, the assassinations of JFK, RFK, MLK, and Malcolm X, and the fights for civil rights and to end the Vietnam war.

As for dynamical systems theory, our work, sometimes called the Smale program, was devoted to the basic ideas of generic properties, structural stability, and bifurcations. Eventually, some of our optimistic predictions were foiled by clever counter-examples, and the experimental discovery of chaotic behavior by Yoshi Ueda in 1961, and Ed Lorenz in 1963.

After a summer-long conference in Berkeley in 1968 our group splintered as people returned to the drawing board, browsing various sciences for fresh ideas. And I left Princeton to return to California. In the first half of 1968-69, my conversations with Fred resumed, and contact with Steve Smale as well. The second half of that year I spent at Chris Zeeman's new institute, the Maths Research Centre, at the University of Warwick in Coventry, UK. Most of the dynamics gang reconvened there, in a sort of wake for our failing program, and desperate search for new directions, Thom's catastrophe theory leading the way.

In the following years, catastrophe theory fell by the wayside. Dynamical systems theory became known as chaos theory after influential articles by Robert May in 1974, and Li and Yorke in 1975. In the early 1980s, my dynamics picture book, joint with Chris Shaw, became a learning opportunity for scientists in various fields, including the neurosciences. Fred leveraged this work into texts specially tuned for psychology, and these became influential, along with his Society for Chaos Theory and Psychology.

After a short wave of popularity around 1987, chaos theory followed catastrophe theory into the twilight.

Brain Science, Primitive Thoughts

Fred, meanwhile, had created a large lab at the UCLA Brain Science Institute devoted to EEG analysis involving human brains as well as simpler organisms. I was excited by ideas involving large-scale synchronization of electrical and chemical activity. At this early time, around 1971, I identified physical states of the biological neural network with mental states and thoughts, and tried to apply ideas of chaos and catastrophe theories to these states.

Besides Fred's influence in the early 1970s I had made the acquaintance of Walter Freeman, who had arrived in Berkeley in 1959. Computer graphic technology became available at UCSC in 1974. With this new technology I created images and animations of chaotic behavior for my classes, and for science conferences in the US and Europe. Dan Sunday, a mathematician with computer graphic skills, came to Santa Cruz to work with me, and then moved on to Berkeley to work with Walter. Together they made computer graphic animations of Walter's EEG data showing waves of electrical activity on the olfactory cortex of cats or rabbits, which were very stimulating to my fantasies of chaotic dynamics in neural networks. These would be around 1980 I believe.

Mind Philosophy, Some Experiments and Fantasies

After teaching catastrophe theory in Amsterdam, 1971-72, I spent the rest of 1972 in India. There, through experiments with LSD and meditation in the Himalayan ambiance of the guru Neem Karoli Baba, I began to think of the mind as distinct from the brain, but still behaving as a complex dynamical system. These ideas followed from my studies of Sanskrit literature such as *Yoga Vasistha* and other classics of Vedanta which were provided by Neem Karoli's ashram. The ideas in this tradition included dynamical metaphors such as vibration and resonance, that I later found fully expressed in Kashmiri Shaivism.

As I followed the evolving ideas of Walter Freeman and his joint work with Christine Skarda in the 1980s, I felt there was a convergence of chaos theory and mind philosophy that epitomized the potential benefit of mathematics to science and philosophy.

Conclusion

If I am correct in this thinking, then the courageous use of chaos theory by Fred and Walter are precious examples of the best of applied math. Hopefully these developments will continue in future, to advance the life sciences, to inspire young scientists to follow new mathematical discoveries, and to apply them creatively in their work.

PART 1
PHYSICAL MODELS
1972-1982

Chapter 4
Psychotronic Vibrations

Abstract

A scientific model for parapsychological phenomena is proposed, based on vibrations of the psychotronic field, coupled to biochemical oscillations in living material.

Publication

Ms #14, written 1973. Originally published in the *Proceedings of the First Intl. Congress of Psychotronics and Parapsychology*, Prague, 1973.

Contents

Introduction
A Mathematical Scheme for Kymatics
Biokymatics
Psychokymatics
Parapsychology

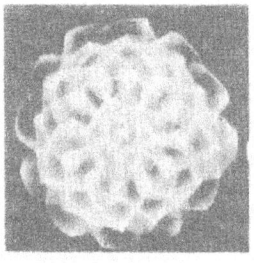 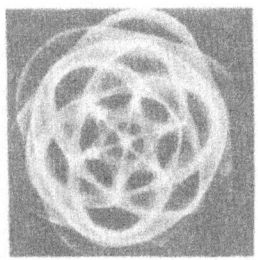 

Introduction

Vibratory mechanisms for material phenomena, especially the evolution of form in living material (biological morphogenesis) and its interaction with the physical universe, was proposed in the Rg Veda, and has fascinated scientists ever since — Pythagoras, Aristotle, and Goethe for example. Now called kymatics (also cymatics,) this circle of ideas has been given a firm mathematical foundation in the revolutionary work of Alan Turing (1954) and René Thom (1966). Recent results in biological morphogenesis reveal specific vibratory (biokymatic) mechanisms in embryology, plant growth (phyllotaxis), social amoebas (chemotaxis), insect swarms (ecotaxis), colored dappling of plants, animals, oyster shells, fingerprint patterns, and many others. Here I propose similar mechanisms for mental functions such as memory and perception (psychokymatics), and speculate on the role of psychotronic vibrations in parapsychology. I am grateful to Neem Karoli Baba, René Thom, Hans Jenny, Dick Bierman, Emilia Hazelip, and Fred Abraham for many discussions, and Hans Jenny for the photographs.

A Mathematical Scheme for Kymatics

This section is for mathematicians, and can be omitted

harmlessly. A simple geometric formalism, suggested by the ideas of Thom, Ruelle, and Takens, may be visualized as follows. Let S denote the spatial domain of the process, of dimension three or less. Let T be the temporal domain, a line. And let V be the space of possible vibrations of the process, an infinite-dimensional space in general. Imagine the product space $S \times T \times V$ as a simple triaxial scheme, with S and T as horizontal axes, and V as the vertical axis. Over each "event", or point (s, t) in $S \times T$, record all vibratory states of the process at that point by marking the appropriate point in the triaxial scheme, $(s, t, v(s, t))$. After recording all the states at all events, the vibratory history of the process represents the graph of a function (possibly multivalued) from $S \times T$ to V. If variation of the event (s, t) causes a discontinuity, or radical change, in the vibratory state $v(s, t)$, then (s, t) is called a *catastrophe point* of the process. The *catastrophe set* is the set of all catastrophic points in $S \times T$ and may be visualized as a family of curved planes of dislocation, or faults, in the space-time domain. The noncatastrophic points are divided by these faults into various connected pieces, each characterized by a single mode of vibration. These pieces are the space-time domains of irreducible units of the vibratory process, and in various contexts are called wave-packets, chreodes, particles, crystals, psychotrons, and so on. In general, I will call them *crystals*, and think of a crystalline structure produced in the space-time domain by the vibratory process.

 Another basic concept of the kymatic scheme is synchronicity. When two crystals, although separated in space-time, exhibit the same vibratory mode, they are called *synchronous crystals*. In physical systems, synchronicity is usually produced by an external coupling of two separated vibratory processes, each represented by a single crystal. Resonance produces essentially identical vibratory modes in

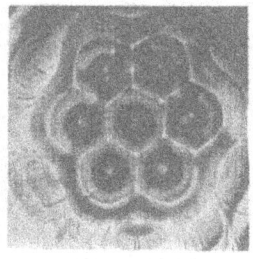 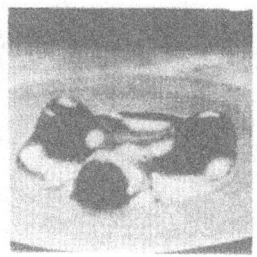 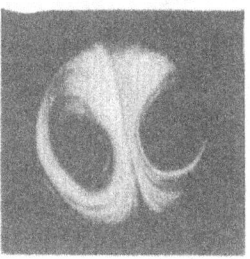

each vibrator. Most physical vibrators are extremely sensitive to very weak coupling to another vibrator.

Biokymatics

By *mechanical vibrator* I mean a physical material — gas, liquid, liquid crystal, or solid — in a state of vibration, or periodic flow. A chemical vibrator is a mixture of diffusing chemical reagents, in a state of periodic reaction. An electromagnetic vibrator is a periodic wave-form of the electromagnetic field. Coupling between chemical and mechanical vibrations in the same medium takes place when hydrodynamic flow combines with diffusion to transport the reagents. Coupling between mechanic and electromagnetic vibrations occurs if the physical medium is charged (plasma), a conductor (magnetohydrodynamics), or molecularly electroactive (solid or liquid crystals). Coupling between chemical and electromagnetic vibrators occurs by ion transport, for example.

A fully coupled mechanical, chemical, and electromagnetic vibratory process is characteristic of biological materials and life processes, so I call this a *biochemical oscillation*. Many such vibratory processes have been photographed in laboratories, and reveal highly symmetric and beautiful space-time waveforms, or biochemical crystals, recalling the morphology of many biological forms. This is the basis of the biokymatic theory of pattern formation of Turing and his successors.

Psychokymatics

To date, most psychobiological theories of mental function, both local and non local, are connectionist; that is, they involve only the neural network. Here I am speculating that a thought, or memory (engram), is a biochemical crystal in the brain body, and the neural network functions mainly as a metabolic energizer for the maintenance of the biochemical oscillation and a coupling device to other vibrators in the organism, such as the muscles and organs of perception. Similarly, I propose that perception is a resonance phenomenon between the brain and external vibrators. The skin, eyeball, and cochlea are intermediate vibratory transformers. Electromagnetic registration and chemical disturbance of neural activity give some support to this idea. There is little doubt that biochemical crystals exist in the brain body, but it is not yet established whether these are functionally significant, or epiphenomena.

Parapsychology

If we accept, for the moment, the psychokymatik hypothesis — a thought is a coupled mechanical, chemical, and electromagnetic wave-form in the brain body — then the resonance phenomena of coupled vibrations immediately provides us a mechanism for many parapsychological phenomena of short distance by electromagnetic coupling, without invoking the existence of a psychotronic field. But if we suppose, in addition, that the psychotronic field exists, supports vibratory activity, and is coupled to biochemical oscillations by some unknown mechanism, then the combined psychobiochemical crystals in living material, and especially the brain, provide mechanisms for all parapsychological phenomena. Especially, cosmobiology, psychometry, primary perception in plants, telepathy, and clairvoyance are easily understood as crystal resonance phenomena. Rather than detail these models, I would like to end with a plea for more experimental data. Oscillatory mechanisms have largely been ignored in psychotronic research. It would seem valuable, in all experiments involving electromagnetic registration, to monitor the power spectrum in the principal range of biochemical frequencies, 0 to 200,000 cycles per second, using techniques such as those of Volkers and Candib.

Chapter 5
Vibrations and the Realization of Form

Universal Form and Harmony were born of Cosmic Will, and thence was Night born, and thence the billowy ocean of Space; and from the billowy ocean of space was born Time — the year ordaining days and nights, the ruler of every movement.
 — *Rig Veda X 190*

Abstract

Application of vibration theory to mental fields.

Publication

Ms #15, written 1975. Published in *Evolution and Consciousness: Human Systems in Transition*, Erich Jantsch, Conrad H. Waddington (eds.) 1976; pp. 134-149.

Contents

1. Introduction to Macrodynamics
    Simple Macrons
    Complex Systems of Macrons
    Geometry of Macrons
    Techniques of Macroscopy
2. Applications to Morphogenesis
    Cosmology
    Geology
    Biology and Neurophysiology
    Noology
3. Conclusion
Acknowledgments

1. Introduction to Macrodynamics

Macrodynamics is a synonym for kymatics. My preference for Anthony's (1969) nomenclature over Jenny's (1967) is just personal taste. If any of this part seems too technical, skip directly to Section 2.

Morphogenesis, the evolution of form from chaos, has a high priority in the philosophical literature of many cultures: the *Rig Veda*, *I Ching*, Heraclitus, Cabala, and others. Up to this very volume, phenomenological descriptions of morphogenesis in various spheres abound in our literature. On the other hand, *morphodynamics* — the study of the mechanics of morphogenetic processes in the context of hard science — is just beginning. It has been born of two recent developments: a suitable mathematical foundation, the theory of catastrophes of René Thom (1973), and an adequate observational tool, the macroscope of Hans Jenny (1967, 1972). Here, then, is a very concise introduction to experimental morphodynamics, including a preliminary report on our own macron observations through the first color macroscope. This chapter is dedicated to Neem Karoli Baba, late of Uttar Pradesh.

72 Vibrations and Forms

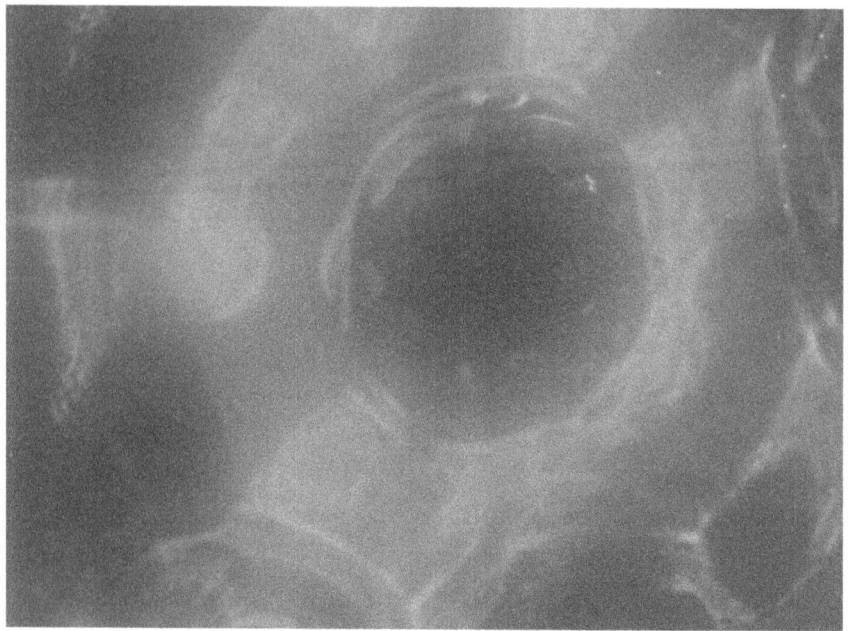

Figure. An elastic macron.

A typical elastic macron, as seen with the macroscope of the University of California at Santa Cruz. This is 175 H_z in a thin layer of glycerol. The original color image is shown on the back cover.

Simple Macrons

Macrodynamic processes in nature take place in hierarchical systems of compound (heterogeneous) macron organisms. To understand these processes, we try to dissect them into fictitious categories of simple (homogeneous) macrons. The three basic categories are physical (P); chemical (C); and electrical (E). The physical macrons are further subdivided according to the material state of the macron medium: solid (PS), isotropic liquid (PL), liquid crystal (PX), and gas (PG). Here we discuss examples of these six types.

Physical Solid (PS): A flat plate is vibrated transversally by an external force, usually electromechanical transducers coupled either directly or through an intermediate fluid. A stable aspect of the system is a spiderweb of motionless curves, the Chladni nodal lines, originally observed by sprinkling sand on the plate. The complete vibration pattern of the plate is best revealed by laser interferometry. This pattern is the *macron* in this example. It depends upon control parameters of two types: *intrinsic controls*, such as dimensions and elasticity of the medium; and *extrinsic controls*, such as frequency and amplitude of the driving force. Of course, this example is very special, as the medium is more or less two-dimensional. For a generic example in this category, consider a rubber ball in place of the thin plate. Stable modes of vibration are characterized by symmetric distortions of shape, separated by motionless nodal surfaces. If the medium is magnetic or piezoelectric, driving forces may be applied directly with electromagnetic fields.

Physical Isotropic Liquid (PL): Beginning once again with a two-dimensional approximation, suppose a round dish is filled with a thin layer of isotropic liquid, and the bottom of the dish is heated. Soon the liquid will begin to *simmer*.

Careful observation will reveal a spiderweb of nodal lines (actually, parallel lines — *rolls* and packed hexagons called *Bénard cells* — are combined in patterns), within which the liquid convects toroidally (up at the boundary of the cell, down in the center).

This *Bénard phenomenon* is a macron. Another type is observed by vibrating the bottom of the dish in a (PL) macron. As the amplitude is gradually increased, the liquid layer first behaves as a solid — the *elastic macron*; then, after a certain critical amplitude is reached, the *simmering point*, a convection or Bénard-type simmering fluid flow begins — the *hydrodynamic macron*. The macrons, or stable modes, depend on intrinsic controls such as shape, compressibility, and viscosity; and external controls such as frequency and amplitude of the driving force. In the general case of a thick layer of liquid, the elastic and hydrodynamic macrons are three-dimensional generalizations of these effects. But there occurs at least one effect of a different type. If the dish is rotated or the liquid is stirred, there may arise toroidal partitions, within which a ring of fluid — a *Taylor cell* — flows spirally. These rings are also seen when a drop of fluid enters another mass of fluid, as in smoke rings. Hierarchical repetition of Taylor cells may be observed by dripping ink into a glass of very still water. The *Von Karman vortex street* also belongs to this class.

Finally, we include in this category *isotropic powder*, that is, dust made of spherical solid particles of identical size. Jenny (1967, 1972) has produced Bénard cells in powders of moss spores.

Physical Liquid Crystal (PX): If the medium is in a liquid crystal metaphase, any macrons of elastic or hydrodynamical type may be induced in it. But two additional phenomena have been observed which are peculiar to this phase, and other simple macrons will undoubtedly be discovered which belong especially to this category. If a thin layer of fluid is exposed to a transverse electrostatic field, simmering is induced in approximately hexagonal cells — the *Williams effect*. Presumably, an elastic macron is induced below the simmer point. In an oscillating electromagnetic field, piezoelectric waves are induced — the *flexoelectric effect*. In this category we might also include *anisotropic powder* — dust of identical aspheric solid particles.

Physical Gaseous (PG): In gases, we observe the macrons of isotropic liquid, as well as (presumably) additional pattern mechanisms belonging specifically to this category. Perhaps these gaseous macrons are unique combinations of elastic and hydrodynamical macrons of the (PL) category, possible in this context because of the high compressibility and low viscosity of the usual gases. The enormous dimensions of these macrons make them hard to observe, and at present it is not known whether or not exclusively gaseous macrons exist.

These four classes of macrons compose the category (P) of simple physical macrons. This is the context of most of the research in experimental morphology up to now. The remaining two categories, (C) and (E), are therefore very embryonic at present.

Chemical (C): There are various macrons, or basic pattern phenomena, which are fundamentally chemical in origin. These occur in heterogeneous media, amid chemical reactions. Included are mechanisms of change of state, such as patterns of precipitation, Liesegang rings of crystallization, and opalescences like abalone shell. To this class also belong the classical diffusion patterns as well as the newly discovered patterns of periodic chemical reactions (see Chapter 5 by Prigogine). This is a little-studied category, which will undoubtedly be explored more thoroughly.

Electrical (E): The description of basic electrical macrons is included here for the sake of completeness — in spite of being based almost entirely on speculation — and because of my belief that it will figure vitally in the understanding of the brain and in the engineering of artificial intelligence, sometime in the future.

Consider a heterogeneous medium of smoothly changing physical properties, especially electrical conductivity, and possibly containing sources of charge. This is an *electronic spacework*. An electronic network may be thought of as a spacework with discontinuities, or as a retraction of a spacework onto its skeleton of dimension one. A semiconductor device is an example of a genuinely three-dimensional spacework. However, this concept must be allowed to include matter in all phases, especially charged fluid (plasma, ionized gas, etc). Thus, classical magnetohydrodynamics (MHD) is included in this context.

In an electronic spacework, subject to controlled external electromagnetic fields or to controlled charge exchange with the environment, macrophenomena of categories (P) or (C), as well as other unique phenomena, may be observed. Those macrons occurring uniquely in the context of spaceworks include category (E). For example, the Störmer orbits and Alvén waves of magnetogasdynamics and northern lights are macrons of type (E). As in ionized fluids, rolls comprise transformers, Bénard cells are toroidal inductors, Taylor cells combine linear and toroidal induction, membranes are capacitors, and so forth. It may be expected that an entirely new discipline of engineering could be based upon a full understanding of macrons in specific spaceworks. The idea of a liquid crystal transistor, combining fluid, electronic, and MHD technologies, is not too far-fetched.

Macrons of type (E) will be known better in the future,

when the development of specific MHD machines will make systematic observation possible.

Complex Systems of Macrons

The macrodynamics of a real event is complex in two ways. First, a single organic structure may exhibit a macron in which physical, chemical, and electrical modes are combined. This is especially the case with biological organisms. Second, two distinct structures may be weakly coupled, forming a larger, compound organic unit. Here we discuss compound modes and coupling separately.

Since basic macrons are of three types, (P), (C), and (E), there are only four types of compound macrons: (P-C), (P-E), (C-E), and (P-C-E).

Physical-Chemical (P-C): A typical situation of this type is a mixture of fluid reagents. While a stable pattern of chemical origin exists, an elastic or hydrodynamic macron is excited. Since convection is faster than diffusion, the hydrodynamic macron dominates the patterns of reagent concentration and reaction rate. For example, Lew Howard and Nancy Kopell (1976) observed Bénard cells with purple hexagonal boundaries and red central cell bodies in the Zhabotinsky reaction, when the surface of the fluid was cooled by evaporation. The separation of the reagents is accomplished by a *separation mechanism*, which, for this *Howard-Kopell phenomenon*, is undoubtedly centrifugation of the reagents. The separation mechanism is also well illustrated by an analogous experiment carried out by Jenny (1967, 1972): Sand is sprinkled on a vibrating plate; it gravitates, very slowly, to the Chladni nodal lines. These motionless curves outline cells of transverse vibration, each with a center, or nucleus, of maximum motion. Now spore powder is sprinkled on the vibrating plate. This moves to the nuclei, forming small piles of powder at each nucleus. Furthermore, each pile can be seen to roll constantly in a toroidal eddy, exactly as in a Bénard cell. In the latter case, I believe the separation mechanism is differential response of the reagents to flotation in invisible Bénard cells excited in the air over the plate by the vibration.

Physical-Electrical (P-E): As in the previous discussion of basic macrons of type (E), we can only speculate on this case, which is exemplified by *plasma*. The production of a toroidal inductor in a fluid spacework by intentional excitation of a Bénard cell is an example of a compound (P-E) macron. The generation of electromagnetic waves by physical vibration of a cholesteric flexoelectric liquid crystal is another.

Chemical-Electrical (C-E): Spaceworks designed specifically to separate ionized components into a particular spatial pattern could be used to grow semiconductor crystals, specialized lenses, or any frozen, precipitated, or crystallized solid in a given pattern. These media are *electrochemical spaceworks*.

Physical-Chemical-Electrical (P-C-E): Physical macrons in fluid reagent mixtures, including liquid crystal and solid components, some of which are charged or otherwise electroactive, comprise the patterns of living organisms. Embryology provides countless examples. This general case may therefore also be called *bioplasma*.

Whereas in the laboratory, macrons of a pure, basic type can be created, in the real world of phenomena only the general case is found. Suppose now that two single systems of bioplasmic (P-C-E) type are at hand, and their separate stable modes are known. Let these two now be weakly coupled, by physical contact, chemical mixing in small exchanges, interaction through the electromagnetic field, or a combination of these means. The coupled system will now have its own stable modes. How are the combined macrons related to the original separate macrons? This relation, which we call the *algebra of macrons*, is the most intriguing problem of morphology. The classical ideas of resonance, sympathetic vibration, and so on, serve as clues. The experiment of Jenny (1967, 1972), showing the vibrating plate and the overlying air in related macrons (revealed by the eddying piles of powder at the nuclei of the plate macron), gives a more useful example of macron addition.

In fact, there are no pure macrons. In order to study the stable modes of one system, we must couple it to another. Thus, all experiments in morphology are actually examples of coupled macrons, and because the number of organic units in a coupled system of the phenomenal universe is always large, we shall one day be led to a probabilistic, or statistical-mechanical theory of complex macrons for hierarchical systems. However, this is far off at the moment. We have, at present, only a very rudimentary preview of the mathematical theory of basic macrons.

Geometry of Macrons

A full understanding of the mathematical description of macrons would require a knowledge of the theory of dynamical systems up to the current research frontier and beyond. For those who wish to pursue this exciting hobby, the introductory book of Hirsch and Smale (1974) provides a good starting point. For our presentation, we shall require but a single concept of that theory, that of *attractor*, which is easily grasped on an intuitive level.

Suppose that a particular medium is to be studied, for example, a bowl of salty jelly. We have to assume (1) that a suitable mathematical space has been described, called the *phase space*, such that each point in the phase space corresponds to a completely satisfactory description of a configuration, or geometrical posture, of the jelly; and conversely, that each posture of the jelly corresponds to a unique labeling point in the phase space. Therefore, jiggling the jelly defines a curve: a point in the phasespace, moving along a path, Next, we have to assume (2) that the particular experimental situation of the jelly — for example, if it is stirred in a precise way — is described by a *dynamical system* in the phase space. This is a mathematical structure with the following properties:

(a) The phase space is divided into a number of different zones, called *basins of attraction*.
(b) In each basin there is a distinguished set, its *attractor*, which is a sort of atomic, or basic, representation of a dynamical system.
(c) If the jelly, in the chosen experimental situation, is set going in any original state, its corresponding curve or successive states in the phase space will proceed in a unique fashion toward a final equilibrium motion near the attractor of the basin in which the curve started.

If we ignore here the nonequilibrium states — which is justified for structures for which the approach to equilibrium is very swift — then all we need to know about dynamical systems is their attractors, which is excellent, because all dynamical systems may then be represented by the same types of "atomic" attractors, in different "molecular" clusters. Further, these common attractors are classified by a system which begins with a simple sequence, starting with the simplest. Here are the first three attractors in this sequence:

1. A single point, corresponding to static equilibrium — the jelly ceases to jiggle, or dies;
2. a circle, with a parameter, corresponding to a cyclic repetition of states, an oscillation in the jelly with a single period, or frequency;
3. a two-dimensional torus, with a curve spiraling indefinitely around it, as in toroidal inductors — corresponding to an *almost periodic motion*, a compound oscillation with two independent frequencies, irrationally related.

This sequence continues with tori of increasing dimension and more complicated compound oscillations, until very chaotic motions are included. The full description of this list of attractors is, in my view, one of the great achievements of mathematics in the twentieth century.

This completes our excursion into dynamical systems theory, and its concept of attractor. By now, the intention of this excursion is probably clear: *the mathematical description of a macron is an attractor*. In itself, this does not help us much to understand macrodynamics or morphogenesis. It is actually the theory of *transitions of attractors*, or *catastrophes*, as developed by René Thom (1973), which is the basis for the geometry of macrons, as it has developed so far.

Here is the concept of catastrophe, as used in dynamical systems theory.

Returning to our original experimental situation, we have supposed that the medium of the experiment — salty jelly (or an economy, an electronic black box, or whatever) — is described by a phase space; and that the specific experimental situation — comprising the fixed values of the various intrinsic and extrinsic control parameters — is described by a particular dynamical system, with its molecular cluster of basins and attractors. It follows, then, that changing the values of the controls will change the dynamical system, the basins, and the attractors, which correspond to observable states, or macrons. Thus, as the controls are smoothly changed, the attractor under observation must be expected to change. But the attractors belong to a discrete list, and can only change in jerks. These are the catastrophes and they may be considered as boundaries of particles, providing a mathematical (nonlinear spectral theory) version of particle-wave duality. In fact, an esoteric quantum field theory based on this analogy has been suggested by Thom, and may one day be developed.

Dynamical systems theory provides us, in addition to the classification of attractors — point, circle, torus, and so forth — with a classification (not yet complete) of catastrophes, or allowable (i.e., generic) transitions of attractors. This classification also begins with a discrete list of increasingly complex phenomena. We end this mathematical aside with a description of the two simplest types of catastrophes: the *leap* and the *wobble*.

Suppose the system is observed in a certain macron (attractor) and the control parameters are gradually changed. The macron is gradually distorted, but undergoes no definite change of type. Suddenly, at a critical value of the controls, it changes instantaneously into a completely different macron. This is a leap. In the simplest case, it is a point (steady-state) attractor which leaps. The steady state suddenly changes to a radically different steady state. For example, the onset of Taylor cells in rotating fluids is a leap catastrophe.

The wobble is a subtle catastrophe, almost unnoticeable. In the simplest case, called *Hopf excitation*, a point attractor changes into a circular attractor, as the control parameters are changed through a critical value. At first, the circle is very small, corresponding to a *wobble* or oscillation of very small amplitude. As the controls continue to change, the circle (and wobble) grows until the oscillation becomes noticeable. For example, the fluttering of the boundaries of Taylor cells in rotating fluids is an example of a wobble catastrophe.

It is possible to organize all the attractors and catastrophes, referring to a given experiment with controls, in a single geometric model. This is called the *logos*. The structure of these models, the *geometry of macrons*, is the triumph of Thom's theory of catastrophes. Unfortunately, it is unapproachable without technicalities. In an experimental situation, however, it is possible to construct a map of the logos more or less empirically by exploration. The confusing feature is a kind of *hysteresis*: the observed state, for a given control setting, may depend on the direction of approach to that control setting. For each control value (such as rate of stirring of the salty jelly) many attractors may exist. The geometry of macrons can be a great help to the experimenter at this point. This will become clearer in the context of the example discussed in the next section.

For those who would like to know more of macron geometry, the basic references are included in the bibliography. My *Introduction to Morphology* (R. Abraham, 1972) includes some helpful illustrations. *Warning*: The classical literature of catastrophe theory (Thom, 1973, and Zeeman, 1971) assumes that the phase space is finite dimensional. This is not the case in macron theory. The extension to the infinite-dimensional case, technically very difficult and not completely satisfactory, is discussed by Ruelle and Takens (1971) and by Marsden and McCracken (1976).

Techniques of Macroscopy

The study of macrodynamics must be founded on the

observation of basic macrons of types (P), (C), and (E), and their coupling behavior. Here we describe the construction and operation of the *macroscope*, a universal tool for the observation of transparent macrons of physical (P) types based upon prototype instruments built by von Békésy (1960), Jenny (1967), Schwenk, Settles (1971), and others.

The instrument combines five units (see Figure 6.1): (1) a color schlieren-optical system of Settles-Toeplitz type, with a four-inch field of view, terminating in a rear-projection screen; (2) a transparent vibrating dish, driven by a high-fidelity loudspeaker outside the field of view; (3) a sine-wave generator, controllable in the rectangle 0-1000 Hertz by 0-15 watts; (4) a control rectangle monitor, including a cathode-ray tube and two digital meters; and (5) a xenon arc lamp, capable

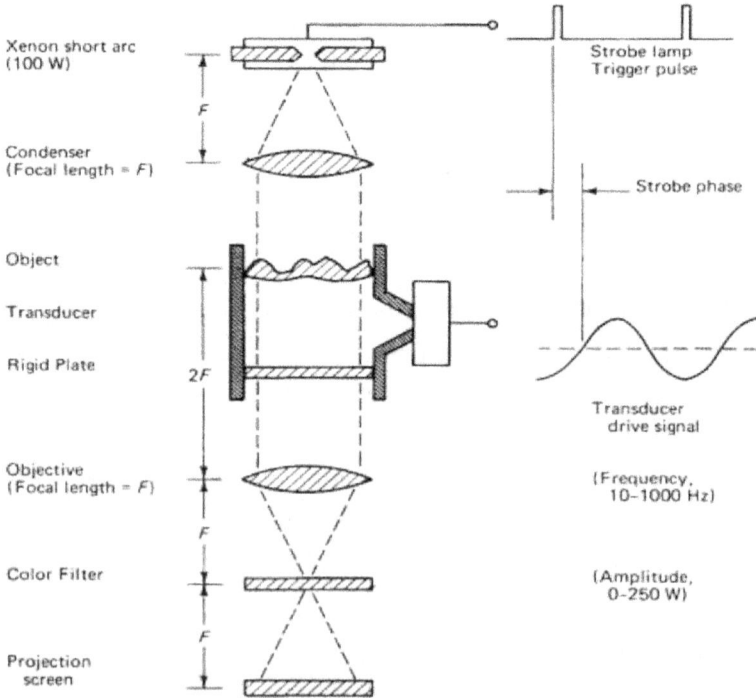

FIGURE 6.1. Schematic view of the four-inch macroscope of the University of California, Santa Cruz. (Diameter, 4 in.; F, 48 in.)

of microsecond flashes up to 1000 Hertz at 100 watts average power, triggered by (i.e., synchronous with) the sine-wave generator, with adjustable phase lag.

In operation, the fluid or elastic medium (which must be perfectly transparent) is placed in the transparent dish. The instrument is switched on, and the experimenter steers the control parameter around the rectangle with two knobs, while watching the colored image on the screen. Leap and wobble catastrophes are readily observed, and can be plotted on the face of the CRT control monitor with a wax crayon. The geometry of the logos is easily discovered by exploration. The exploration of different media indicates the effect of the intrinsic control parameters; for example, physical dimensions and viscosity, upon the logos.

But what is the relationship between the colored image on the screen, the physical macron within the medium, and the mathematical attractor which describes it? Theoretically, the physical parameter represented on the screen is the *horizontal gradient vectorfield of the index of refraction of the medium, expressed in polar coordinates of color and intensity.* In practice, interpretation in macroscopy, as in radiology, is learned by experience. Two separate causes of coloring must be distinguished: deformation of the surface of the medium (lenticulation) and pressure waves within it (pressurization). Normally, two separate images are superimposed on the screen, the λ-image (due to lenticulation) and the π-image (due to pressurization). Fluid flow within the medium is not revealed, but can be observed directly by the usual technique: dusting the medium with aluminum powder. Also, rapid Bénard cells (boiling) cause concentric rings in the λ-image, and discs in the π-image.

The image, with the control parameters left fixed, is usually moving. In fact, it is full of fast action (e.g., like boiling) and also presents a slow progression through different forms. The slow motion repeats itself periodically. This is a toroidal attractor. Counting the dimensions of the torus strains the human space-time pattern recognition facility, and justifies the warning of Anthony (1969) that macroscopy causes brain damage. But when the driving signal is very small, the image may be still. This does not mean that the macron is a point attractor (stable equilibrium), because the illumination is stroboscopic, and stops all periodic motion at the driving frequency. At this point, the phase between the driving signal and the arc lamp must be adjusted through a full cycle to determine whether the macron is a point or circle attractor.

Macroscopy is impossible to describe verbally or photographically. Color cinematography and videotape are the appropriate media for registration of experimental data in this field, and in experimental morphodynamics in general. Moreover, by using your imagination freely, you may think of countless experiments to do with a macroscope, the results to be stored on videotape. Also, many different macroscopic devices are feasible, including one under development at present, in which video equipment itself is used as an analogue device to generate macrons and catastrophes.

2. Applications to Morphogenesis

A long series of applications of catastrophe theory to morphogenesis already exists, thanks to the inspired works of Thom (1973) and Zeeman (1971); see also Isnard and Zeeman (1975). The majority of these applications belongs to static theory and shows that the geometry of point macrons alone is adequate to model a fantastic variety of morphological phenomena in the real world. Therefore, in this section, I shall give a selection of sample applications which are essentially nonstatic, or vibratory, in nature. These are from the traditional four levels of the phenomenal universe.

Cosmology

There is not much to say on this level beyond the basic observation of Jenny (1967, 1972): sand patterns on vibrating plates are analogous to galactic patterns of stellar material. If this analogy is pursued further, there arises a classical conundrum: What cosmic driving force corresponds to the plate, and how is it coupled to the galactic dust? This is the basic problem of the priority of the *word* in the philosophy of the Cabala, or the *tapas* of the *Rig Veda*, which I have transliterated as Cosmic Will in the preface. In any case, it is beyond mathematics, I think.

Geology

Here I can cite a few sample applications from each of the three basic planetary spheres. Regarding the morphogenesis of the *geosphere*, a basic morphogenetic situation is presented by the condensing sequence of gaseous, liquid, and solid phases, which could be studied in the macroscope. I suppose the conservation of the vorticity inherited from the initial motion of the cosmic material determines a certain macron in the sphere of mixed phases, combining elastic lenticulation of the crust determining the location of continents, floating mountain ranges, ocean basins, and perhaps a network of global rifts along the nodal surfaces with Bénard cells of convection in the hotter liquid core. These cells may be the driving force of continental drifts and earthquakes.

In the *hydrosphere*, I suspect that global ocean currents are toroids of the Taylor cell type. Local temperature gradients must produce Bénard cells, some of which may be very stable. Perhaps these are responsible for sculpting the conical projections of the ocean floor. On a smaller scale, Bénard cells are obviously responsible for the honeycomb patterns on the bottoms of icebergs observed by the Jacques Cousteau group.

Macrons in the *atmosphere* are manifest in the wind patterns of the weather map. Bénard cells cause honeycombs in sand dunes and sun cups on glaciers. It is not unlikely that the prevailing westerly winds contain Taylor cells girdling the equator. Hydrodynamical macrons around spinning spheres probably deserve closer study. The macroscope is an ideal tool for such practical investigations.

Biology and Neurophysiology

Much has been written on biological morphogenesis (see Waddington, 1968-1972) and undoubtedly there is much more to come. The book of D'Arcy Thompson (1945) has become a modem classic. Comparison of the nature drawings of Haeckel (1974), or of the photographs of Strache, with the macrophotos of Jenny (1967, 1972) is very suggestive. Turing's (1952) revolutionary article on phylotaxis was perhaps the starting point of modern mathematical morphogenesis. The mechanisms of chemotaxis and ecotaxis are active areas of research. Macrodynamic explanations of nongenetic heredity, orgasm, telepathy, and many other phenomena are easily proposed. I shall confine myself here to two applications which are the subject of current empirical study: the ear and the brain.

The process of audition is more or less understood, except for the mechanical to neural transducer, the cochlea. This is a closed vessel of fluid (perilymph) with a mechanical input piston on one end, and a very complex pressure-sensitive organ stretched within the fluid and comprising a flexion sensor (organ of Corti) embedded in a jelly (endolymph) bound by two membranes (Reissner and basilar). Obviously, this is a natural macroscope. Realizing this, von Békésy (1960), the great pioneer of perception research, made a transparent model of the cochlea and looked at the macron produced in the perilymph. He observed an eddy current which, now bearing his name, has dominated speculation on mechanisms of the cochlea ever since. Recently, Inselberg (Inselberg et al., 1975) has suggested that the eddy of von Békésy is artifactual. On the basis of our macroscope results, it would seem that the elastic macron — which was invisible to von Békésy — is more likely than the simmering macron he saw to be the mechanism of hearing. This question is the subject of current research.

We shall now consider the brain from the macron point of view. As a physical object, it is apparently a bioplasmic spacework with hierarchical structure. Its very physical structure suggests an elastic macron with clearly defined nodal surfaces. Its various segments support compound physical (elastic), chemical, and electrical macrons — which are coupled through the dendritic surface. So far, there has been no discussion of a functional role for the elastic vibrations of the brain body. But from the macrodynamic point of view, the elastic behavior is coupled to the electrochemical state through known plasma mechanisms, and probably also through liquid crystal (flexoelectric) mechanisms as well, so the possibility of a functional role cannot be ignored. In any case, what can be said at this stage is just a conjecture: *a thought is a macron of the brain bioplasma.* This suggests a physical mechanism for a holistic approach to brain function. For example, the transfer from short-term to long-term memory might be explained as follows: A short-term memory is a brain-body macron, metabolized (or driven) by the neural network. This macron maintains a spatial pattern of various biochemical and ionic particles, as in the Howard-Kopell phenomenon. As this pattern is maintained through repeated neural activation of the macron (thought), some molecules within this pattern become attached to membranes and thus immobilized. This physical realization of the engram (macron) pattern is the long-term memory. Recall is effected by a macron resonance phenomenon; and so forth.

The juxtaposition of these two examples of macrodynamic processes, hearing and thinking, suggests that the whole information-processing chain can be interpreted as a flow of macrons extending, through coupling, across different media. This idea has been carried to extremes by Thom (1973), in his psycholinguistic theory.

The morphodynamic conjecture for brain function is not about to be established by any current research program. Yet there is some work on electrical macrons in the dendritic surface — that is, spatial patterns of EEG potentials. Various results (F. Abraham, 1973; Adey, 1974; Brazier, 1969; Freeman, 1975) suggest that brain macrons have functional roles. As a last laugh, we propose that the classical salty jelly experiment of Kennedy (1961), supposedly ridiculous, has serious implications.

Noology

Probably the macrodynamic brain theory has eliminated all but the most credulous readers. If there are any survivors, we may as well dispose of them now by discussing the macrodynamics of consciousness. Actually, this is not impossible, as there exists a (quantum) mechanical theory of consciousness, thanks to Walker (1970), which admits of a macrodynamic formulation. However, let us ignore the question of mechanism. Suppose a human being can be identified with a conscious unit, a particle in the noosphere. Suppose, furthermore, that these macrodynamic units are coupled by communication, a macron resonance phenomenon, as described in the brain speculation. Then, the noosphere may be described as a complex system of macrons. Actually, this idea can be formalized mathematically, so that an archetype in the collective unconscious becomes a stable elastic vibratory state of the noosphere (the Big Salty Jelly in the Sky). This provides macrodynamic mechanisms for astrology, telepathy, clairvoyance, synchronicity, and so forth, as I have proposed in *Psychotronic Vibrations* (R. Abraham, 1973). The existence of a new force, the psychotronic field, is a separate question.

3. Conclusion

In this introduction to macrodynamics and its applications, there is admittedly an inordinate amount of speculation. I regret this sincerely, but as many have discovered, speculation is much faster than experimental work. I must therefore single out especially the hardware projects, described in the section on techniques of macroscopy, as terra firma in this ocean of dreams. And I confess that my goal in these hardware projects, in addition to my own curiosity, is a political one: to stimulate a wave-conscious, morphological orientation in scientific research.

Acknowledgments

My interest in morphology, over the past four years, has been inspired by the ideas of many other dreamers. Here I must acknowledge the most significant of these influences: Hans Jenny and René Thom.

In connection with the construction of the four-inch color macroscope during the past year, we are indebted to the Academic Senate of the University of California at Santa Cruz for financial support, to the technical staff of its Division of Natural Sciences for every kind of moral and material support way beyond duty, and especially to Stephen Furnald and Paul Kramerson, amateur scientists, for donating their time and energy to the task of constructing the macroscope. My thanks to you all.

Chapter 6
The Function of Mathematics in the Evolution of the Noosphere

Abstract

A model for the noosphere is proposed, in the spirit of geometry and dynamics, in which sociodynamics and information flow cause bifurcations, while mathematics is responsible for synthesis. The concordance of the noosphere is embedded in the model, all illustrated by recent events in mathematical physics. Some speculations on the future, including the impact of computers, are presented.

Publication

Ms #20, written in 1980. Published in *The Evolutionary Vision: Toward a Unifying Paradigm of Physical, Biological, and Sociocultural Evolution*, Erich Jantsch (ed.), Westview press 1981; pp. 153-168.

Contents

Bifurcation and Synthesis
Geometric Models of the Noosphere
Concordance
Mathematics and the Natural Sciences:
    An Exemplary Bifurcation
Geometry and Physics:
    An Outstanding Concordance
Dynamics and the Sciences:
    Concordance on a Larger Scale
A Platonic Confession
The Evolutionary Roles of Mathematics and
    Informatics
The Future
Acknowledgments
Notes

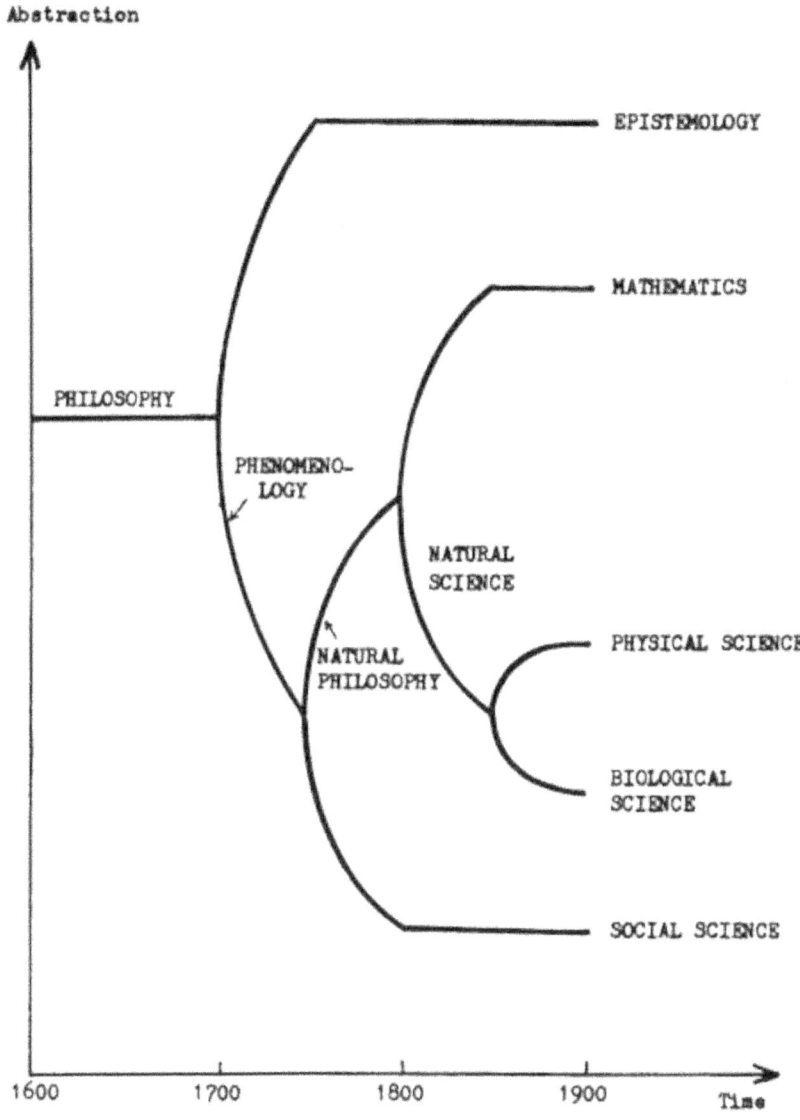

Figure 1. Bifurcation sequence of the noosphere in the 17th, 18th and 19th centuries. The bifurcations shown are "socio-informatic" — they indicate a separation of the scholarly community into subgroups which intercommunicate poorly (or, a reunion of such), as indicated in the text.

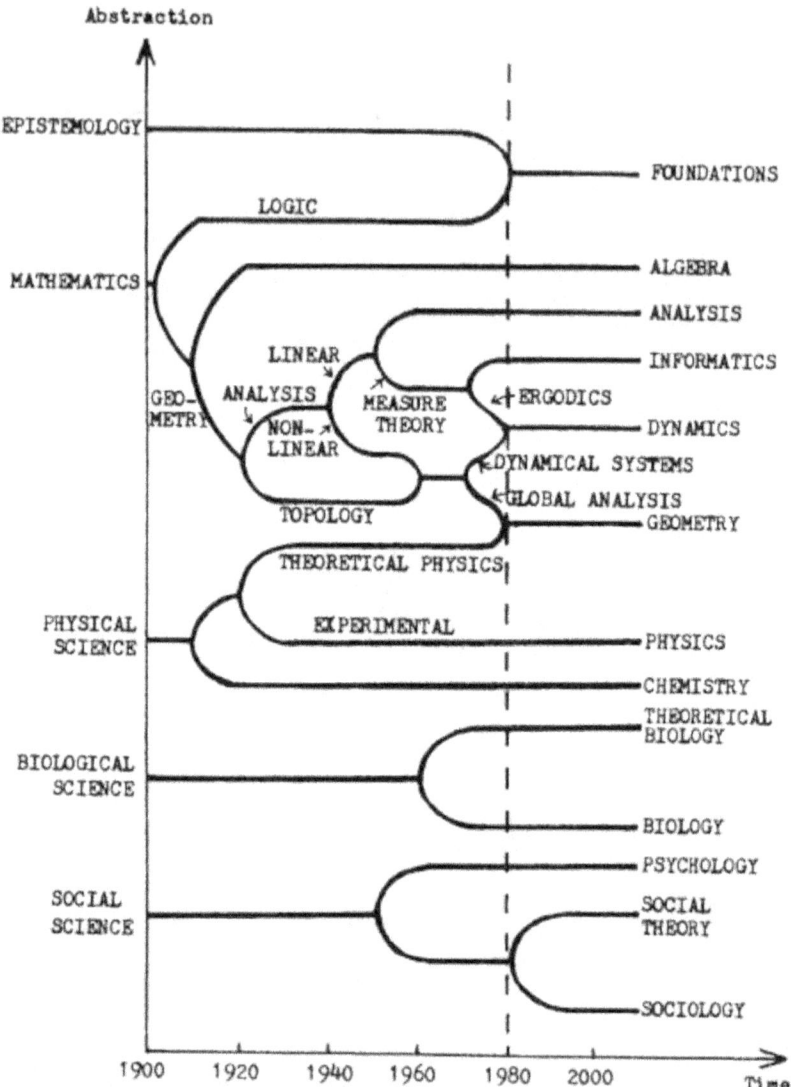

Figure 2. Bifurcation sequence of the noosphere: Philosophy in the 20th century.
Fine structure shown here in the mathematical zone only.

Bifurcation and Synthesis

The world of ideas — evanescent bubble of knowledge, inflated by millenia of human thought, attached to our fragile culture, maintained on paper and in consciousness by words and drawings — is too vast to grok. Our languages scarcely have words for it. So let us call it the *noosphere*, and distinguish it from the world of ideas of Plato — if there may be such a universal store of form, beyond the emergence of knowledge into the consciousness of our planetary society. The noosphere evolves and bifurcates into independent domains, as required by the limited capacity of individual humans for the storage and manipulation of information. (A version of the recent history of the noosphere of our own culture is shown in Figures 1 and 2.) The very dynamics of this process of growth and bifurcation itself evolves, as the culture develops information and communication technology such as printing, photography, electronics — which extends the capacity of the individual servants of the noosphere. Thus it may occur, in the history of knowledge, that independent domains recombine and synthesis occurs.

We may think of bifurcation and synthesis as opposed forces in the evolution of the noosphere, like the masculine and feminine principles of evolutionary dynamics. And our time is one of the domination of the noosphere by the masculine force, in this sense. But the computer revolution currently in progress may extend the information capacity of the servants of knowledge, if they succeed in adapting the emerging technology to this purpose, and thus enhance enormously the forces of synthesis. It may be that the future history of the noosphere, in fact, demands synthesis soon, to avoid dispersion of knowledge into superstition, or the knowledge death of the Egyptian, Chinese, Arabic, and Mayan cultures described by White (1979).

On the other hand, it may be that the rigidity of society will resist the emergence of the feminine principle (synthesis) or that counter-evolutionary forces will monopolize the new technology, and our cultural noosphere is doomed to follow these examples. My own experience as an extreme specialist in the world of ideas, attempting syntheses on a minute scale, has been discouraging. One feels pressures of all sorts, pushing backwards towards the security of specialization, conventional work, easy appreciation. It is thus with the greatest trepidation that I now put forward these trial ideas on evolution, the role of mathematics, the potential of information machines, and the future of our noosphere.

Geometric Models of the Noosphere

We may visualize the world of ideas divided conventionally into subjects, as in a library or university catalogue. Alternatively, we may view the noosphere sociometrically: a "subject" or domain is defined by a group of scholars, and we distinguish subjects as disjoint areas when the scholarly groups defining them intercommunicate poorly. Taking this latter point of view, a portion of the noosphere corresponding to "philosophy" is shown schematically in Fig. 1. As time progresses through the period 1600-1900 (roughly), the subject bifurcates successively into disjoint areas in the sociometric sense. The corresponding schematic diagram for the past century, Fig. 2, reveals numerous syntheses as well as bifurcations. These occur when two specialized groups get interested in each other, learn to intercommunicate, and combine as an informatic organism.

These schematic diagrams are not yet geometric models. We must imagine a representation of the noosphere with more dimensions, within which each "subject" is a surface (of two or more dimensions), and among which the "bifurcations" are such as those of catastrophe theory, or some other classification even more general. For example, the earliest bifurcation of Fig. 1 is represented in Fig. 3 as a cusp catastrophe — see Thom (1972), Zeeman (1977) or Poston

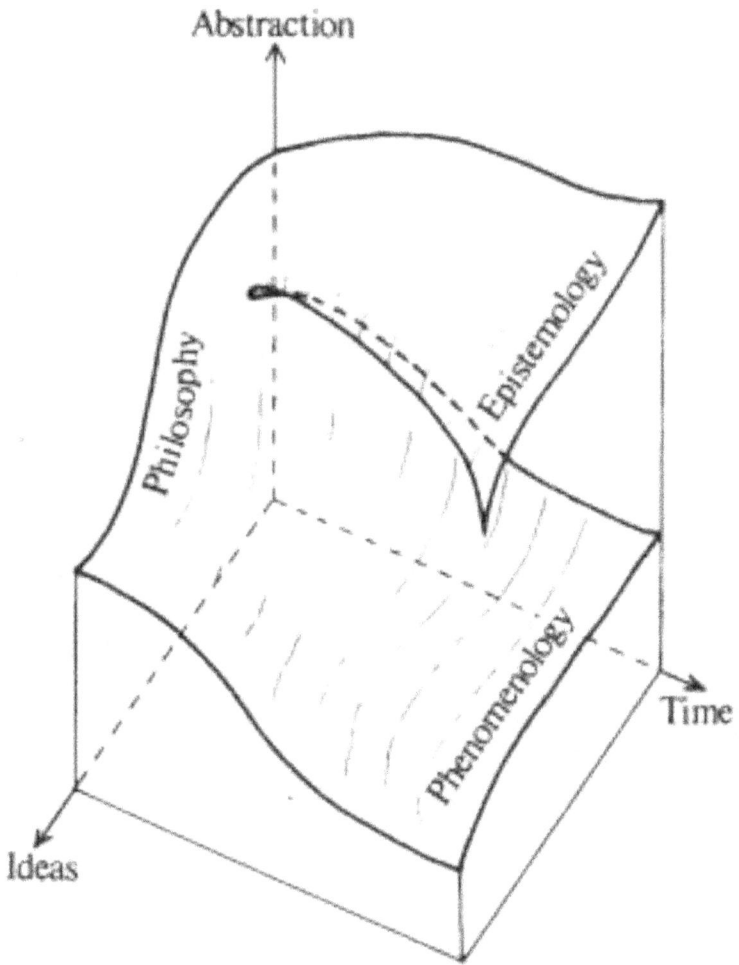

Figure 3. Representation of a bifurcation as a cusp catastrophe.

and Stewart (1978) for the concepts of catastrophe theory. With the whole history of philosophic scholarship represented in such a pictorial scheme, we would have a geometric model of the noosphere.

We proceed now, without an actual geometric model, but as if we had one. Then a small piece of the model, a typical

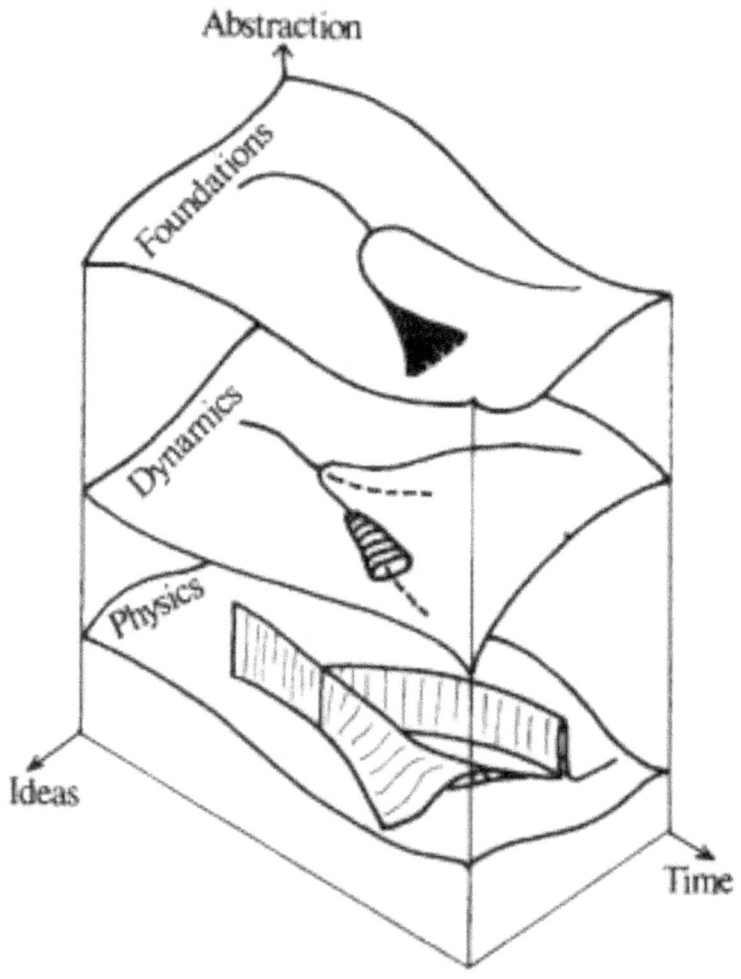

Figure 4. Morphogenesis of data, shown as concordant bifurcations on parallel sheets of the sociodynamic substrate.

piece, would consist simply of a finite stack of surfaces of various dimensions. Such a "neighborhood" of our fictitious geometric model of the noosphere is shown in Fig. 4. Here, parallel small pieces of three "subjects" are depicted as surfaces of dimension two. A local chart of coordinates - abstraction, morphology, and time — is shown. We imagine that, if our geometric model was fully described (as it is not), then these local coordinates would likewise be exactly defined (they are not.) But these vague coordinates are introduced in Fig. 4 just to give intuitive sense to this neighborhood in the world of ideas.

These surfaces represent the evolution in time of a subject defined by intercommunicating groups of scholars. This is the substrate of the information (data, texts) of their scholarly discourse, not the actual content of it. So we further imagine — defined upon these "surfaces" or substrates — some geometric objects which model (no matter how crudely) the informational content of the subject (field, area of knowledge.) And these geometric data structures also evolve in time, so that differentiation and morphogenesis occur on each surface. This morphogenesis of data, on the sociometric substrate of the model of the noosphere, is shown in Fig. 4.

Such a composite picture — bifurcation sequence, geometric representation, and data structures including morphogenesis — is what we mean by a geometric model of the noosphere.

Concordance

We suppose now that a geometric model is at hand, that it bas been determined from the historical record — the libraries of our culture — according to a constructive algorithm, and that the geometric dimensions are at least intuitively meaningful to future historians. If this seems far-fetched, remember that this is done daily by applied mathematicians, at least for very small neighborhoods. For examples, see Poston and Renfrew (1979), or Thompson (1979). What is proposed here is no more than a certain enlargement of scale. Let M denote the substrate of this model — the geometric surfaces without the data.

For the sake of further discussion, we now make a restrictive geometric assumption about this model: the layered structure shown within a small neighborhood in Fig. 4 exists throughout the model. To be more precise, we assume there is a certain "master substrate", or space, S, and a map from the substrate of the model, M, into $S \times R$ (here, R denotes the real numbers)

$$\pi : M \to S \times R$$

The master substrate, S, is an extension of the coordinate called "morphology" in Fig. 4, and the real line, R, represents historical "time." We further suppose that the layers of M are each divided into a finite number of pieces by reasonable boundaries, and that, restricted to any of these pieces P, the map $\pi : P \to S \times R$ is regular (that is, approximately a linear projection locally) onto an open subset of $S \times R$. The map $\pi: M \to S \times R$, together with such an assumption of piecewise regularity, is a *concordance* of the model.

The idea behind our assumption of a concordance is this: we want to relate different descriptions of the phenomenal universe, perceived by the different disciplines, as if these were an objective reality beneath phenomena. Thus, the mathematical, physical, chemical, and biological descriptions of an "event" are imagined to correspond. The concordance of the model, π, represents this correspondence. Thus two different points of the model — m_1 and m_2 in M — which have the same labels assigned by π:

$$\pi(m_1) = \pi(m_2) = \pi(s,t)$$

are supposed to locate data structures describing the same event. We may suppose, in addition, that the data structures of the model are such as to allow comparison at different points. Thus we could say: the data at m_1 are similar to those at m_2, or they are not. How this comparison may be accomplished is very difficult to describe in general. But we have excellent examples in the history of mathematical physics, which we will soon describe.

Mathematics and the Natural Sciences: An Exemplary Bifurcation

Our proposal for a geometric model of the noosphere is not solely a cognitive device. We have in mind a causative dynamics — a sort of force field on the sociometric space to account for the bifurcation and synthesis of "subjects" in the course of time. As viewed here, this is a psychosocial process, due to the migration of interest of scholars, and their capability to communicate with each other. The coupling of intrinsic properties of subject areas with psychological and social factors are involved in the migration, and thus in the dynamics. We now consider, from this point of view, the bifurcation of natural philosophy into mathematics and the sciences.

We must characterize the differences between mathematics and physics from the scholar's point of view. Formerly, one used to say that mathematics is more abstract — a formal (axiomatic) system, its truth absolute and decidable while physics is based on phenomenal reality — a conventional system, its truth relative and empirical. Lately, the emphasis on the empirical process in mathematics, by Lakatos (1976), inclines some to identify mathematics with physics.

This is a sort of materialism, like the identification of mind and body. But from the psychological point of view, the feeling of truth of a mathematical theorem is based on faith in its proofs — its conformity to the formal (logical) system at the foundation of mathematics — which increases with time, as trusted workers check the logical proofs repeatedly, and testify to their completeness and accuracy. This is well described in Manin (1979).

In contrast, the feeling of truth in a physical theory depends upon faith in its tests — its conformity to the phenomenal universe — which increases with time, as trusted workers check the empirical tests repeatedly, obtaining consistent results. In spite of the similarity in these faith mechanisms, there is a difference of polarity. Mathematicians look upward, and physicists downward, for the impression of truth. Thus individuals attracted to natural philosophy will be polarized towards mathematics or the sciences, according to their tendency to believe in inner (upward, logical, mental, personal) or outer (downward, empirical, physical, social) reality. This dynamics polarized the natural philosophers into two parties, Inwards and Outwards. Yet this polarized group of scholars is to be considered a single "subject" in our model for the noosphere, as long as the two kinds are each in mastery of the entire subject. When this ceased to be the case, in the history of our own culture, is difficult to pinpoint in time. In Fig. 1, we have set it rather arbitrarily around 1800CE. In any case, the post-bifurcation subjects are identified with two groups of scholars (mathematicians and scientists) which intercommunicate poorly, and suffer mutual suspicion, jealousy, and competition.

These two subjects eventually provide an excellent example of the sociodynamics of synthesis as well. In Fig. 2, a synthesis between global analysis and theoretical physics is indicated around 1980, that is to say, at the present time. We have seen a decade or two of struggle by individuals within these groups to learn the language of the other group, for pursuit of their own goals. The progress of global analysis, within its own domain, produced simplification to such an extent that its language became learnable by theoretical physicists. Meanwhile, successive generations of theoretical physicists learned bits of global analysis, and rewrote their subject in this language, making it accessible to the mathematicians. As these physicists seek a theory of a mathematical type, the psychological conditions for synthesis are favorable, and so it progresses at present.

Geometry and Physics:
An outstanding Concordance

Now, that the basic concepts of our essay — sociometric domain, bifurcation, and synthesis in the universe of ideas have been illustrated with mathematics and the natural sciences we return to the supplementary notion of concordance.

If two subject areas are actually a single organism in our sense — as, for example, mathematics and natural science (that is, natural philosophy) before the 19th century (see Fig. 1) — one would not be surprised by a correspondence in their morphology. In fact, an inconsistency in the data structures of two parties (such as the Inwards and the Outwards) would undoubtedly produce a bifurcation. However, after a bifurcation, the concordance of two disjoint subjects is a cause of awe, wonder, and the suspicion of miracles, divine works, and Platonic ideas.

Two outstanding examples from the literature of our century are provided by Einstein and Wigner. A century or so after the separation of mathematics and physics (according to the very rough scheme of Fig. 1), the success of general relativity theory as a geometric model for the solar system prompted Einstein (1921) to address the Prussian Academy of science thus:

> At this point, an enigma presents itself, which in all ages has agitated inquiring minds. How can it be that mathematics, being after all a product of human thought which is independent of experience, is so admirably appropriate to the objects of reality? Is human reason then, without experience, merely by taking thought, able to fathom the properties of real things?

And more recently, inspired by the success of group representation theory in modeling elementary particle physics, Wigner (1959) wrote:

> Mathematical concepts turn up in entirely unexpected connections. They often permit an unexpectedly close and accurate description of the phenomena in these connections... It is difficult to avoid the impression that a miracle confronts us here...

These two examples of the successful application of mathematics to physics are outstanding for the independence of the mathematical discoveries (tensor geometry, classification of representations of Lie groups) from the physical data (motion of Mercury, hadron multiplets) and for the precision of the concordance. But we should note that applied mathematics — the art of exploring concordance — had many other success stories in its history, and the high technology of our culture is based upon them. The concordance of geometry and physics continues to grow, for example, with the Ruelle-Takens (1971) model for turbulence.

Dynamics and the Sciences: Concordance on a Larger Scale

As a branch of mathematics, dynamics was born with Newton, launched into prominence a century ago by Poincaré, and became an autonomous subject, in our sense, within the past decade or two — as shown in Fig. 2. The basic concepts of dynamics — attractors (simple and chaotic), basins, separatrices, robustness, and bifurcation — are described, in historical perspective, in Chapter 8 of Abraham and Marsden (1978). An unusual feature of this area is the role played by computing machines, which emerged (along with information science) as a distinct subject in the same period of time (again, see Fig. 2).[1]

This concomitance has polarized the dynamics community, which (unlike other branches of mathematics) has an essential experimental subgroup. Eventually, dynamics may bifurcate into theoretical and experimental camps. For example, one of the central ideas of dynamics is that of a chaotic attractor. This was discovered by experimentalists, but came to the specific notice of the theoreticians only a few years later. In fact, it received explicit attention neither in the influential survey of Smale (1967) nor in the futuristic book of Thom (1972). At present, the polarization of dynamics is not yet a bifurcation, as the two groups intercommunicate well. The information load may soon overwhelm the communication channel, or the storage capacity of individual dynamicists, and create a separation.

We may divide theoretical dynamics into three branches, considering the already extensive and rapidly growing application literature. These are:

- Dynamical systems (DS) theory, dealing with the classification of attractors, the characterization of robustness, and generic dynamical properties, as described in Smale (1967) or Abraham and Marsden (1978).

- Elementary catastrophe (EC) theory, the classification of general bifurcations of static attractors, see Zeeman (1977) or Poston and Stewart (1978).

- Dynamic bifurcation (DB) theory, the classification of generic bifurcation of attractors, outlined in Thom (1972).

These three theories may have the most impressive and extensive concordances in the history of applied mathematics. The lists of "admirably appropriate" applications and "unexpectedly close and accurate descriptions" is extended daily in the rapidly growing literature. By now there are exceptional concordances of:

- DS theory with electronics, game theory, meteorology;

- EC theory with sociology, naval architecture, mechanical engineering, linguistics, optics; and

- DB theory with hydrodynamics and elastodynamics;

to list just a few. The pioneering text of Thom (1972) suggests a very novel correspondence of the metaphors of DB theory with numerous fields. And in fact, we have hinted here at a DB-theoretic model of the noosphere, in which DB theory would model itself, amid all the rest of our evolving knowledge, social structure, and psychohistory.

A Platonic Confession

We acknowledge the incredibility of so vast a concordance in the world of ideas. Some of the early publications of EC applications have been criticized as "wild claims," most notably in the epistomological megalith of Fussbudget and Znarler (1979). We admit a bias in favor of concordance, and moreover toward a Platonic idea reality — an additional sheet in Fig. 4, high above philosophy, hidden from consciousness by clouds, yet pinned through to the fabric of the noosphere by an extensive concordance, as a pattern for life. Yet we come out of this closet — like Plato, Einstein, Gödel and all other revealed believers before us — in full confidence that extreme specialists and conservative informalists in great numbers will confirm the concordance of mathematics and all the sciences beyond question.

This Platonic faith obviates logical difficulties as well. It assumes that the exploration of mathematical reality and the discovery of its secrets by our society are a matter of revelation or creative intuition, as described by Hadamard (1964). The extent of this discovery process, being limited by the structural evolution of the inquiring minds of our times, yields a poor sketch of the terrain, expressed as a formal (logical) system. But the full flavor of Platonic reality is harmonious and consistent beyond the capability of our formal languages.

Thus, the inward faith is essentially unassailable. Yet our view of the *role* of mathematics, in the evolution of our noosphere, inspired by Whitehead (1929), is independent of this bias. The outward view — that concordance grows from roots in phenomenal (ordinary) reality beneath the lowest sheets of the noosphere (as represented in our geometric model, for example, below Fig. 4) and that mathematics results from the abstraction process, applied to human perception of the real world, and carried to extremes — equally admits the growth of a culturally determined, concordant noosphere. In fact, Inward and Outward scholars work side by side, harmoniously, unconscious of their faiths. Tirelessly serving the shared principle of concordance, they jointly erase conflicting data. So it is no wonder that our cultural noosphere is concordant.

When in the future, however, an Alexandrian library might be unearthed by archaeologists, or a Mayan Codex overlooked by Bishop da Landa, or if a UFO were to land at a terminal of the galactic library in the sky, might we not be amazed by an Outwardly inexplicable, cross-cultural concordance? We might look first for the mathematical leaf of the alternative noosphere, seeking a correspondence with our own.

The Evolutionary Roles of Mathematics and Informatics

What is this special role of mathematics in the evolution of cultural noospheres? Mathematics is abstract enough to be central to an extensive concordance and yet precise enough for these to be meaningful, even amazing. Its own morphogenesis,— whether Inward or Outward directed, or a random process — leads the corresponding morphogenesis in scientific domains. In this way, Ricci calculus preceded Einstein relativity, Cartan classification preceded Gell-Mann quarks, and the Lorenz attractor preceded Ruelle-Takens turbulence. But beyond this temporal leadership, in which metaphors emerge into the evolving consciousness of our culture on an abstract level and are mirrored on the more concrete planes a few years later, mathematics serves the feminine principle, synthesis, in a functional way.

As described above, specialization and bifurcation in the world represent an informational defect in the sociodynamics of the scholarly community. The limits of individual information handling capacity mandate the separation of a scholarly group into special subgroups. The subgroups drift apart, from the communication point of view, as the local language of a subgroup expands to fill its vocabulary capacity, thus pushing the vocabulary of the complementary subgroup out of local memory.

Mathematics, as a higher-order language which grows vertically, provides ever more compactification and efficiency in the technical languages it serves. Thus the "chaotic attractor" of mathematics may replace "turbulent, broad spectrum, stochastic, aperiodic, ergodic, noisy" and a host of other concordant concepts of the sciences. The compactification reduces memory requirements, permitting groups to learn some different words of each other's vocabularies.

And the commonality of the mathematical metaphors allows a limited intercourse in a universal language, among all groups knowing some mathematics. Thus, mathematics decreases the informatic distances between scholarly groups at the same time that their intrinsic efforts tend only to increase them.

In fairness, we must admit that the growing role of computing machines, and the associated scholarly domain of information science, share exactly the same evolutionary roles in the future growth of our noosphere. First of all, mathematics itself relies increasingly on machines for proofs, management of literature, and experiments with algebraic, geometric, and dynamical systems. Further, the use of machines by the various disjoint scholarly groups increases their information capacity, and thus their power to intercommunicate. Similarly, the use of machines for communication networks will increase the information capacity of channels interconnecting these groups. And finally, and most importantly, the new concepts of information science, like those of mathematics, are highly compactive and efficient as linguistic elements for scientific use. In fact, we have used some in describing the role of mathematics above.

In both cases, mathematics as well as informatics, we have described qualitative utilitarian roles *in addition* to the obvious quantitative one: computation. So let us note here that computation has played a primary role in the growth of the natural sciences in the past and will remain important in the future, but the qualitative function of conceptual morphogenesis has in both cases, surpassed computation in its evolutionary importance. Thus we have emphasized here qualitative (especially geometric) mathematics, informatics, and machines.

The Future

We have looked at the noosphere from the coarse point of view of sociodynamics, and seen its morphogenesis — including the special role of mathematics and informatics, in promoting syntheses, to balance the inevitable tendency toward fragmentation — in the visual metaphors of dynamics and catastrophe theory. To this picture, a mathematical formulation of "concordance" has been adjoined and we have proposed that a vast concordance of unprecedented scale is presently emerging in our noosphere. This is an occasion of tremendous excitement in the scholarly community. Projecting into the future (if indeed the planetary political reality admits one) we see thus a catastrophic struggle between the masculine principle (fragmentation) and the feminine (synthesis). In our view, the future evolution of our noosphere will be possible only with a balance of these forces. At present, scientific patriarchy (specialization) dominates, and synthesis is oppressed. Thus, to nourish our future, extra fuel should be provided mathematics, informatics, the access of mathematicians to computing machines, the applications of mathematics to all fields, the intercommunication devices such as computer networks and interdisciplinary conferences, and the entry of feminists into the scholarly community. Yet the social climate for this nourishment of synthesis in the noosphere appears cool. The feminine principle in the scholarly world is starving. Perhaps the mathematical-informatical community should take more responsibility in the field of public education and aggressively seek support.

Our idea in this essay on sagacity theory, or psychohistory, is to begin the development of a model for the noosphere, aided by mathematics, with which in the future we may pick up the reins of evolution and choose our own future history.

Acknowledgments

We gratefully acknowledge aid in collecting these ideas from Alan Garfinkel, Terence McKenna, Tim Poston, and Ray Gwyn Smith.

Notes

1 (Stein and Ulam, 1964)

PART 2
SPIRITUAL MODELS
1982-2005

Chapter 7
Dynamic Models for Thought

Abstract

Here, we introduce a complex dynamical model for the brain, and present some trial mechanisms for the abstraction and application of ideas. These, based on the concept of the holonomy of a bifurcation diagram, are intended just to indicate the range of possibilities, not as definitive models.

Dedicated to Aharon Katzir-Katchalsky (1914–1972)

Publication

Ms #25, written November 18, 1981. Published in *J. Social Biol. Struct.*, 1985; pp. 13-26.

Contents

Levels of Abstraction
Interactions Between Levels
The Field Scheme for Organs
The Complex Dynamical Scheme
The Field Scheme for Thoughts
Absolute Programs
Integrative Programs
Holonomy Programs
Abstraction and Application
The Geometric Model
Special Purpose Cells
Conclusion
Acknowledgements
Notes

Levels of Abstraction

In *The function of mathematics in the evolution of the noosphere*[1], we proposed a model for a noosphere, an aggregation of conscious organisms. Here we will retreat one step, and consider a single mind. But as this organism is viewed as an aggregation of organs, the model described here is very similar to those proposed previously.

In our geometric model it is convenient to discretize one preferred dimension — abstraction. This strategy, explicit in classical Sanskrit (Upanishad) philosophy, replaces a model of dimension n by a finite stack of parallel models, say k planes of dimension $(n - 1)$. If $n = 3$, this is like a deck of cards. A more extreme version of this strategy — division of the geometrical model into a finite set of cells — reduces in one step from dimension n to dimension zero. The cellular structure of biological organisms is an important example of the extreme strategy. We will return to this example later. Now, we consider a stack of k parallel planes of dimension $(n - 1)$ as a model for a single conscious mind. Although the dimension must be large for a reasonable model, we will set $n = 3$ here for the sake of visualization. Likewise, the number of planes, to approximate a continuous scale of abstraction, should be large. The Sanskrit philosophers frequently take $k = 7$. Following Plato, we will take $k = 4$. According to Shear (1977), this structure of consciousness coincides with the development stages of Piaget for the growth of consciousness in children. The four levels of Plato's hierarchy are:

G. The Good — universal archetypes;
M. Mathematics — abstract images of archetypes;
S. Science/theories/models — representation of sensory experiences;

P. Phenomena — data of sensory experience of the phenomenal universe.

We would like to embed this hierarchical structure in a dynamical model for the mind, so we choose to use *complex dynamical systems* as the basic unit in constructing the model.[2] We have proposed a model of this type for the mammalian brain, in *Vibrations, the realization of form*.[3] Eventually, our goal in this paper is to study the interaction between two adjacent levels. The model for each level will be based upon a familiar mathematical object; *a simple dynamical scheme*, or in other words, a *dynamical system with controls* (albeit, with a very large number of dimensions). Our theory of interaction would equally well apply to the serially-coupled adjacent levels of any complex dynamical system. But for this exposition, we use Mathematics and Science, levels M and S of Plato's model of the mind.

In summary: We construct a partial model for mind with two levels of abstraction:

Level M: Mathematics.
Level S: Science.

In this model, we study interactions based on two-way communications between levels.

Interactions Between Levels

The movement of information between these two adjacent levels of the model are *abstraction* and *application*. We consider these, one at a time:

Abstraction: information moves from level S to level M in the emergence of an abstract mental image in M, based upon

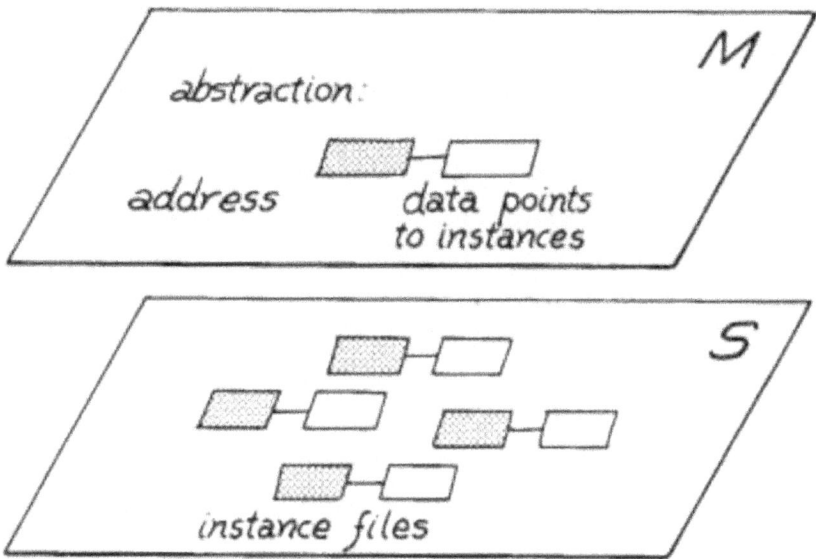

Figure 1. Informatic metaphor for application.

the association, or *aggregation*, of several special cases existing in consciousness on level S.

Application: information moves from level M to level S, through *diffusion* of an abstract image into a region of experiential (or experimental) data to which it can *apply*, or *associate* as shown in Fig. 1.

We may describe these two interactions through metaphors, without an explicit scheme for the representation of an idea in a new physiological model for the mammalian brain. In this section, we describe them in mechanical and informatic metaphors. In a later section we will interpret these metaphors in a specific neurophysiological model.

First, we consider *abstraction*. In the *informatic metaphor*, each instance of a similar theory or model in S may be considered as a *file*, or movable package of information, with a *name*. Actually, the name is a *pointer*, a program which finds the file. The aggregation of these instances into a single concept, or file, on a higher level of abstraction, only requires moving the files into a common *directory*. The directory is just another file, which contains the names of (instructions for finding) the instance files. The structure of this system is a tree of information. The abstraction operation is the creation of a new directory of level M, containing pointers to all the instance files on level S, which still live there. They have not moved.

Although this metaphor for abstraction is reasonable for a hard-wired computing machine, it is obviously inappropriate for a dynamical network like the mammalian brain. We now transform it into a *mechanical metaphor*. We customarily use this metaphor even when thinking about computer systems, because it seems more natural.

In the mechanical metaphor, we think of each instance (model on level S) exhibiting a given concept (model on level M) as a file folder lying on the desk, rather than as software, attached to an immovable physical address. We associate the files into a directory by moving them physically, into a stack. This stack is not the directory, for it still occupies level S. But as the instances are physically associated to a common address, the coordinates of the pile of file folders, we may use this common address on level S as a name for the abstraction. Thus, the directory is a filename (or pointer program) on level M, which points to a physical address on level S, at which all the instances may be found. This is like the subject catalog in a library.

In the informatic metaphor, the process of forming an abstraction consists of making a list on level M of instance addresses on level S. In the *mechanical metaphor*, the process consists of moving the instances around on level S, to a common location, and noting its address on level M.

Next, we will describe the *application* process in both

metaphors. In the informatic metaphor, we suppose we have an abstraction on hand, as a directory on level M, containing the names of instances on level S. These instances are files of information, and the names are programs which find these files. The *application process*, for an old application, requires just recognizing the name of the instance, and running the program to link the abstraction to the instance file. But suppose we want to create a new *application*. We must *recognize* (or guess at) an existing abstraction which the instance exhibits, and then name the instance within the abstraction directory. That is, we must create a program linking the abstraction to the new instance. In the mechanical metaphor, we must recognize the abstraction (the address on level M of a pile of file folders on level S), and then move the new instance onto the pile.

The next few sections will elaborate the informatic metaphor for both processes into a non-local neurophysiological model, and elaborate the mechanical model into a local geometric model. The neurophysiological and the geometric models may be directly related, without the metaphors described above, which are for explanatory purposes only.

The Field Scheme for Organs

A precise model for a mammalian brain, in the context of complex dynamical systems theory or any such discipline, is beyond us at present. What we do have now is an emerging scheme. We have written of this previously[4] as have Kolmogorov *et al.* (1937), Rashevsky (1940), Turing (1952), Rosen (1970), Arbib (1972), Katchalsky and Neumann (1972), Hoffman (1977), Zeeman (1977 : 293), Freeman (1981), and many others. In this section, we review and expand the field scheme described earlier.[5]

We think of a biological organ (for example, the hypothalamus) at once as a three-dimensional continuum of biophysical matter, and as an aggregation of cells. We carry along both of these images simultaneously, as in the wave/particle duality of physics. We suppose that each cell is reasonably well modeled by a simple dynamical scheme (dynamical system with controls). Admittedly, this is an extreme oversimplification. Beginning with an *excitation*, control metabolites (hormones, neuro-transmitters, morphogens, etc.) diffuse and react slowly in this continuum. On a shorter time scale, convection currents within the cells average the momentary concentrations of these control metabolites. On yet a shorter time scale, the cell dynamics move the physiological state of each cell through a brief transient, to the attractor determined by the average control metabolite concentrations, the states of neighboring cells, and its initial condition (previous attractor) at the time of excitation.[6]

There may be different types of cells interspersed and matted in the aggregation.[7] Even though this may be essential for our scheme, we will suppose now, to simplify the discussion, that they are all of one sort. (This might be justifiable in the case of slime mold, or the liver.) Later, in Section 10, we will relax this restriction. With this simplifying assumption, we may visualize the instantaneous state of the organ in our scheme as follows.

1. Choose a simple dynamical scheme modeling the standard cell of the organ, the *standard scheme*.
2. Discretize the domain, choosing a point *centrum* in each cell.
3. Represent the continuous distribution of control

metabolites throughout the organ by a map from the physical domain into the control space of the standard scheme. This *continuous control field* may be regarded as a vector in an infinite-dimensional state space of the control system, in the language of complex dynamical systems.

4. Dually represent the control metabolite levels at the center by a map from the center (actually, a finite set of indices identifying them) into the control space of the standard scheme. This *discrete control field* may be regarded as a finite-dimensional state of the reduced control system. At this point we visualize the organ, its cellular decomposition, and its center, all imaged in the control space of the standard scheme by these two maps. We proceed now by interpreting the dynamics of each cell in the standard scheme.

5. Choose an initial state for each cell, and visualize it in the standard scheme, hovering over the image in the control space of the centrum of that cell, under the control field. These choices, together, comprise the *initial field* of the organ, in this modeling scheme.

6. Start up the cellular dynamics, in a separate copy of the model for each cell, and wait for dynamic equilibrium in each.

As the transients die away, one attractor is occupied over each centrum. We obtain an image of the organ on the locus of attraction of the standard scheme, representing the instantaneous state of the organ. The initial field has evolved to the final attractor field. During this process, we have assumed that the control fields have not changed, or at least, that *they change very slowly* with respect to the internal dynamics of the standard cell.

To visualize the instantaneous state of the organ, we use the trick of Zeeman, and *observe the control fields and attractor fields in the standard scheme for a single cell.* If the control metabolite levels in the organ slowly change, the control and attractor fields move about in the standard scheme. Thus, the attractor field will shlep along the locus of attraction. Whenever the control field transits the bifurcation set in the control space of the standard scheme, the attractor field will transit a bifurcation (subtle or catastrophic) of attractors, in the locus of attraction.

In summary, under all these assumptions, the current state of the organ is represented by the attractor field. This is a map from the cell center to subsets (attractors) of the locus of attraction. This map *covers* the discrete control field. That is, to each centrum is assigned an attractor of the dynamical system determined by the control levels of that centrum.

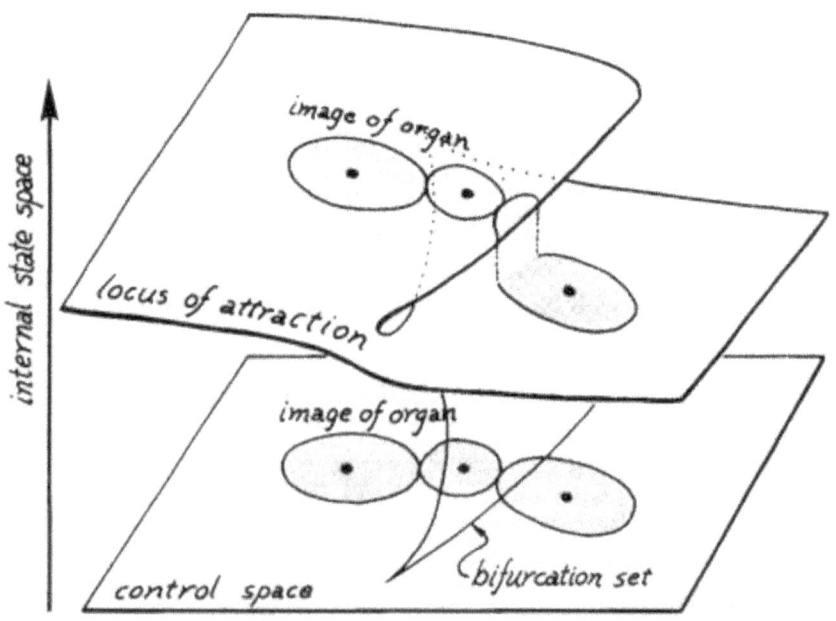

Figure 2. Images of the organ in the dynamical scheme.

In Fig. 2 one is drawn in three dimensions, assuming:
(a) the number of control metabolites is 2;
(b) the number of internal state variables of the standard cell is 1;
(c) the bifurcation diagram of the standard scheme is the cusp catastrophe, as used by Zeeman for his heart model;
(d) the dimension of the physical substrate is 2;
(c) the number of cells is 3.

The Complex Dynamical Scheme

At this point we may draw the connection between this field approach, and the specifics of complex dynamical system theory.

The actual dynamical scheme for the finite set of cells is a Cartesian product of identical copies of the standard scheme, one copy for each cell. The dynamical evolution, and the single attractor representing the dynamical equilibrium of the combined system of all the cells belongs to this, which we will call the *big scheme*. The discrete control field determines a single point in the control space of this combined system. The continuous control field is an instantaneous state of another dynamical system, of infinite dimension, which models the diffusion and reaction of control metabolites in the physical domain. This is the *executive scheme*. The discrete control field represents the static scheme, coupling the control metabolite diffusion system to the big scheme for the cellular organ, which is the *subject scheme*. The production of control metabolites by the cells represents a feedback from the subject scheme to the executive. Thus, we have a serially bicoupled network scheme for the total system, as shown, in Fig. 3.

The serial bicoupling between the executive scheme for the control metabolite system and the big scheme for the cellular

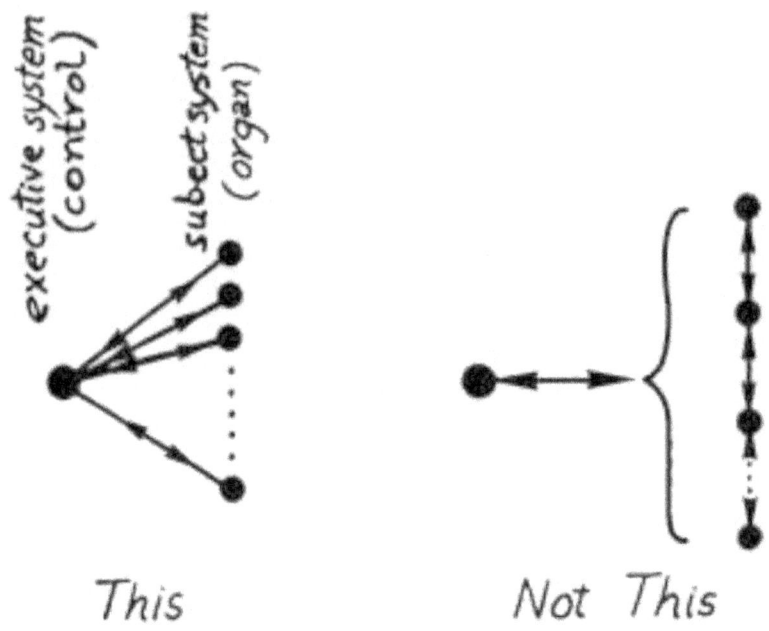

Figure 3. Schematic of the serially bicoupled network.

organ replaces the usual idea of a direct parallel coupling between the cells. It can easily accommodate different types of coupling, such as diffusion through tissue, blood circulation, pipette systems such as the portal-hypophyseal ventals, and synaptic junctions.

Our strategy in this paper is to fasten upon the attractor field, and forget about the actual attractor in the big scheme. This is reasonable, if the cells are not dynamically coupled to each other. This is not realistic[8] but it will allow us to visualize the concepts under discussion, all of which apply equally to the more general scheme. A more realistic model for the organ would allow spatially modulated coupling between cells. Thus, the subject scheme would be a serially bicoupled network, as suggested by Kolmogorov *et al.*[9] And now, as this model is too large to visualize, we return to the field approach.

The Field Scheme for Thoughts

We suppose that we now have at hand a field model for the mammalian brain. An instantaneous state, a *thought*, is controlled by a control field, and is represented by an attractor field. Unlike our simplistic three-dimensional example in the preceding section. this one may have many control metabolite dimensions, and many internal state variables. Thus, the typical attractor will not be static (a point) or even periodic (a cycle), but most probably chaotic. Nevertheless, as multiple surfaces terminated by catastrophic bifurcations abound in typical bifurcation diagrams, hysteresis will be a principal feature of the standard scheme. Our emphasis here is on *the geometry of the locus of attraction*, not on the qualitative features of the individual attractors.

Thus, an attractor field is a thought. A thought covers a control field. Different thoughts can cover the same control field. Changing the control field will change the thoughts in a deterministic way. The (discrete) control field belongs to a finite-dimensional space, and its change should be thought of as a curve in that space. But in the spirit of control theory, we will also think of such a curve of control fields, in discrete approximation, as a finite sequence of points. And beginning from the same initial control field, different sequences of intermediate control fields may end at the same final control field. And the same initial thought, shlepped along the locus of attraction by these different sequences of intermediate control fields, can end up as different thoughts, covering the same final control field. This is because there is *hysteresis* in the standard scheme. We think of the controlling sequence of control metabolite maps as a *program*, which means something like this in information theory. And we refer to this dependence of the change in the attractor field upon the program as *holonomy*, which means something like this in differential geometry.

Absolute Programs

Note that the bifurcation set divides the control space (of virtual control metabolite concentrations) into a number of disjoint regions, *supposed finite*. Over each region there is a fixed set of attractors, also supposed finite. These are called competing attractors by Thom. Here, generic means that there is no centrum in the bifurcation set. Thus, for a fixed generic control field there is a finite number of attractor configurations possible, and in fact, a finite number for any generic control field. We regard them here as the *gamut of thoughts* possible over a generic control field. This is the basis for the following informatic metaphors.

An *address* is a generic control field. The *data* at that address is an attractor field (thought) covering it. A program, as defined above, is a sequence of addresses, regarded as the discrete approximation to a curve in the control space. We will call this an absolute program.

But to *copy data* to a final address, one must start with the right initial data at the initial address, and run the right program from the initial address to the final one. Changing either the initial data (thought, attractor field), or the program (sequence of addresses, control fields) ends at different data, although at the same address.

Integrative Programs

But now to complete the connection between the neurophysiological model and the informatic metaphor, we must allow for the process of feedback from states (attractor fields) to controls (control fields), for *the cells may produce (or destroy) control metabolites*. Thus, we will generalize the idea of a program as follows. We introduce now a new hypothesis: *the control space of the standard cell is a vector space*. Thus, control fields comprise a finite-dimensional vector space, and we may add them. This hypothesis can be easily generalized, by introducing a nonlinear map in place of addition, but this would only complicate the discussion unnecessarily.

Further, we introduce a new structure, to represent feedback from the subject system to the executive system. This is (in its simplest version) a function from the internal state space to the control space of the standard cell. We assume that in a given instantaneous state of the standard cell (represented by a point in the internal state space) control metabolites are produced at a constant rate. The new function, the *rate function*, specifies this rate.

Further, we assume that each cell (represented by a given concentration of control metabolites, and an attractor of the associated dynamical system) produces control metabolites at a constant rate, averaged over the fast variation of internal parameters along the attractor. Next, we suppose that sequential programs are run according to a strict clock. Thus, in each unit interval of time corresponding to one instruction of the program, a cell in a given attractor (data) over a given control metabolite level (address) will produce an increment of control metabolite which is the integral of the averaged rate function over the clock interval. Thus, given an instantaneous state of the entire organ, each cell produces increments of control metabolite. The contribution of each cell results in an increment to the control metabolite concentration for itself, and also its neighbors. So, finally, we must have in the scheme a spatial rule to specify how an increment of control metabolite concentration in the original organ will change the control field.

This should be expressed as a *dynamical system* on the finite-dimensional vector space of control fields, such as reaction-diffusion equations. In this case, we have this situation: there is a control field (original address) at an attractor of its own dynamic on the control space, a fast perturbation arrives, the control-space dynamic relaxes the perturbed state to the appropriate attractor (new address). If the perturbation does not push the instantaneous control state into a new basin, it relaxes to the original attractor-no address increment. In any case, we assume now such a rule: at each state of the organ, an increment to the control field is determined. We call this the *address increment* of the given state of the entire organ.

A program now will consist of initial data at an initial address, and a sequence of *relative addresses*. Each step of the program goes to a new address (control field on centra) determined by adding the current address, the address increment from the current state (assumed to be a constant) and the relative address at the current step of the program. Now, the same program, with different initial data, *can end at different addresses*. We will call this new kind of program an *integrative program*.

Holonomy Programs

Finally, imagine an integrative program which begins and ends at the same *end field*. Its effect upon all the attractor fields (thoughts) covering its end field is to *map* them among themselves, generally in a many-to-one manner. This map is analogous to the holonomy concept of differential geometry. It is caused by the catastrophic bifurcations in the standard cell model.

We shall have use for some of the language of holonomy, from differential geometry. The invertible holonomy programs, at a given end field, comprise the *holonomy monoid* of that address. And for a given file (data, attractor field) at that address (end field), the set of all files obtainable from it by the operation of invertible holonomies upon it comprise the *holonomy orbit* of the original file.

The holonomy of bifurcation diagrams could (and perhaps will) be studied in the abstract. Meanwhile, it will be fundamental in our application of the field scheme for the brain to cognitive processes, in the next section.

Abstraction and Application

Now we are ready to apply our scheme to the abstraction and application processes described in a preceding section, in the informatic metaphor. The main idea is that *the abstract concept* on level M, in the hierarchical model of consciousness described previously, is all an initial data file (thought, initial attractor field) at a given address, as described in the preceding section. This is a filename, or pointer program; that is, it is a dynamical state generating an integrative program leading to a key state on level S. Its instances (thoughts, as final attractor fields) on level S *are the files of the holonomy orbit* of this *key state*. The *name* of an instance on level S is the holonomy which creates it from the key state, which represents the abstraction on level S.

The *old application process* just requires running the appropriate holonomy program, its name, starting from the correct initial address and data of the abstraction. The *new application* process is a little more difficult. It requires the recognition of an existing abstraction, of which the new file is an instance. That is, an initial file (key of the abstraction) must be found from among those already learned and ensconced on level M, and a holonomy program from key to instance. Thus, recognition is carried out, in this scheme, by running trial holonomies, hoping to strike the key of an existing abstract model of level M. If found, the recognition problem is solved. (The difficulty in finding one is resolved in the next section.) The successful holonomy program must now be *inverted*, to name the new instance.

Two problems are encountered here:
1. How to determine, within the neurophysiological model, the close approach of two files. That is, while moving a file by a holonomy program, when is it close to another file (for example, an existing abstract model), and converging to it. We call this the *convergence problem*.
2. Having found an interesting holonomy program, how can we find an inverse holonomy, if there is one. We call this the *inversion problem*.

The *abstraction* process is even more difficult. From several instances on level S, one seeks integrative programs with identical final addresses, uses these programs to copy all the instances to this new address (this moves the file folders into a common pile), and operates on these transposed instances with the holonomy monoid of the common address. If possible, an abstraction (file on level M) will be found after enough trials, in the orbit of which lie all of the several instances. This presents, again, the two problems of *inversion* and *convergence*. In the next section, we describe a transformation from this scheme to another (the local geometrical model) in which the convergence problem is solved.

The Geometric Model

What we wish to do now is to simplify programs as much as possible, by standardizing the addresses. We observe that, although there is a continuum of addresses (vector space of control fields), most of them are equivalent. That is, any address can be deformed into another without essentially changing the data (attractor field) as long as *no centrum crosses a hypersurface* of the bifurcation set. We choose, thus, a *standard control point* in each component of the regular set (complement of the bifurcation set) in the control space. At the end of each program, we deform the final address into a standard one, by standardizing the control metabolite concentration at each centrum. Thus, if a centrum has control metabolite concentration in one of the components,

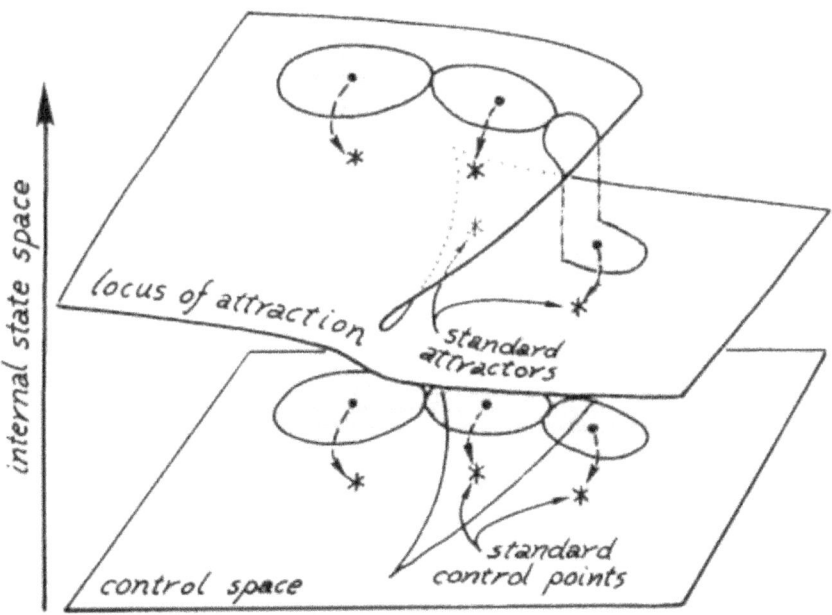

Figure 4. Deformation to a standard.field.

136   Vibrations and Forms

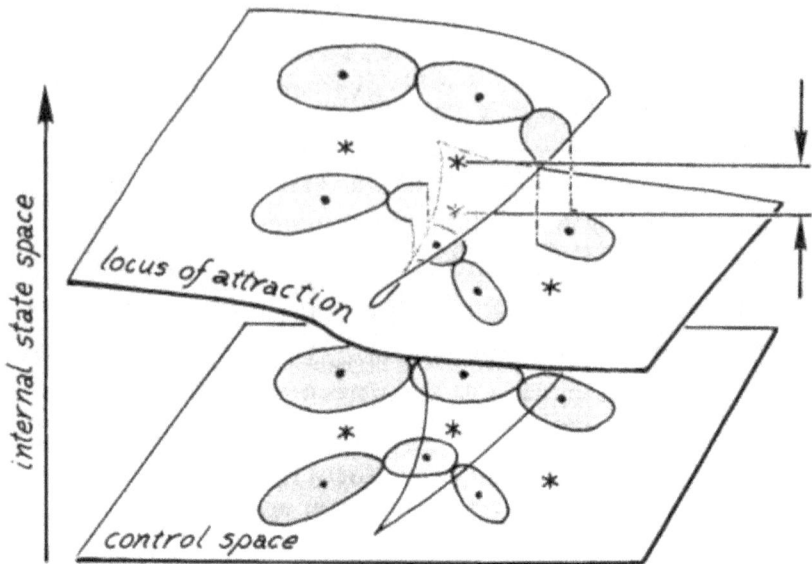

Figure 5. Distance between two fields.

we deform this concentration to the standard one, *within the same* component, as shown in Fig. 4. For the moment, we regard this as a mathematical transformation only. Later, we will propose a neurophysiological mechanism for this, inspired by Hoffman.

A *standard field* is identified by two labels attached to each cell: the component of control space occupied by its (standardized) control metabolite concentration , and its attractor. These comprise a *standard state* for that cell. What we have achieved, through standardization, is a physical location, in the state space of the cell, for each of the possible attractors of a given regular component of control space. In fact, choosing one point in each basin (we think of this as the *average state* of the cell for the given attractor) we may define the distance between two standard fields, as shown in Fig.5. And thus, we can try to minimize this distance. For standard configurations with separate addresses, we say the distance is infinite.

Now, at last, we can imagine a possible algorithm for the abstraction process. Given several *instances*, we standardize them. In the simpler cases, they comprise different data over the same address. Otherwise, we copy the data to the same address with an integrative program. If there is no integrative program from an instance to a common address, it must be abandoned.

Now, as described in the preceding section. we experiment with our favorite *holonomies*, integrative programs which begin and end at the same address. From all the different initial data, we are seeking common final data. So for each instance file, we run all of our holonomies, generating its instance orbit. Files (attractor fields) in the intersection of these instance orbits are candidate abstraction keys for these instances. They must be tried, one at a time.

For each candidate, we apply the holonomy monoid to create its orbit. Then, the distances from each instance to the orbit must be added to measure the value of the candidate

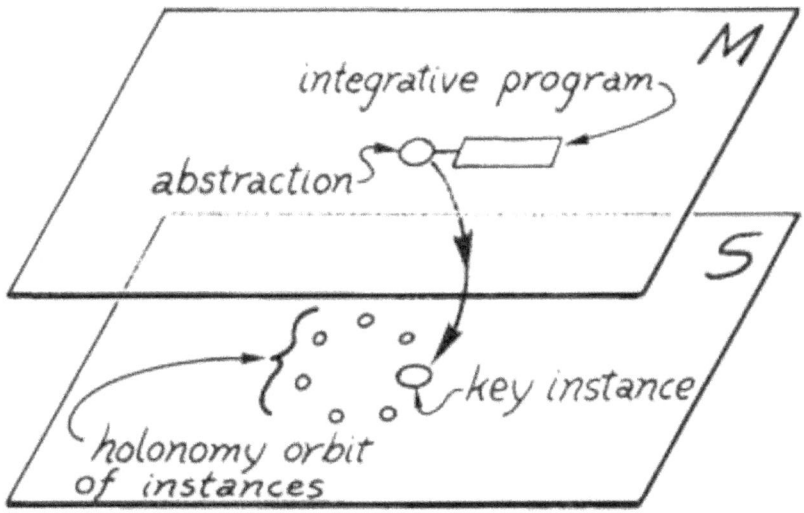

Figure 6. Abstraction, key, and instance orbit.

abstraction. Varying the candidate, we seek to minimize this distance. If successful, we have found an abstraction for the given instances. The abstraction on level M is an integrative program leading to the key.

We think of the instances, standardized to the same address, as the pile of file folders, in the earlier mechanical metaphor. But in this case, it is not the address which is the abstraction, but the file on level M, which points to a key file in the pile, as shown in Fig. 6.

Special Purpose Cells

Finally, we will describe the Hoffman-inspired neurophysiological mechanism for the standardization of addresses. This requires adding some auxiliary cells to the neurophysiological scheme. Thus we will have a complex dynamical scheme for the brain which has a simple standard cell, inhomogeneous cell-types, and nonuniform control metabolite distribution, in the framework of organic resolution.[10]

First, there must be *buffer cells*. Their purpose is to sense nearby control metabolite concentrations and buffer them, simultaneously inhibiting any efforts of uniform cells to change the address (control metabolite concentration) as if in response to excitation. They have to steer away from the bifurcation set.

We may imagine a gradient-like dynamical system in the control space, moving away from the bifurcation set toward a distinguished central point of each component (see Fig. 7). But recall that an address is a control field, and the effect of buffer cells is to pull the image of the (cellular) physical substrate into these sinks. The image is stretched tight across the bifurcation set (see Fig. 8). The high gradients between cells on these boundaries will overpower buffering, and limit gradients will exist. A typical control field is shown as a graph in Fig. 9. So we propose an additional distribution of special purpose cells, the sample-and-hold cells. These sense a region of essentially constant control metabolite levels, sample these levels, and hold them. The geometric evaluation of candidate abstraction programs, described above, is accomplished by the sample-and-hold cells.

Conclusion

Here we have described a hypothetical scheme for communication between adjacent levels in an hierarchical information structure of a conscious mind. In informatic and mechanical metaphors, we have described the processes:

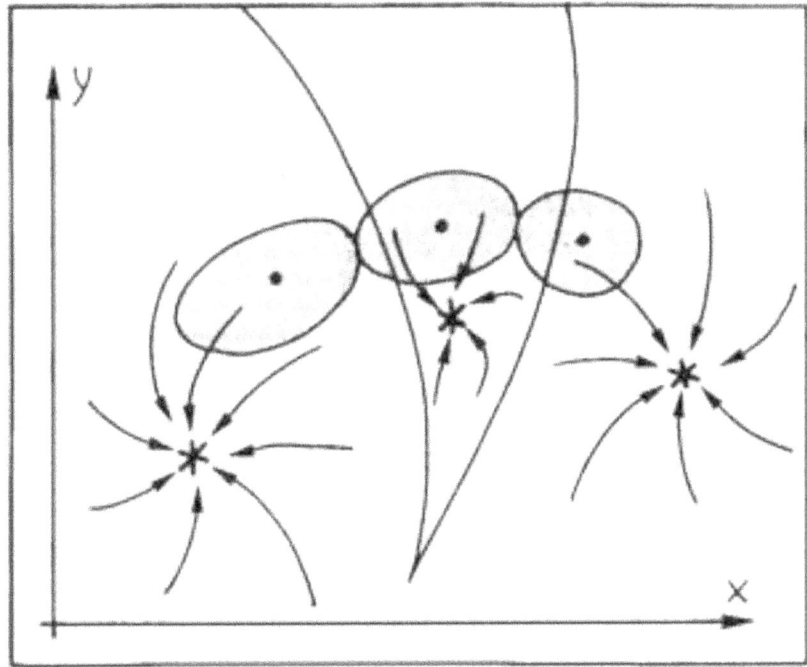

Figure 7. Standardization of control field, in progress.

140   Vibrations and Forms

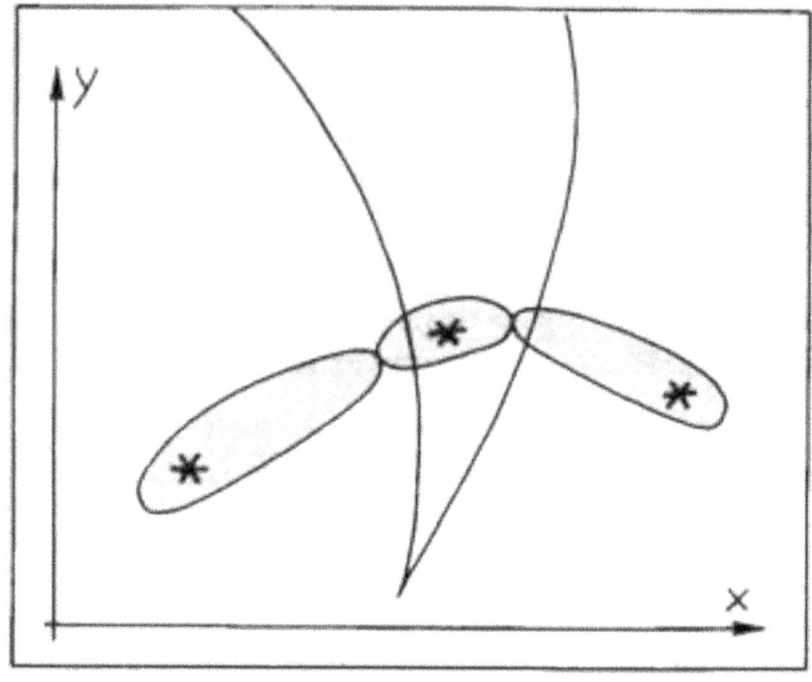

Figure 8. Standardization of control field, completed.

(a) *old application* of an existing abstraction to an existing instance;
(b) *new application* of an existing abstraction to a new instance; and
(c) *new abstraction* of similar instances into a new abstraction.

The informatic metaphors developed here are:

(1) *address* as a standard control field;
(2) *data* as an attractor field;
(3) *data comparison* by a geometric distance;
(4) *program* as a sequence of relative address moves, integrating data at each incremental address, according to a

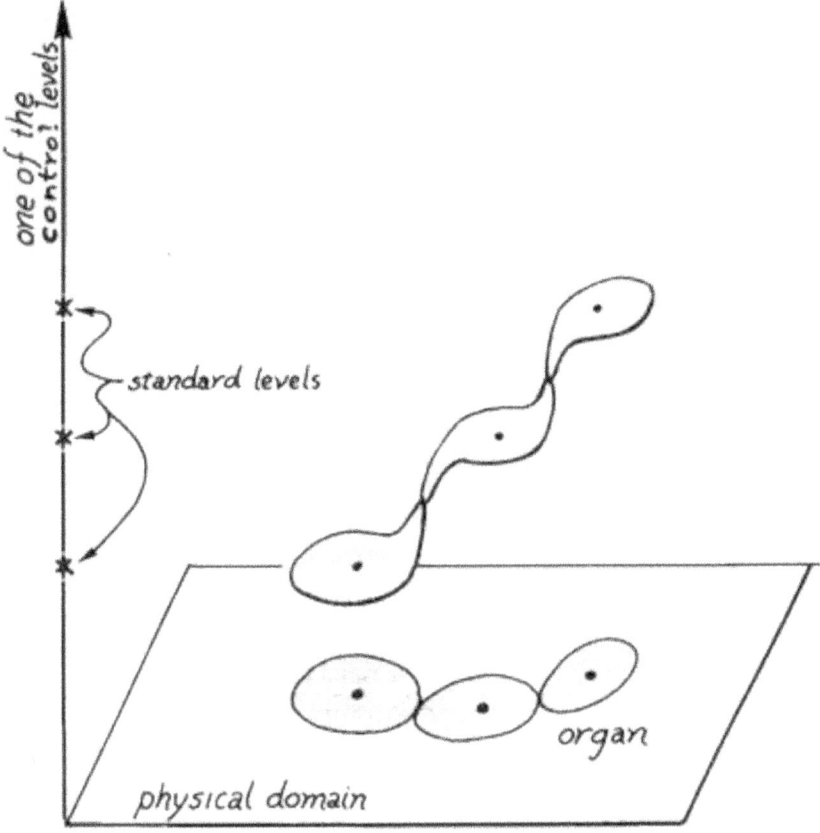

Figure 9. Graph of standard control field.

dynamical system on the address space, and dragging the data along the locus of attraction of the dynamical scheme for the standard cell, and

(5) *filename (pointer)* expansion by a integrative program.

Further, an homogeneous neurophysiological model has been proposed for the realization of these processes and metaphors in mammalian brains. The application process is simple and direct in this scheme, based on the informatic metaphor. The abstraction process is more complicated. For this, we have introduced two supplementary distributions of special cells: buffer cells and sample-and-hold cells. In this inhomogeneous neurophysiological model, the mechanical metaphor (aggregation of files to a pile of a common address) becomes simple and direct as well.

All this is based on the theory of complex dynamical systems, developed in the earlier papers, and developed in the context of the bifurcation diagram of an imaginary neuron model. This theory provides some guidance, even when the actual dynamical model is unknown. For this reason, we call it a scheme, rather than a model, for thought.

Nevertheless, one could go much further with this theory if explicit dynamical models (for a single neuron, for example) were known. In addition, the existence of buffer and sample-and-hold cells is hypothetical here. This part of the theory is inspired by the work of Hoffman, which goes much further in studying the function of special distributions of cells. We should like a more concrete neurophyslological proposal for these cells. The structure of the glial body, as a bundle over the cortex, is suggestive here. We propose these problems to neurobiologists.

Acknowledgements

This paper, written on 17 October, 1981, on the train from Paris to Amsterdam in a moment of revelation, is the translation into the new language of complex dynamics of some old ideas, familiar to visionaries of the past and present. In particular, Arbib, Freeman, Hoffman, Katchalsky, Kolmogorov, Plato, Rashevsky, Rosen, Thom, Turing, and Zeeman are mentioned in the text. Here I would like to recognize the particularly seminal work of Aharon Katzir-Katchalsky, which appeared shortly after his death, at the beginning of my interest in this subject. Finally, I would like to acknowledge the influence of important conversations with Fred Abraham, Walter Freeman, Alan Garfinkel, William Hoffman, Tim Poston, Dan Sunday, René Thom, and Christopher Zeeman, the support of the Institut des Hautes Etudes Scientifiques, particularly Nicolaas Kuiper, during the preparation of this work, and valuable feedback from the referee on expository matters.

Notes

1. (See Abraham, 1981).
2. See (Abraham, 1983*b*) or (1983*c*) for the definitions.
3. See (Abraham, 1976).
4. See (Abraham, 1973) and (1976)
5. See (Abraham, 1983*c*)
6. See (Abraham and Shaw, 1982) for an introduction to these concepts of dynamical systems theory, and (F. Abraham, 1983*c*) for their application in this context.
7. See Hoffman (1977) for an interesting classification of those in the visual cortex, based on Lie algebra theory.
8. See (Abraham, 1983*c*) sections BS, C4
9. See (Abraham, 1983*c*)
10. See (Abraham 1983c).

Chapter 8
Vibrations in Math, Music, and Mysticism

Abstract

Transcript of a presentation for the International Synergy Institute, at the American Film Institute in Los Angeles. The five M's: Music, Movies, Math, Mysticism, and Meditation. Proposal for a computer graphic animation project at the Visual Math Institute.

Publication

Ms #42, written January 6, 1985. Published in *IS Journal*, #0, David Dunn (ed.), International Synergy, 1986; pp. 7-8.

Andra Akers, the late film actress and intellectual, founded the International Synergy Institute in Hollywood around 1983, to confront the social challenges of the time. She greatly supported my work, and arranged several lectures for me in Los Angeles. This paper, from one of these talks, was published in her journal.

Vibrations and Forms

Contents

Background
Vibrations Made Visible
Two Dolphins
Visual Music
A Hinge of History
Restoring Integrity
Sacred Art
The Five M's

Background

I come from a very obscure background: thirty-three years studying the mathematics of vibrations. In the middle of this career there came a holiday of some three years when I went off the professional track. When I returned from the Himalayas about eleven years ago, I found to my surprise that I was still interested in vibrations, but not just the mathematics. I was interested in the real thing. And so at that time, in 1974, I built a machine named the Macroscope. A name inspired by a science fiction novel. Some of you know it. The idea was to make vibration visible.

Vibrations Made Visible

The metaphor of vibration occurs in traditional literature about the higher things. So, what we are seeing is fluid a little thicker than water, a transparent fluid, being seen through a Macroscope which makes its vibration visible. This is, I have no doubt, what a dolphin sees in his melon, receiving vibrations created by himself or others. So this is fairly simple. No computer graphics. No analog computer. No digital computer. A very cheap machine. It makes the real vibration in a transparent medium visible. Even in air this machine is so sensitive that if you light a match, it will show the heat waves. So we're seeing extremely subtle vibrations in the fluid caused by the music that you hear. It is the nature of fluids to make these patterns when vibrating — a droplet, a biological cell, a liver, a stomach, the ocean. When you look through the swimming pool at the bottom, this is what you're seeing.

Two Dolphins

Eventually, this led to my swimming in a tank with the Lillys' two dolphins, Joe and Rosie. During this swim, I did try to communicate with them in this fashion using different kinds of clucking sounds which I had tried out and found made a certain pattern in this machine. They both became extremely excited. The people who watch the tank there admitted that these dolphins had never been so excited. So something happened and indeed we fell in love. It was an alien love, extraspecies love.

Visual Music

Then eventually it led me here, four months ago, to a talk where I spoke about visual music, a very established medium into which computer graphics has recently arrived. And as we have seen this morning, there are many things that computer graphics can do in the area of visual music. For me there was a different significance to the arrival of computer graphics as a reasonable partner with visual music, and that is that it makes possible the incorporation of mathematical ideas: visual mathematics. If there's one thing that computer graphics is good for it's making mathematics visible, particularly the mathematics of dynamics. That's very important, because we previously have had no way to make visible to the outside world moving mathematical images in the mind of a mathematician, not even to each other. Now the possibility is not only to put them in with music to use them as the backdrop of a film or something but use them as artistic elements in intentional creation, because the mathematical algorithms are not only visible on the screen but are, in fact, the easiest way to create new imagery.

A Hinge of History

If there is a hinge of history then it folds between a future and no future. That is what many of us are feeling now. Can our evolution continue? We want to create the future, a beautiful one, not necessarily according to our own design, but according to some better design that we will help pattern. To go over the hinge of history toward yes, we want to raise the intelligence of society. Do you know about Luis Machado? He was the Minister of Intelligence in Venezuela. He was the only Minister of Intelligence in any government of the world. He got this idea that intelligence is our birthright and that our manifest destiny is to be intelligent and to have the pleasure and wealth of that. Unlike many people who may have had this idea, he happened to be a personal friend of the president of Venezuela, who liked this idea. So he was made Minister of Intelligence. He is using the best techniques of the most radical educators around the world in public media programs, and retraining the teachers in the schools, effectively raising the intelligence of the populace of Venezuela. His goals are maybe national or beyond. Our goals are planetary and solar. We want to create a society with the stars as our manifest destiny, so let's go. We've got to raise intelligence because this whole trip now is just too stupid. We could be more optimistic if this intelligence was trainable. I'm using the word 'raise' because I want to suggest something which I think Luis Machado is not talking about. I want to raise intelligence vertically, not just learn how to solve physics problems better. I want to increase the connection to the divine plan, so that we can receive whatever is necessary to get past that hinge in history.

Restoring Integrity

Return to Center is the name of a book by Father Bede Griffiths. He is this guru in the south of India who is also a Catholic priest and monk of the Benedictine Order. His idea, like many people but he says it so well, is that we have our terrific society here with these things like computer graphics, but they're all peripherals of some master computer which has unfortunately been turned off. So these peripherals can't actually do anything. There's no center. You could call this a lack of integrity. Sometime in the recent past, it might have been only five or ten years ago, the last person with integrity died. Society is totally without a center. Father Griffiths has written a little algorithm for regenerating the center. No matter how much intelligence is raised, unless we have some kind of integrity, this technology will not only be used for what we see now, but some people will use it for what some people would say is bad. These bad uses, for everything which we manage to create, enormously outnumber the good uses, which gives us a feeling that there is a downward spiral. We need a return to center. Could this technology be used for that? This is a balancing act because the thing is sort of on tilt.

Sacred Art

Jose Arguelles is coming from this super-scholarly art history direction, looking at the whole history of art through all of the cultures on Terra, from the perspective of a traditional Buddhist. He says that there are certain artists who are special: sacred artists. Sacred art is some sort of thread which always existed throughout time, and what those people are doing is a certain absolutely essential something without which evolution can't happen. Sacred art is the evolution of a planetary society according to a design, which has not only a future but a beautiful and paradisiacal one. Those computer graphics and visual musics we create could contribute to a planetary art. Is that a possibility? Can we get money from the National Science Foundation to further that? Will that solar society be lovingly beautiful or military — *Star Wars, Starfighter, Tron* or what? I loved *Tron* too, but let's face it, — on the content level there's a certain lack of center. It needs a return to center.

The Five M's

For the five M's I want to suggest a possible way in which we could relate the technology at hand to the questions that have been raised. Just one of many possible bridges we could try and build in our minds.

M #1 is MUSIC. That's the music we're all familiar with but there is a theory, particularly in Indian music, about the emotional values of notes, scales, and sequences. I want to suggest that the emotional, the intellectual, the physical, or whatever content of music, is specifically our goal because it has vibrations. It resonates with different aspects of being and consciousness. It has an effect upon a person even without words, and when you add words, when the lyrics are properly coordinated, then the effect of each is enormously enhanced through the recruitment of different centers of the brain, according to a common something or other. This integration of different aspects of consciousness into a coordinated activity, as I have described, is specifically our goal.

M #2 is MOVIES. Something more like Vibeke Sorenson where we have music, maybe with lyrics, and images coordinated sufficiently well so that there is a resonance of three different centers.

M #3 is MATH. I want to use the fact that artists doing this can't resist using computer graphics anyway. They're available, affordable, programmable, and happen to be supremely suited for presentation to people of dynamical mathematical images.

Music, movies, and math would then be coordinated into a combined medium from the viewpoint of raising intelligence and discovering if it is possible to influence the return to center through the presentation of some kind of content with this medium.

M #4 is MYSTICISM. We have in our history this species called mystics. It's a default category for people who can't be called anything else.

Finally, M#5 is MEDITATION, a very important M. Mystics, by one means or another have a direct experience of some other reality, but their efforts to communicate, to us who are left behind, are unsuccessful. So the philosophers argue about whether or not they saw what they were seeing. In the writings of these mystics there are always — even when they come from completely different cultures — a commonality of themes like vibrations, for example. I have my own experience with this reality. It appears and sounds simultaneously as a continuously, infinitely everywhere-extended field in which vibration is taking place. Words insult it. The Tao that is spoken is not the true Tao. You cannot fit it into words. There is this injunction in every tradition. If the reality of mysticism is a dynamical one, and words refer to fixed constants, then it's impossible to wrap into words the simplest experience of the divine. It's not hard to remember the last time you visited there, but it's very hard to say in words. Could it be that this technology will allow us to go beyond where words can never go in communicating with each other?

Chapter 9
Mechanics of Resonance

Abstract

This article is based on a talk given at the Esalen Institute in June 1986.

Publication

Ms #44, written June 5, 1986. Published in *ReVISION*, Vol.10, n.1, Summer 1987; pp. 13-19

Contents

Oscillation and Vibration
    Examples of Oscillators
    Nonlinear Resonance of Oscillators
    Nonlinear Resonance of Vibrations
        Morphic Resonance
        Physiological Resonance

Recently, my greatest pleasures have occurred in the company of some beautiful older books I came across while studying the history of vibrations. Chief among them is the history of mechanics from Galileo to Lagrange by Truesdell (1960), in which he points out that *mechanics* belongs to our perennial wisdom. It was associated with our highest pre-modern knowledge, and is not just a bad habit of the modern period. When our post-modern science emerges (if it ever does), I believe we will come to see mechanics resume the place of importance it held in Ancient and Renaissance times.

In particular, the *discretization* of continuous systems for the sake of understanding them in mechanical analogy, was introduced by Leonardo da Vinci around 1500. Discretization denotes the modeling of a continuous system by a finite number of discrete ones. It is a cognitive strategy inverse to interpolation. For example, a length of flexible cable may be modeled by a length of chain. In fact, this was essentially Leonardo's earliest example of the discretization strategy.

Later, the disenchantment of the Renaissance reduced this cognitive strategy to dogma. This happened in 1600 with the burning of Bruno, according to Berman (1981), or perhaps in 1627 with the dream of Descartes, according to Davis and Hersh (1986). Leonardo's strategy reappears in 1646, in Huyghens' study of suspension bridges, and again in 1675, in Huyghens' study of the vibrating string (Truesdell, 1960, Ch. 1, pp. 45-49). By this time, the degeneration of mechanics from cognitive strategy (in the spirit of Hermeneutics and verstehen) to dogma (as in Physicalism, Reductionism, etc.) was well under way. Truesdell tells us that the phenomena of resonance was known to the ancient Greeks; that Leonardo resumed its experimental study early in his career; and that Fracastoro gave its correct explanation in 1546 (Ch. 1, pp. 16-22).

In this article, I try to give the basic idea of the *nonlinear resonance of vibrations* by extracting a few episodes from the history of mathematical physics in the three-century period beginning with Galileo. One immediate goal is that you should understand how to break a plate of glass by singing, worrying it around its resonant frequency. You might be able to do this without knowing how. The person who figured out how to do this was Duffing (1918), an Austrian engineer. His discovery is the fundamental phenomenon of nonlinear resonance, the *double fold catastrophe*, and it is this which breaks the plate of glass. If you understand this, you can apply it to many other things, such as morphic resonance. A few such applications are suggested in the last sections.

Oscillation and Vibration

Oscillation and vibration are two different things. An oscillator is something like a clock; it reproduces its states in a cycle, traversing each cycle in the same period of time. The prototypical examples of oscillation are the rising and setting of the sun, the phases of the moon, the tides, the mammalian reproductive cycle, and the cycle of the seasons. The modern nonlinear resonance concept applies primarily in the domain of oscillators, as studied by Duffing. If two oscillators are nearby and influence each other, a resonance phenomenon may be observed between them. But here, I wish to extend this concept to the classical context of resonant vibrations of strings, for example.

Vibration is a spatially distributed field or family of coupled oscillators. In a vibratory field, cooperative behavior might give the appearance of a wave traveling. Actually, nothing is moving, only individually oscillating up and down, like the surf. The cooperative behavior of a field of coupled oscillators is a vibration. The prototypical vibrations are, of course, strings, water waves, and sound waves. No others were known until the relatively recent discovery of wave phenomena in the electromagnetic field, quantum mechanical oscillations, biological systems, and so on.

Resonance between vibrating fields is an extension of the resonance of oscillators. Imagine a vibrating guitar string for example. If you have another vibrating string near it, the resonance phenomenon between these two vibrations or fields of oscillators is a cooperative phenomenon among the individual resonance effects between the oscillators of the one and the oscillators of the other, collectively composing the individual vibrations. This is a much more complex phenomenon than the simple resonance of oscillators. Our goal is to understand this by means of a mechanical analogy or model.

Examples of Oscillators

I think that the first man-made oscillators were models of the natural oscillators. For example, the ancient Egyptian water clock and the pendulum clock of Galileo and Huyghens are self-sustaining oscillators made in imitation of the natural prototypical oscillators.

A pendulum is oscillatory, yet it is not an oscillator in the strict definition I am using here that of requiring self-sustaining motion because the widths of the swings of a pendulum die away in a short time. However, a pendulum is oscillatory in the sense that with every pendulum there is associated a certain natural frequency. Around 1588, Galileo had noticed that this frequency is roughly independent of the width of the swing, the so-called isochronous property of the simple pendulum. So, although the swinging dies away, as

158 Vibrations and Forms

long as it persists one may keep time with it. In fact, Galileo timed his astronomical observations in this way.

To make a satisfactory pendulum clock, what was required was a mechanism that would automatically keep winding up the pendulum. Such an escape mechanism was invented by Galileo (who never made it work) and applied by Huyghens (who did).

In fact, Huyghens made a great number of clocks. He had a machine shop in downtown Amsterdam make clocks for him, and they were all over the house. He noticed that even though the clocks in separate rooms were keeping time differently one gaining time every day, another losing time every day when he put them in the same room, close together, they would

Name	Born	Died	1400	1600	1800	2000
Leonardo da Vinci	1452	1519	---A---			
Geronimo Fracastoro	1483	1553	----F			
John Dee	1527	1608	------			
Giordano Bruno	1548	1600		---B		
Francis Bacon	1561	1626	------			
Galileo Galilei	1564	1642		--H-----		
Isaac Beeckman	1570	1637		------		
Johannes Kepler	1571	1630		------		
Marin Mersenne	1588	1684		--------		
Rene Descartes	1596	1650		--C--		
Christiaan Huyghens	1629	1695		--DIE		
Isaac Newton	1643	1727		------		
Joseph Saveur	1653	1716		---M---		
Leonhard Euler	1707	1783			------	
Jean d'Alembert	1717	1783			--K--	
Joseph Lagrange	1736	1813			------	
Ernst Chladni	1756	1827			---N--	
Joseph Fourier	1768	1830			---	
Sophie Germain	1776	1831			------	
Baron von Helmholtz	1821	1894			--J---	
Lord Rayleigh	1842	1919			---L--	
Georg Duffing	1861	1940?			---G--	
Christopher Zeeman	1930					---O--
			1400	1600	1800	2000

Figure 1. The principal participants and events, in order of appearance.

keep time at the same rate. If they had an error, it would be the same error. But more than that, the pendulums would actually swing in phase. This is the *entrainment phenomenon* discovered by Huyghens in 1665. It is an aspect of resonance.

The tuning fork interruptor, or door buzzer, is another example. Like the pendulum, a tuning fork is oscillatory but is not an oscillator. One of the first electrical oscillators was

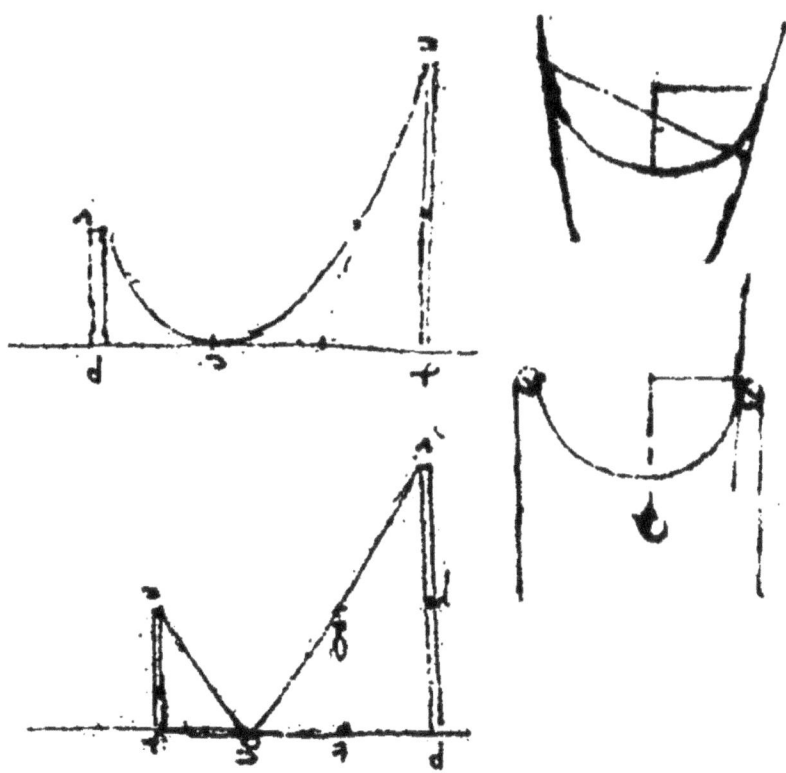

Figure 2. These sketches from Leonardo's notebooks, about 1500 A.D., show the weight of the string concentrated in a single heavy bead near the center. This is the earliest known example of a discrete model for a continuous mechanical system.

160   Vibrations and Forms

Helmholtz's invention of the door buzzer, about 1850. He took a tuning fork, put a nail close to one of its bars, and when the

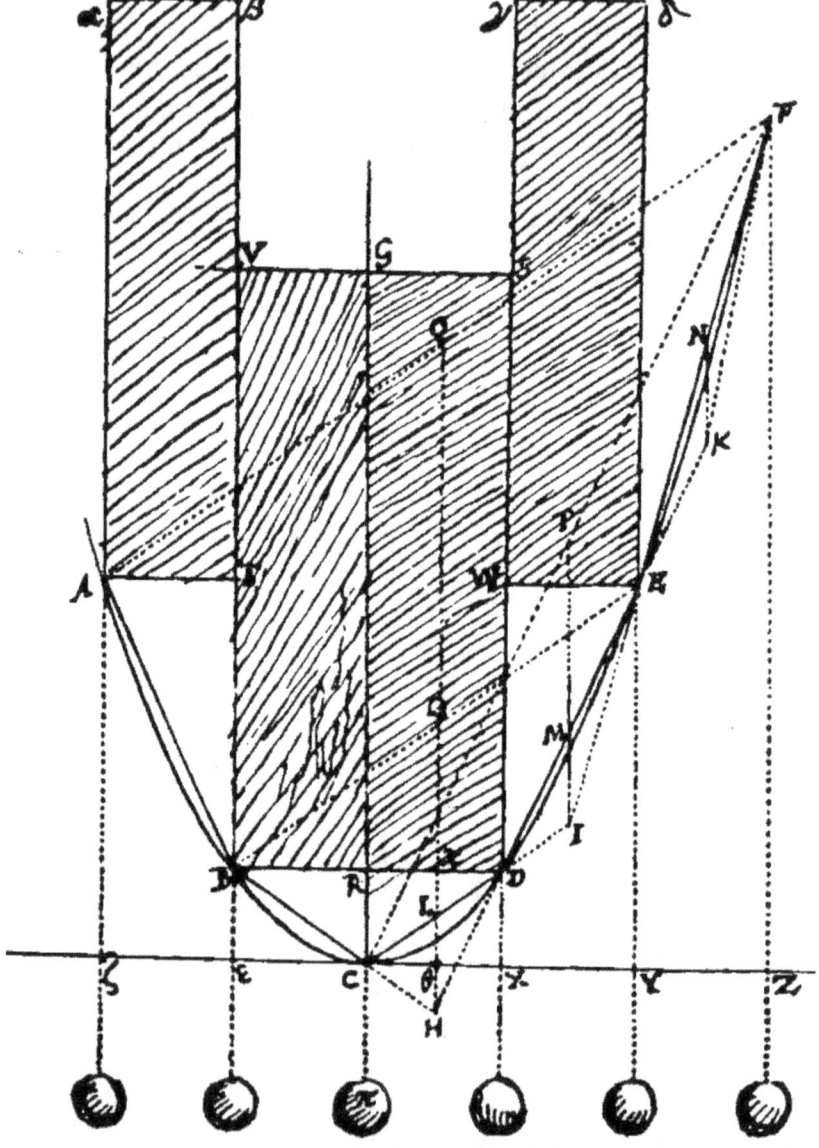

Figure 3. In this study of a suspension bridge from 1646 CE, Huyghens employs the discretization strategy of necessity.

tuning fork vibrated, contact with the nail would complete a circuit with a battery and a coil; the electromagnetic field of this coil would give the impetus to strengthen the vibration. The door buzzer would keep on buzzing.

Nonlinear Resonance of Oscillators

First of all let us consider linear resonance, a fiction of the imagination because nothing in Nature is truly linear. A tuning fork, for example, might be a linear oscillator if it were infinitesimally thin. A pendulum might be one if all of

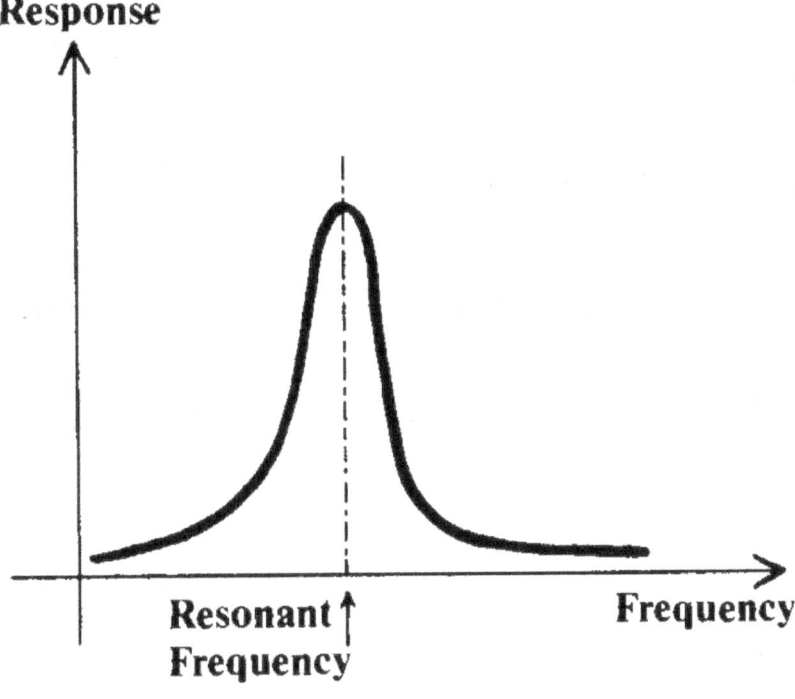

Figure 4. This graph shows the response of the sympathetic oscillator (pendulum, string or fork) concentrated at single frequency, the resonant frequency. This is the response diagram for the linear resonator.

its mass were concentrated in a small bob at the bottom of a weightless string, if there was no air in the room, or if it swung only slightly, and so on.

The idea of the linear resonator, in the case of a thin tuning fork, is that you sing at it, and that tends to put it into vibration. But if you are at the wrong frequency, its response is nil. When you sing at the right frequency (the natural frequency), the fork will almost instantaneously go into a relatively large oscillation. That is resonance. If you raise the pitch of your voice gradually from below the resonant frequency to above it, the fork will respond only at the one frequency. This behavior is shown by the response curve (see Figure 4).

What happens with a nonlinear (that is to say, real) tuning fork is that this response curve is bent, as shown in Figure 5. Duffing studied this by modeling the forcing oscillator (that is, the nearby voice) as a large pendulum moving very slightly, and modeling the responding oscillator (tuning fork, or whatever) as another (smaller) pendulum. The mechanics of each pendulum are inherently nonlinear. For the coupling between them, he hung the smaller pendulum from the bar of the larger one. He was interested in the effect on the little one of the forcing oscillation of the driving pendulum. This one was so big that it was essentially unaffected by the motion of the smaller one.

Recall that a simple pendulum has a natural frequency at which it likes to swing when left alone. Suppose the big one is forcing the small one at a frequency slightly lower than its natural frequency. Then the small one might respond with a very small oscillation at that same frequency. Now repeat the experiment, increasing the forcing frequency. In the linear case, there would be no significant response of the driven oscillator until the forcing frequency reached the natural (resonant) frequency of the driven oscillator.

But in the nonlinear case, the resonant behavior of the pendulum is bent over; the whole response curve is bent over. As the driving frequency increases, the sympathetic response increases gradually until the driving frequency reaches some critical value well past the natural frequency of the follower. Then abruptly, the response falls to a much natural lower

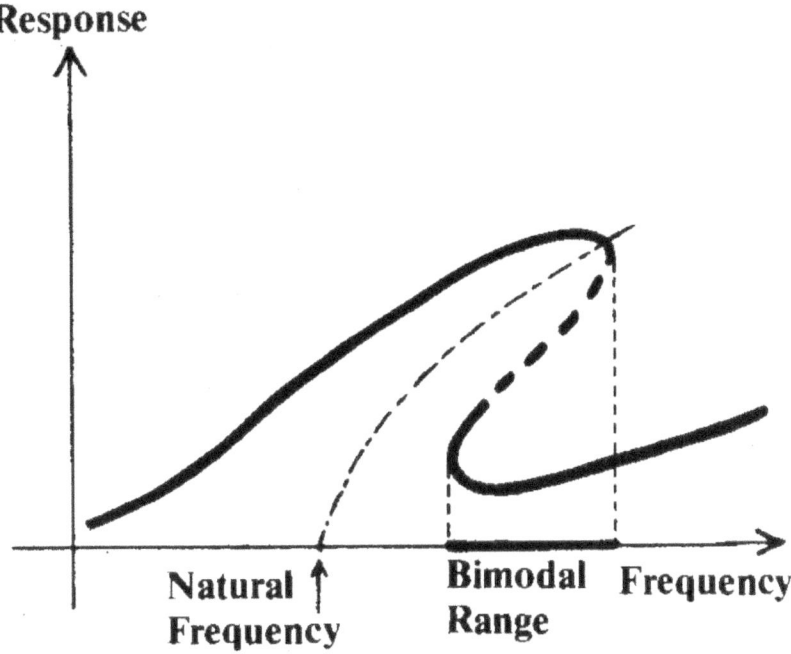

Figure 5. This is the response diagram for a nonlinear resonator. The response curve has been bent over towards the higher frequencies. The solid curves represent attractors, the dotted curve indicates the separatrix between the basins of the two competing attractors. Within the resonant interval there are two sympathetic responses, a loud one and a softer one. At the boundaries of this interval are found the double fold catastrophies, in which one or the other of the sympathetic vibrations disappears.

level. Decreasing the driving frequency again, the smaller response persists until the driving frequency gets to a critical value somewhat above the natural frequency of the follower. Then, again abruptly, the response increases. This complete sequence is called an *hysteresis loop* (Abraham & Shaw, 1982). The interval between the two critical frequencies is called the resonant frequency interval or, the bimodal regime. This is the nonlinear analogue of the resonant frequency in the linear context.

This is what Duffing discovered with the small pendulum hanging from the bar of a larger pendulum. He examined the complex motions of the system by taking very careful observations with a stroboscope. (According to Lord Rayleigh, the stroboscope was invented by a pendulum scientist, Foucault.) Extended vibrating systems (string, tuning fork, wine goblet, etc.) behave similarly.

You may try this with your own wine glass. You sing at a low frequency, and the glass is not vibrating very much in sympathetic response. You increase your pitch at the same loudness, and it vibrates a lot. You can see it and also hear it, because the glass essentially functions as a speaker cone. The sound of the sympathetic vibration gets much louder, although you are changing only the frequency of the forcing sound and not its loudness. When the responding sound gets much louder, you have identified the natural frequency, the resonant interval. You can raise and lower your pitch, keeping the same loudness. When you go *down* through the lower endpoint of the resonant frequency range, there is a snap up in the loudness of sympathetic response of the glass. It is this snap or popping that can actually break the glass. As you pop it again and again, the glass weakens. If the glass were a linear vibrator (for example, a very thin plate of glass), you could probably break it by forcing it at the resonant frequency, although you might have to use a somewhat louder forcing sound.

We may now apply these concepts of resonance of nonlinear oscillators to a field of oscillators or vibrators. To do this, we may use the discretization strategy invented by Leonardo about 1500. In the case of the tuning fork bar or guitar string, we have to replace it with a discrete mechanical model. We saw one bar of the tuning fork into pieces about an inch long and then put these pieces back together again with springs. There is not much room for the springs, so we take each chunk of aluminum and compress it into a tiny bead of enormous density without losing any mass. Now we have spaces of about an inch between adjacent beads in which to put the springs. This becomes a discrete model in the style introduced by Leonardo and much used in the corpuscular mechanics of the 18th century. We have a discrete mechanical model for one bar of the tuning fork, as a string of dense beads, essentially pendulum oscillators, coupled with small springs.

This model was used by d'Alembert at the dawn of mathematical physics in 1749. He made a model for the vibrating string by discretizing it in this way, imagining that springs came between discrete heavy beads. He then wrote down $f = ma$ (Newton's equation for this discrete model), and continued as though there were more and more beads, lighter and lighter and closer together, making a better and better approximation to the vibrating string. For details of this analysis, see Buckley (1985).

The extreme case of this conceptual simplification of Leonardo is exactly what Rayleigh (1960) did in his analysis of the clarinet reed, in his fundamental book on acoustics in 1882. He replaced the reed by a single heavy bead at the top that was connected to the base of the mouthpiece by a

166   Vibrations and Forms

weightless leaf spring. Then it is a simple kind of nonlinear oscillator, like a pendulum.

Nonlinear Resonance of Vibrations

If you place two tuning fork bars or two vibrating strings side by side and you discretize each in this extreme way into a single bead, and the coupling between them is modeled by another small spring, then you have almost exactly the situation of Duffing's experiment. So the response diagram of Duffing's catastrophe, Figure 5, applies here.

Now consider more realistic discrete mechanical models for the two strings, in which each is modeled by a string of dense beads connected by weightless springs. We may model the coupling between the two strings, the medium for the sympathetic response of one to the motion of the other, by an additional row of even smaller springs, as shown in Figure 6.

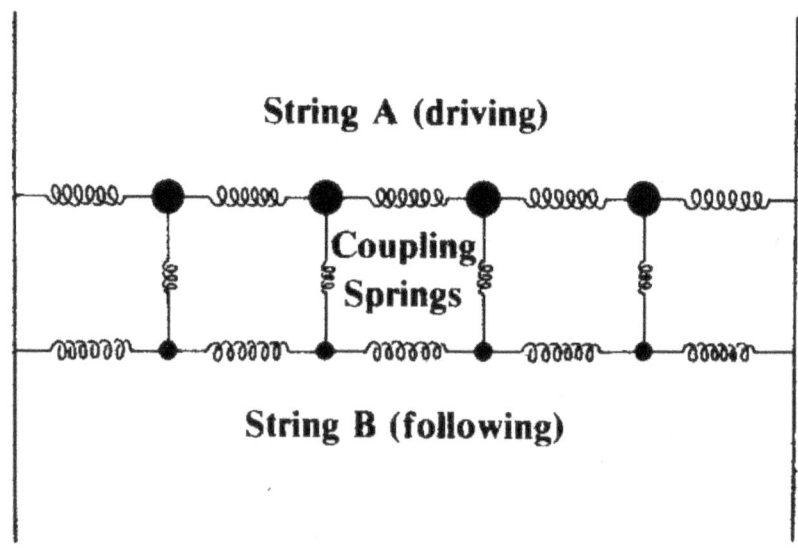

Figure 6. The discrete mechanical model for two coupled vibratory fields.

This is the final goal of our exercise in mechanical modeling. Some adaptation of Duffing's response diagram still applies, as each pair of beads (one from string A, the corresponding one from string B, and the very weak coupling spring between them) has its own double fold catastrophe.

Morphic Resonance

If you want to understand, for example, the phenomenon of memory in the vibratory field, how to store and retrieve memories using *vibratory resonance*, this is how you might do it.

Consider our basic discrete mechanical model for two coupled strings (Figure 6). We will suppose that string A is heavier: it is the *driver*. And string B is lighter; it is the *follower*. The coupling springs between the two strings are weightless and very weak. Imagine each string in a state of vibration. Thus, each bead is oscillating across the direction of the parallel strings. The cooperation of the string of driving oscillators might make the appearance of a traveling wave, a standing wave, or whatever. But below is string B, the follower. Each oscillating A bead is forcing a corresponding B bead into a sympathetic, resonant oscillation. And the resonant response is subject to the Duffing diagram (Figure 5). Maybe Pythagoras did this experiment; I don't know. But Saveur did it by 1700 (Cannon & Dostrovsky, 1981). The driving string is above, the following string below. You pluck the upper one (the driver) and observe the effect on the target string (the follower) below. At a constant amplitude (loudness) of the driving string, you change its frequency (pitch). The lower string will suddenly, at certain places, snap up to the larger amplitude, the second state observed by Duffing.

If you could observe piano strings carefully after they

are struck, you might see discrete disjoint segments of the string where it is in the bigger mode or the smaller mode, which differs only by fractions of a millimeter. This is the *memory of a pattern*. Within the vibrating wave, there are two states possible, almost identical, but one has a slightly larger amplitude than the other. Of all the oscillators comprising the coherent phenomenon of vibration, some will be in the loud state, others in the quiet state. If you color the loud beads blue and the quiet beads green, you would see a blue pattern on a green background. That pattern is remembered in the vibrating string as long as it continues to resonate.

The pattern in the following string might have been created by intentionally programming the activity of the driving string, by changing its frequency and amplitude patterns. This mechanism would achieve the storage of a selected pattern within the vibratory field of the follower string. To retrieve a vibration memory stored in this way, you would have to drive the system with a very sensitive device that is able to detect which beads are in the loud state and which are in the quiet.

This is a mechanical model for morphic resonance: a pattern in one vibratory field creates a related pattern in another coupled, vibratory field. This particular scenario is an application of just a single phenomenon of nonlinear dynamics, the double fold catastrophe. (There are many others.) With it you can break the glass, or if the glass is more· flexible, like an automobile fender, you can impress in it a memory in the shape of a dent, and then retrieve that memory and get its shape out into another vibratory medium. This application was envisioned by Chladni, the father of acoustics, around 1800. He played plates of glass with a cello bow, observing patterns in a thin layer of sand on the plates.

Physiological Resonance

This has been an arduous metaphor to follow, and perhaps not everyone wants to know how to break a wine glass by worrying it to death. However, I believe that this mechanism of morphic resonance may enable us to understand many phenomena involved in brain and mind functions. In fact, it was proposed explicitly by Zeeman (1977), around 1970, as a mathematical model for memory traces in the brain.

To understand the occurrence of this kind of vibratory pattern in physiology, we must observe that Nature has designed biological organs somewhat in the style of Leonardo's discrete mechanical model. Take a liver for example. The liver is a mammalian organ that consists primarily of one kind of cell. (Most organs have many different types of cells.) There is a lot of structure besides a homogeneous mass of liver cells. We will just try to imagine what kind of behavior we would expect from a mass of liver cells.

First, there may be an oscillatory process in each cell. Second, these oscillatory processes may communicate with each other through different kinds of messages (which are not entirely understood) passing between cells. There is a whole universe of life in the extra-cellular space, involving electrolyte physics and biomolecular processes. Third, the response diagram of each cell to an exogenous forcing oscillation may contain double fold catastrophes or even more complicated behavior. Thus, there may be amplitude patterns spread over the liver. Finally, there is a cooperative mechanism among the cells, which is more or less predictable from this kind of dynamics of coupled populations of oscillators, based upon phase regulation (Abraham, 1986). The oscillations are of approximately the same frequency for the different cells, and their relative phases organize into patterns. In sum, there may be amplitude patterns, phase patterns, and frequency patterns, as in radio communication.

If you observe phase patterns in the right way, for example, the cells in phase with each other would all appear blue to you, and the cells out of phase with these would seem green. Some cells would change from blue to green and back again according to their phase relationships, under the influence of some external driving field of bioelectrochemical vibration. Then you would observe this as a green pattern moving on a blue background. This is how physiological vibrations might be mechanically modeled. A lot of functions might be understood this way, particularly of the pituitary, where clocks have to be in phase; or in the reproductive cycle, where there is the mysterious phenomenon of the luteinizing hormone (LH) spike.

In the middle of the reproductive cycle, before ovulation, the luteinizing hormone (LH) concentration in the blood suddenly rises to astronomical levels. This LH is released by the pituitary on receiving a message from the hypothalamus of LH releasing hormone (LHRH). Now imagine you are a pituitary cell, and you have around your periphery a bunch of vesicles full of this LH, which you have been saving up for your moment, your place in history. You must release your whole store at the proper time and synchronously with all your sister pituitary cells. If all these pituitary cells let go their LH stores on the same day, then your owner has a proper LH spike and ovulation is possible. If you get it a little bit wrong then there is no LH spike and no ovulation and no subsequent reproduction. Life itself depends on strict cooperation!

How do all these pituitary cells know their exact circumstances? Is it simultaneous arrival of the LHRH message? If so, how does the hypothalamus know how to do this, and so on? I am suggesting that the answers to these questions may be sought in the behavior of discrete mechanical models, particularly in models of resonant vibrations. The mechanisms of morphic resonance, applied to physiological models, may increase our understanding of life processes.

There is a universal strategy in mathematical modeling, including all of mathematical physics, mathematical biology, and mathematical sociology up to the present time, with very few exceptions (Abraham, 1984). It is the exercise of this strategy, in combination with participatory experiments and observations that advances our grokking of the world of phenomena and process. This is the hermeneutical view of the history of the mathematical sciences, from Cro-Magnon times to the present.

Applied to the vibrating string, following Leonardo, Galileo, Huyghens, d'Alembert, and Euler, it is *mathematical physics*. Applied to the pituitary, the liver, and the other organismic vibrators (populations of oscillating cells) it is *mathematical biology*. Applied to social structures and ecosystems, it is *mathematical sociology*. *The certain sure sign of life is vibration*, and the mathematics of vibration (including mechanical models for morphic resonance) is a valuable strategy for grokking life.

Chapter 10
Visual Music Instruments and Chaos

Abstract

Chaos theory has given birth to new visual musical instruments. Here I trace the genesis of the MIMI projects.

Publication

Ms #47, written October 22, 1988. Published in *High Frontiers*, Fall, 1988.

Contents

My Walkabout in Chaos
The Vibration Metaphor
The Macroscope
The Visual Math Project
The MIMI Project
Acknowledgments
Box 1: The History of Visual Music
Box 2: The History of Acoustics

Visual Music Instruments

Readers of James Gleick's *Chaos* will recall the quixotic Ralph Abraham and his Chaos Cabal nestled in the witchy-woods of the Santa Cruz Mountain. For years they met secretly in catacombs under the UCSC campus tinkering on rusty icons like the Systron-Donner analog computer. The Dynamical Systems approach was initially seen as a dangerous mind parasite by both the physics and mathematics departments.

Yesterday's heresy or dangerous sectarianism is today's — well, if not exactly orthodoxy — let's say: *hottest new way of looking at the universe.* Now two of his experimental projects in chaos and vibration theory have finally evolved into a digital-video based instrument. Here he traces the genesis of MIMI or *Mathematically Illuminated Musical Instrument.*

— Queen Mu

My Walkabout in Chaos

Once upon a time, I worked on a single mathematical problem for six years. The project culminated in two books, written simultaneously. When the manuscripts were done, I looked up to see what was happening in ordinary reality. It was Princeton University in 1967. The Sixties were happening. A full-bore revolution was on. A lot of people were departing ordinary reality for one-day trips. Like Joseph Knecht, I decided on the spur of the moment to try it out. For me, this was no one-day trip. When I came down, it was 1973.

During this six-year walkabout, I moved from Princeton to the University of California at Santa Cruz (UCSC), toured spiritual groups and techniques, saw my family expand and contract, took leave to explore Europe hippie style, searched the Himalayan foothills for traditional knowledge, trekked to the borders of Tibet. In Santa Cruz there were rock concerts with light shows. In Amsterdam there were esoteric books and video artists, and floors to sleep on. In India there were yogis, gurus, classical North Indian music teachers, Sanskrit texts in English translation, and caves to sleep in.

Reentry was difficult. After a cooling-off period in Tahoe, supported by mathematics applied to blackjack, I returned to my post at UCSC in January, 1974. I tried to integrate what I had gained from my journey with my work as a professor. I gave seminars on vibrations, combining Vedic concepts with European mathematics. My goal, inspired more by desperate need to communicate than the ideals of Boddhisatva or Toynbee, was to share the essential visual aspect of the vibratory field I had seen in my travels. The whole experience of the Logos could not be shared, but perhaps a visual representation would excite the full field in the viewer's mind through morphic resonance.

The underlying idea was a vibration analogy for mind, brain, and human behavior. At present, similar ideas have become widespread and familiar, in the form of neural nets, excitable media, cellular automata, and complex dynamical systems. But at the time, they belonged to the fringe. Further, the edge of the chaos revolution wave had just arrived at the shores of the physical sciences. Some students, still under the influence of the lost Sixties, were attracted. Together, we began the macroscope project.

The Vibration Metaphor

During the European phase of my walkabout, in February, 1972, I was invited for a short visit at the Institut des Hautes Études Scientifiques near Paris, the French equivalent of our Institute for Advanced Study. This is the home institution of René Thom, who invented catastrophe theory in 1966, and David Ruelle, who brought chaos theory to the attention of physicists in 1973. Thom showed me Hans Jenny's book, *Kymatics*. I was immediately struck with a feeling of urgent importance. I called Jenny in Basel to arrange a meeting. Soon I was at Jenny's home, where he showed me slides and films of his work, and shared his ideas on the significance of vibrations and Chladni patterns in human physiology. He was a follower of Rudolph Steiner.

Later that year in India, Jenny's ideas were echoed in my reading of the *Vedas* and the teachings of the yogis and gurus, especially Neem Karoli Baba. My own experiences, repeated during regular inward journeys over the five years, provided further teachings on the vibration model for mind and consciousness. My study of Indian music furthered my understanding of the wave metaphor, which is basic to the Samkya philosophy.

Dynamical systems theory, including catastrophes and chaos, provides a mathematical framework for the elaboration of the vibration model. Indeed, this elaboration was already underway in the work of Thom. In fact, Christopher Zeeman described his own explicit model for memory based on catastrophe theory and excitable media to me in Amsterdam, shortly before I flew to India. However, it was Jenny's work, providing visual representation of the basic concepts and phenomena, which seemed to me to have the greatest potential for furthering our understanding of human consciousness.

The Macroscope

With the aid of students from my UCSC seminar, I reproduced Hans Jenny's kymatic device in my lab. Our device was larger and less precise than Jenny's. We used a four-inch dish for the water/glycerol solution, four-inch telescope mirrors loaned by Lick Observatory, and a color Schlieren filter developed by Gary Settles. An analog electronic tone synthesizer was built especially for the device, and an industrial xenon arc lamp provided the illumination. When finished, I aligned the optics, approximating by eye, turned everything on, and glanced at the screen. I was astonished to see a perfect Jenny-style Chladni pattern, in full color. The experience overwhelmed me, and I retired to the corridor outside the lab to recover my composure.

An official opening was planned for the lab, renamed the JENNY FOUR-INCH MACROSCOPE, in July, 1974. On impulse, I asked my Indian music guru, S. D. Batish, to sing at the opening. We attached a microphone to the amplifier that vibrates fluid in the dish, in place of the pure tone generator. This event provided my first experience of visual music based on Chladni patterns, the essential forms of vibration in three dimensional media. It connected, all at once, my experience with Indian music, Samkya vibration theory — Thom's catastrophe theory, and the light shows of the Sixties. Math, music, mysticism — all are one!

Subsequently, we made systematic use of the instrument (with the tone generator, not my master's voice) to study the bifurcations of chaotic motions of vibrating waves until 1979. A video describing the instrument and the experiments is available from Aerial Press. No other direct reports have been published in scientific journals, but the understanding gained from my experience with the Macroscope has illuminated all of my writings (especially those collected in my books *On Morphodynamics* and *Complex Dynamics*). Recently we revived the macroscope to record a "music video" of Jill Purce's overtone chanting. The routine use of such a device for visual music is inconvenient but highly recommended, and this direction has been developed by Gary Settles.

ERNST CHLADNI. A contemporary of Mozart and Beethoven, he founded modern acoustics while trying to improve the tone of Ben Franklin's glass harmonica.
— Reproduced from Mary Waller (1961), Plate 1.

The Visual Math Project

Soon after beginning the Macroscope Project, computer graphics arrived at UCSC. In 1975, with computer scientist Evan Schaffer, I taught a special section of calculus using computer graphics for demonstrations. This grew into a state- and federally-funded project to develop a massive teaching system for beginning math courses, called VISMATH. It ended in 1982.

Part of our VISMATH program was an annual film show, at which almost all computer graphics films on mathematics were shown. Each year it was longer, and eventually multiple shows were necessary. As film artist John Whitney and his family, co-workers, and followers were using mathematics in their works, we added a number of art films to the programs. In this way we became familiar with the visual music medium, as used by frame-by-frame film animators. We also got to see Tom Banchoff's great classic of mathematical animation, *Hypercube*, and Nelson Max's all-time great *Inversion of The Sphere*, and to meet their authors. In these two films, in particular, I recognized actual images from my own inner experiences during my walkabout. Some were so accurate that a prior experience in 1969 might almost have been a precognition of sitting in the film show in the UCSC auditorium in 1975. Patiently, I waited for computer graphic hardware to evolve the capability to create and manipulate these images in real-time, so that I could use it to share my own inner visual experiences with other people. Meanwhile, I tried to create suitable images with video feedback. Although these efforts failed, they did provide some fundamental concepts relating dynamical systems theory (especially bifurcation theory and chaos theory) to the visual music context.

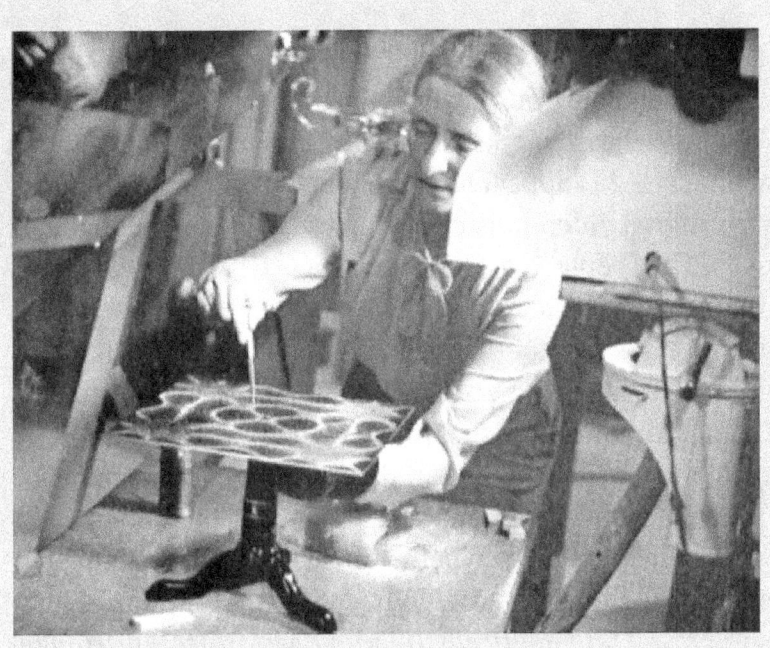

MARY DESIREE WALLER.
Here she demonstrates her method, an extension of Jenny's work, for television. The sand pattern is formed on a square plate, under the action of vibration maintained by dry ice.
— Reproduced from Mary Waller (1961), Plate 2.

Some of these are illustrated in an excellent video made by Jim Crutchfield with an analog video synthesizer, available from Aerial Press. But we wanted affordable, programmable digital video.

The MIMI Project

In the early 1980's, satisfactory digital video hardware became available. The Fairlight *Computer Video Instrument* (CVI) was an early application. Soon, a Cellular Automaton Machine (CAM) appeared at scientific conferences. A new era for digital video music had arrived. For me, this meant the possibility of replacing the Macroscope with a digital clone. This could be *portable, affordable,* and *programmable* .

Further, because of the recent evolution of the MIDI standard for interconnection of digital musical instruments, a digital video-based visual musical instrument could be *playable*, via keyboard, guitar, flute, violin, or even voice.

In 1983, people began inviting me to speak at non-mathematical events. My path along the New Age campsites eventually led to a stage in Hollywood, where I proposed a design for a *Mathematically Illuminated Musical Instrument* (MIMI). This is nothing but a digital-video based clone of the Macroscope, connected via MIDI to a digital keyboard instrument. Sitting at the keyboard, one might sing, play sound, and play picture, all at once. The picture part was envisaged as a modulation upon ordinary reality, in the form of real-time video. This sort of reality hacking is used in the Fairlight CVI. However in MIMI, the operation on a real picture would be defined mathematically, through the algorithms of dynamical systems theory. Among these algorithms are the cellular automata invented by von Neumann to simulate the human brain, cellular dynamata based on the heat and wave equations of mathematical physics, neural nets, excitable media, turbulent fluids, and so on.

For example, with no keys pressed, we might be watching an ordinary video of a dancer or surfer. When pressing a key and holding it down, we get a note. An organ tone *and* a MIMI note. The MIMI note stops the ordinary reality action on the screen, and begins a mathematically defined deformation of the freeze-frame image. In the case of an image processing algorithm based on the heat equation, the picture would fade slowly to grey. This process would continue as long as the key was held down. The pace might depend on key pressure or velocity, pitch wheel, or other MIDI controller. Upon release of the key, the grey would fade back into the ordinary reality of the moving surfer. Similarly, there are different ways to interpret a MIMI interval. Two keys pressed at once could initiate a combined effect, which may be totally unrelated to the individual effects programmed to follow each of the two keys singly. The program attaching a dynamic image process to a key (or combination of keys) runs in a personal microcomputer, and is available to the performer. Finally, the dynamic image process (a mathematical rule followed by the digital video processor) may have parameters under control of the performer via breath controllers or other MIDI devices. Thus, chaotic bifurcations of vibrating fluids such as seen in the Macroscope, may be called up at will by the visual music artist in real-time performance. This may provide a new level of performance for reality hackers of the future.

 The first prototype MIMI is now under construction at UCSC, under a contract from Pacific Shift, a high-tech studio in Santa Fe, NM. It consists of a MIDI keyboard and sound synthesizer, a personal computer with MIDI interface, a real-time digital-video image processor, and a rack of analog video studio gear. All this has cost about $100,000 so far, but prices are rapidly falling for most of the components.

Acknowledgments

In Paris, Harold Rosenberg and the Institut des Hautes Études (especially the director, Nicolas Kuiper) were very supportive. In Amsterdam, Simon Vinkenoog, Judith Schavrien, Thacher Clark, Bill Levi, Jack Moore, and the Matematisches Instituut were most helpful. In Utter Pradesh, Neem Karoli Baba and many Pahari people were very generous. My reentry in Santa Cruz was facilitated by Terence McKenna, Ray Gwyn Smith, the Batish family, and the Abraham clan. It is a pleasure to acknowledge the support of the University of California and assistance of my students over the years in the Macroscope Project (esp. Paul Kramerson) and the Visual Mathematics Project (esp. Peter Broadwell), and the support of Pacific Shift for the MIMI project. Bill Moritz generously shared his rare knowledge of the history of visual music. I am very grateful to all of these people and institutions for their kind support through these many years and changes. Thanks are also due to Hillevi Wyman and Rebekah Levi for their comments on the manuscript.

Box 1: The History of Visual Music

Visual music is a traditional art medium, with an extensive (if little known) history. It probably played a basic role in the arts and rituals of the cave cultures of the European epipaleolithic, and the early civilizations of the Anatolian neolithic. Cave sanctuaries, rituals of Minoan Crete, and the derivative mystery schools of Ancient Greece may have continued this artistic tradition, along with its mystical religious associations. Father Castel's Paris performances of color music created with candlelight and cloths were famous in the eighteen century.

In recent times, visual music reappeared in the Theosophical Revival at the turn of this century. Alexander Scriabin intended *Prometheus: The Poem of Fire* (1910) to be accompanied by a light show. (By the way, it begins in chaos.) Alexander Wallace Rimington performed live color music in London at about this time. Claude Bragdon and Thomas Wilfred in New York created keyboard instruments for live performance of color music in the 1920's. In the same period, Arnaldo Ginna and Bruno Corra in Italy, and Oskar Fischinger in Germany, laboriously made color music compositions in the form of animated films. In 1936 Fischinger moved to California, where he continued his work, influencing John Whitney and other major groups of color music film artists in America.

The live performance of color music survived in the work of Mary Hallock Greenewalt in Philadelphia in the 1940s (she invented the rheostat for her organ). Charles Dockum in New York and California in the 1950's, and of course in the Hip culture of the 1960's.

Box 2: The History of Acoustics

The glass harmonica was invented by Benjamin Franklin in Paris in 1761. It was popular until 1800, and many composers used it, including Mozart and Beethoven. Ernst Chladni was the father of modern acoustics. Born in Wittenberg, Saxony (near Bonn, Germany) in 1756, he earned a degree in jurisprudence at Leipzig in 1782. An amateur musician, he designed and constructed two glass harmonicas. In connection with this work, he developed the technique (now call *Kymatics*) of sprinkling sand or powder on glass plates, and bowing them with a cello bow. The sand would move to filigree of ridges, like ridges of sand dunes, now called the

Chladni nodal lines. The regions between the nodal lines, called antinodes, are responsible for the sound produced by the vibrating glass plate, its pitch, timbre and so on. Chladni searched for a design that would have a specified timbre, like the electronic synthesizer programmer of today. His first report of this research was published in 1787. In addition to pursuing his acoustic researches at home in Wittenberg, Chladni traveled extensively around Europe giving performances and demonstrations of music and sand figures. In 1800, he arrived in Paris and made a presentation to the Academy of Science, at the invitation of Laplace. Chladni had a private audience with Napoleon, which resulted in a prize competition in 1809 for mathematical explanation of the nodal lines. Napoleon's prize was won in 1815 by Sophie Germain, one of the first great woman mathematicians. As women were prohibited from attending university classes at that time, she obtained her mathematical training by impersonating a truant male student, Lucian Leblanc, at the École Polytechnique in Paris. Her prize paper founded the branch of mathematics now known as Continuum Mechanics — the basis for the modern science of acoustics and the mathematical theory of nonlinear vibration.

Chladni's experimental work has been repeated and extended regularly over two centuries, most notably by Mary Waller (London, 1961), and by Hans Jenny (Basel, 1972).

Chapter 11
Cathedral Dreams

Abstract

Over a period of years, the dreams of three men have converged on a radical plan for the renewal of religion, embodied in the largest Gothic cathedral in the world, the Cathedral of Saint John the Divine in New York City. Here is a personal summary of the plan, as conceived at the Lindisfarne Association conference on Friday, the 18th of October, 1991, in New York.

Dedicated to: Hans Jenny (1890–1972)

Publication

Ms #72A, written in 1991. Published in *Annals of Earth*, December, 1992.

Contents

1. Background
2. Jim Morton's Dream
3. Santiago Calatrava's Dream
4. Bill Thompson's Dream
5. Operation Bootstrap
6. The Monitor Project
7. The Animated Stained Glass Window
8. Next Steps
Acknowledgments
Notes

Cathedral Dreams

1. Background

As the synchronistic events of this strange story unrolled, I was eventually called in as a technical consultant on mathematical visualization. Not realizing the magnitude of the phantasy already full-blown, I innocently joined the ship of fools on October 18th, 1991, at a small gathering at Bob Schwartz' home in New York. Trying to understand the palimpsest presented there, I developed a theory. In this report, I share that theory, my own dream, and report the developments which have followed. The theory is based on John Dunne's *An Experiment in Time*, which details a method for discovering precognitive dreams: You must read your dream journal backwards, to fool your mind into recognizing the precedence of the dreamed occurrence over the real occurrence of the event.[1] This book also explains why, if you ask them, the three men might deny having these dreams.

2. Jim Morton's Dream

The Cathedral of St. John the Divine is the largest Gothic cathedral in the world, the second largest church after St. Peters in Rome, and the second most visited tourist attraction on Manhattan Island after the World Trade Center. Under construction for a century, it is yet unfinished. The nave is complete, but the transepts barely begun. James Morton is the current Dean of the Cathedral. Soon after taking office, he dreamt he had a mission to resume the construction of the cathedral, which had lapsed. He envisioned a new style of architecture, which would redefine Gothic architecture for the 21st Century. Later, under the influence of this dream, he organized an architectural competition. This took place in 1979, but the winning design was never actualized. In 1991, a second competition was organized, for the completion of the South Transept.

3. Santiago Calatrava's Dream

Calatrava, a well-known architect in Europe, was invited to compete in the second competition for the completion of the Cathedral. During the planning process, he had a dream of a phantasy cathedral, in which Gothic style was supplemented to include the environment. He saw columns resembling the tallest trees of the climax rain forest, and a mammoth greenhouse full of smaller trees within the cathedral itself. On waking, he actualized this vision in his entry for the competition. And he won, partly because Dean Morton recognized the synchronism of Calatrava's dream with his own. No other entry had transcended the Gothic tradition.

4. Bill Thompson's Dream

Director of Lindisfarne and Scholar-in-Residence at the Cathedral, Thompson had sat in on the first architectural competition but had been unaware of the second. Without knowing about the Dean's dream (or Calatrava's) he became transfixed when John Todd showed him Calatrava's winning designs. Thompson then organized a gathering of the Lindisfarne Fellows for October of 1991 at the Cathedral. And as eighteen of the Fellows were on the podium together before an audience of a hundred or so, in the Common Room of the Cathedral School, he began to explain the "intellectual architecture" which connected my work in the mathematics of dynamical systems to Lynn Margulis' work with spirochetes to Varela's work with neurons and Todd's work with "Living Machines" in bioshelters.

Thompson is a weird sort of Irish-American bard with a gift for gab. He dreams open-eyed as he speaks to an audience. For him, a public lecture is a kind of energy-hit in which he channels things he has never thought of before. So with a backup section of eighteen Lindisfarne Fellows, he took off on a mind-jazz riff on a new kind of "electronic stained glass" that would make the invisible microcosm of Margulis' work visible to people walking through the Cathedral. The sound and wave motion of the flagella of the spirochete would become visible — as children pressed their fingers to a computer screen in a request to hear "the Song of the Spirochete" — on a liquid crystal display screen in the Cathedral.

Margulis and Varela looked along the backup section at each other and laughed. They had been Fellows longer than I and were used to Bill's improvisational raps, but I was astonished. It was as if Bill were reading my mind, picking up an idea I had been wanting to do for a long time. I had proposed electronic murals in 1985 for the Disney EPCOT Center in Florida. But Bill was right: the Cathedral was the appropriate place for it, and "electronic stained glass" correctly captured his sacred intention. The next morning we all got together at Bob Schwartz' apartment in the sky above Central Park West and sat down to work out in earnest the next steps in the design, and for the financing.

5. *Operation Bootstrap*

The 1991 conference resulted in a number of radical ideas for a two-acre Bioshelter in the attic above the Cathedral. Covering the ceiling of the nave and both transepts, it would include giant people-moving elevators, a closed water system in which sewage from the toilettes in the basement would be purified by living machines in the Bioshelter, and of course, the display of many geophysical parameters of the soil, water, and atmosphere. In discussion with Calatrava, a bootstrap plan was developed to realize this phantasy inspite of its enormous cost: it would be constructed one bay at a time. The nave is built in sections, called bays, each about 300 square meters in area. In the bootstrap plan, funds would be raised first for just one bay, at the western (entrance) end of the nave. Operating as a model Bioshelter, this would attract tourists and green pilgrims from the crowd below, and funds would be collected for construction of the second bay, etc.

6. *The Monitor Project*

To make the invisible parameters of Gaian physiology visible, we would make use, as far as possible, of conventional "off-the-shelf" monitors. Here are some of the variables which might be observed.[2] Atmosphere: temperature, humidity, nitrogen, oxygen, carbon dioxide, methane. Water: sodium ions, chloride ions. Soil: biomass, bacteria, moisture, alkalinity, redox potential. In all cases, we would seek to monitor the spatial distribution with an array of identical sensors, sampled periodically by the computer system, and displayed in the graphic style of chaos theory, as in the popular computer game, SimEarth.[3]

7. *The Animated Stained Glass Window*

The displays in the Bioshelter itself might be in occasional booths, in which the interested observer could hunker down to interact with the real data, or with simulated data based on DaisyWorld models, following the work of James Lovelock.[4] But in the proposed new South Transept, a transparent 3D aerial view of the Bioshelter, including a few of the most intuitive parameters (temperature, carbon dioxide) would be on view in the animated stained glass window. Two schemes for the realization of this dream have been discussed: the schlieren scheme, and the LCD scheme.

Color schlieren optical system

This technique requires a huge beam of parallel light rays, such as sunlight through a window. The beam passes through the atmosphere (of the Bioshelter, for example) and then falls on an equally huge parabolic mirror (which could be segmental, like that of the Keck observatory on Mauna Koa). The beam is focused to a point, at which a small, color filter is placed in the optical path. At a distance of one focal length, the beam is projected on a screen, or on the wall. Here, a colored image is formed, revealing the rarefactions of the atmosphere due to temperature fluctuations, or sound vibrations. If infrared light is used, a shadowgraph of carbon dioxide absorption would be revealed.

LCD display

In these days of computer revolution, we have seen brilliant displays of color computer graphics from an ordinary overhead projector. The secret is a miniature "animated stained glass window," an active-matrix liquid-crystal display (LCD). Almost one square foot in area, these respond rapidly to a computer-generated color image, and can follow simple animations at video speeds. We would simply use about 800 of these as panes in a large window. Massively parallel supercomputer technology would enable their simultaneous control by the computer monitoring the data in the Bioshelter.

8. Next Steps

The further advance of the Bioshelter dream requires another meeting of the Fellowship, and a commissioned plan for a small model of the Shelter and monitor system. This small pilot project could be undertaken by a Science Museum, government institute, or private enterprise such as Biosphere 2, or Disneyland.

Acknowledgments

It is a pleasure to acknowledge the generosity of Robert Schwartz for his ongoing enthusiasm and support, the inspiration of the late Hans Jenny for the schlieren glass window scheme, to Jim Lovelock for instruction in the infra-red, to the other fellow dreamers of the Lindisfarne Association, and to the Cathedral administration and staff.

Notes

1. See (Dunne experiment).
2. See pp. 42, 46, Healing Gaia
3. Created by Maxus Software, and sold in computer stores.
4. See (Lovelock healing).

Chapter 12
Cathedral Dreams:
A Synthesis of Music, Mathematics, and Mysticism

Abstract

The Catheral Dreams of the preceding chapter led to an invitation from William Irwin Thompson to perform a concert of animated stained glass by the trio, MIMI and the Illuminati. This took place on October 17, 1992, at the Cathedral. This is a review of that performance. Further details are presented in the following chapter.

Publication

Ms #72B. Adapted from an article in Omni Magazine by Jane Bosveld, December 7, 1992.

It was an odd and spectacular event, even for a crowd used to the visual and audio overload of rock concerts by such luminaries as David Bowie, Michael Jackson, and the comeback tours of the Rolling Stones. The band, so to speak, was as strange as the Cathedral Dreams music and light show that played at the Cathedral Church of St. John the Divine in New York City on a cool October night.

The brainchild of mathematician and chaos guru Ralph Abraham, the concert blended computer images and music with improvised visual effects controlled by human performers. Strange mazes appeared on a screen only to fade into pulsating geometric shapes. Fluid images reminiscent of stained-glass windows — one in the shape of the cathedral itself — changed colors and dissolved. Using a specially designed computer called MIMI (Mathematically Illuminated Musical Instrument), Abraham programmed intricate mathematical formulas which were then translated by a supercomputer into video images. In addition to Abraham, other performers for the event included Ami Radunskaya, a professor of mathematics at Rice University in Houston, whose electronic cello accompanied the visual display, and Peter Broadwell, senior software engineer at Silicon Graphics of Mountain View, California, who designed the concert software.

The Cathedral Dreams, however, was more than academic exercise in the interaction of technology and art. In many ways, it represented the culmination of Abraham's lifelong desire to invest his work in mathematical theory and his love of music with a spiritual dimension. As a member of the Lindisfarne Association, whose twentieth anniversary the concert commemorated, Abraham and his colleagues are dedicated to the serious investigation of the religious dimensions of science. Founded in 1972 by William Irwin

Thompson, other members include microbiologist Lynn Margulis, Gaia hypothesis originator James Lovelock, anthropologist Mary Catherine Bateson, poet Wendell Berry, architect Paolo Soleri, and the dean of St. John the Divine, James Parks Morton.

For Abraham, the renewal of religion is essential for the growth of a vibrant "planetary culture." The old religions, he explains, no longer work. "But we can prune those religions of whatever has inhibited their evolution over the centuries. We need a planetary religion, revolution of religion where there would be a renewal of meaning in rites and rituals."

Abraham's spiritual journey began in the 1960s during a walkabout that took him to India where he met a guru with whom he spent a week on a meditative retreat inside a cave that had been home to yogis for centuries. It was here that he first experienced "visual illuminations," telepathic communications and insights into what the Vedic religious tradition calls the vibration metaphor. Throw a pebble in a pond, and the vibrations ripple out in concentric circles; strike a bell, and it vibrates in waves of sound; meditate on a thought, and it echoes, according to Vedic teachings, through the realm of the collective unconscious, the eternal wellspring of thought. Abraham's training as a mathematician made him wonder if there were a mathematical basis for the vibration metaphor, if human thought could somehow be understood in the same way as ringing a bell.

When Abraham returned to his professorship at the University of California at Santa Cruz in 1974, he began giving seminars on vibration theory, combining Vedic ideas with Western mathematics. To visually represent certain principles of vibration, Abraham had his students build a macroscope — a device that amplifies sound and sends it through a liquid solution, causing it to vibrate in patterns which are then projected via lenses onto a screen. Abraham asked an Indian singer he knew to sing through a microphone that was attached to the macroscope. "His singing produced beautiful patterns on the screen that were suggestive of the music itself," he explains. "It connected, all at once: my experience with Indian music, vibration theory, and mathematics. Math, music, mysticism — all are one."

By the 1980s, video innovations enabled the use of digital equipment in Abraham's experiments with visual music. This work led him to design the MIMI, and later to Cathedral Dreams and the hope that visual vibrations designed in mathematical formulas can be tuned to the pulsating beat of human consciousness.

Chapter 13
MIMI and the Illuminati

Written with
Peter Broadwell and Ami Radunskaya

Abstract

Upon the invitation of the Lindisfarne Association and the Cathedral Church of St. John the Divine in New York City, a concert of audiovisual mathematics/music took place in the Cathedral Church on 17 October, 1992, at about eight o'clock in the evening. Three computers and three persons cooperated in the performance. This is the story behind the event (and its video recording).

Publication

Ms #75, written April 17, 1993. Not previously published.

Contents

1. Visual Music and Math
2. The Performers
3. The Cathedral Concert Setup
4. Mathematics in Music
5. The Pieces
6. Summary
Acknowledgment
Notes

1. Visual Music and Math

Here is a little background on our artistic heritage and orientation.

Visual Music

Visual Music is a traditional art medium with an extensive, if little known, history. One can imagine that it played a basic role in the arts and rituals of the cave cultures of the European epipaleolithic, and the early civilizations of the Anatolian Neolithic. The cave sanctuaries and rituals of Minoan Crete, and the derivative mystery schools of Ancient Greece may have continued this artistic tradition, along with its mystical religious associations. The performances of Father Castel, in Paris, of color music created with candlelight and cloths, were famous in the eighteenth century. In more recent times, visual music reappeared in the Theosophical Revival at the turn of this century. Aleksandr Scriabin intended *Prometheus: The Poem of Fire* (1910) to be accompanied by a light show. Alexander Wallace Rimington performed live color music in London at about this time. Claude Bragdon, and Thomas Wilfred in New York, created keyboard instruments for the live performance of color music in the 1920's. In the same period, color music compositions in the form of animated films were laboriously made by Arnaldo Ginna and Bruno Corra in Italy, and Oskar Fischinger in Germany. In 1936 Fischinger moved to California, where he continued his work, influencing John Whitney and others of a major group of color music film artists in America. The live performance of color music survived in the work of Mary Hallock Greenewalt in Philadelphia in the 1940's (she invented the rheostat for her organ), Charles Dockum in New York and California in the

1950's, and of course in the Hippie culture of the 1960's.

Traditionally, masters of visual music, such as Father Castel or Mary Hallett Greenewalt, gave performances in silence on instruments of their own creation. In the film works of visual music by Oskar Fischinger and by James and John Whitney, mathematics was used as a source of visual musical form for the first time. In the analog video synthesizers and fluid cymatic light shows of the 1960s, visual music — in partnership with aural music — ascended to new heights of popularity and creativity. Our work is further research in this direction, catalyzed by rapid advances in computer science and the mathematics of chaos.

Visual Math is a new development empowered by the computer revolution. Computer graphics has boosted math into an art medium, making mathematical objects visible, and revealing the incredible beauty of the mathematical landscape. In the branch of mathematics known as *chaos theory*, massively parallel models called cellular dynamata, or *CDs*, are routinely observed (running on massively parallel supercomputers) as animated color images. Both spatial and temporal chaos abound in these morphogenetic natives of the mathematical landscape.

The Mathematically Illuminated Musical Instrument

MIMI was first conceived in a talk by Ralph Abraham at the International Synergy (IS) Institute in Los Angeles on October 7, 1984. Actual construction of the first model began in July, 1985, with support from the IS Institute. While this instrument is not yet complete, simulations by supercomputers have been circulating on videotape since 1989. The Cathedral performance in the Fall of 1992, the premiere MIMI concert, was an ensemble of three computers and three humans.

In this concert, the ILLUMINATI TRIO played visual music based on CD models in the supercomputer, and coordinated aural music based on the same models. The aural component is enlarged by an obbligato cello line. The evolution of the CD models themselves is affected by gestural input from the three performers. Beyond the exploration of computer/visual math/music, we are fascinated by the resonance between the two modes. We are extending the domain of Pythagorean harmony, following John Whitney, into an audiovisual and mathematical landscape

2. *The Performers*

(A) The audio performer is Ami Radunskaya, Professor of Mathematics (ergodic theory of dynamical systems) at Rice University in Houston, Texas. Ami has worked extensively at the Center for Computer Research in Music and Acoustics at Stanford University and the Center for New Music and Audio Technology at the University of California at Berkeley. Two of her pieces will soon be released on compact disks on the Centaur Label. She is also responsible for the overall composition of the pieces of this performance.

(L) The linking performer is Ralph Abraham, Professor of Mathematics (chaos theory, computation, and applications) at the University of California at Santa Cruz, founder there of the Visual Math Project and Computational Math Program and author of *Dynamics, the Geometry of Behavior*.

(V) The visual performer is Peter Broadwell, of 3DO. Peter studied computational mathematics in the Visual Math Program at the University of California at Santa Cruz, where he helped create the software of the Computational Math

Lab, earning the degree of Master of Arts in Computational Mathematics in 1988. He was for several years (including the time of the concert) a member of the Technical Staff at SGI, in Mountain View, California, where he created the IRIS software we are now using. He is presently Software Artist at the 3DO Company in San Mateo, California.

3. *The Cathedral Concert Setup*

We used three instruments, one for each performer.

The audio (A) instrument is a Yamaha TG77 synthesizer, controlled by the IRCAM/Opcode program MAX running on an Apple Mac II. The program MAX receives, processes, and sends MIDI messages. It is set up to respond to the (V) instrument (which generates the animation) and also to commands sent from the (L) instrument, and sent from performer (A), with her electric cello, and Zeta MIDI controller.

The video (V) instrument is an IRIS 4D/440VGXT, a 200 MIPS graphics workstation on loan from the manufacturer, Silicon Graphics, Inc. (SGI). It runs programs from the research frontier of chaos theory, the mathematical theory of nonlinear dynamical systems, cellular dynamata, or CDs, and iterated endomorphisms of the plane, or endos. Two CDs were featured in the Cathedral concert: the brusselator and the logistic lattice, and two endos: the twisted logistic and the Henon. All of these are classics of the recent research frontier.

These mathematical systems have parameters which may be manipulated by performer (V). The SGI IRIS workstation creates the digital video stream in real time, that is, as you watch. Performer (V) sends commands to the IRIS with LIGHTNING wands, made by Buchla and Associates of Berkeley, California.

The linking instrument (L) connects the two instruments. This third computer, an SGI IRIS INDIGO graphic workstation, also on loan from SGI, uses algorithms from chaos theory to communicate features of the video (V) to the audio (A) system. The algorithms are controlled by performer (L) by means of LIGHTNING wands.

Hardware

Gestural input device — LIGHTNING. Of course, the most powerful machines won't express anything if you can't give them some input. We wanted the input to be intuitive, and chose a gestural input device called LIGHTNING, manufactured by Buchla and Associates of Berkeley CA, USA. It is designed by and for musicians and interfaces to the computer using the MIDI protocol. We only used a few of the many gestures that LIGHTNING is sensitive to. In particular, we mapped all hits (quick percussive changes in direction) to be point triggers. We also continuously monitored the left and right hand positions and the state of the switches that are on each wand.

Machine 1 — named Morph, an IRIS Indigo from Silicon Graphics, input coordinator. The MIDI signals from the LIGHTNING were fed into an IRIS Indigo R4000 Elan. Here they were bundled up and merged with mouse input from performer (V). The mouse is not as expressive as the LIGHTNING but for simply picking initial conditions and occasional parameter changes, it worked alright.

Machine 2 — named Orbit, an IRIS 4D/440VGX image generator. Morph would then send the bundled inputs over ethernet to Orbit, and Morph. This machine was responsible for calculating the next image. It would then display that image as an RGB signal from its framebuffer. It also kept track of where the interesting trigger points had been dropped and sent the calculated values from those points back to Morph.

Machine 3 — named Point, a Macintosh II sequence controller. The Macintosh was connected to Morph via MIDI, and ran the MAX musical control language. In MAX, incoming time series were processed and mapped to musical parameters in the form of MIDI control, pitch, or velocity values.

4. *Mathematics in Music*

As in the visual arts, mathematics has played an enormous role in the creation of musical forms at every level. Music has, in fact, been defined as structured sound,[1] and mathematics provides the richest vocabulary for the description of structure. The contributions of music to the understanding of mathematics are perhaps more obscure, but nevertheless present throughout history. The Pythagoreans made a religion of numbers and their relationships, and the audification of small integer ratios. The creation of just harmonic relations — for example octaves, fifths, and fourths — contributed to the understanding of the mechanism by which sounds themselves were produced — the creation of standing waves in a string for example. With the advent of computers, and in particular of digital sound, the relationship between numbers and music has become much less subtle and much more intimate: digitally encoded sound is, after all, a list of numbers. The ear is capable of perceiving changes in these lists of numbers received at a rate of 40,000 numbers per second. It is this large band-width that makes the audification of certain mathematical processes intriguing: perhaps the ear can detect patterns which are too long for the eye to process in one pass. In fact, a heart specialist will sometimes listen to an electrocardiogram to detect periodicities and abnormalities that the eye could not: the data is treated as a time-domain representation of an audio signal, and is run through a DAC (digital-to-analog converter) so that the physician can hear it; repeating or periodic patterns can then occasionally be perceived as pitches.

Although the work described here was conceived of and presented as an artistic rather than a scientific enterprise, the same setup can be used to shed light on the mathematical structures themselves. With visualization and audification of an evolving mathematical structure occurring simultaneously, the observer can process more dimensions, and hence has more hope of discovering evidence and justification for any theoretical conjectures which may propose themselves. This bidirectionality — the music as an audification and hence a clarification of the mathematics, and the mathematics as a musical source — is to us one of the more intriguing aspects of this work.

It is important to note that music as structured sound does not necessarily mean ordered sound. The structures in question could be stochastic as well as deterministic. In fact, the particular family of systems discussed exhibit the full spectrum of behavior, from the ordered to the chaotic. The creation and dissolution of order is one of the parameters that is played during the pieces.

The use of random processes as a compositional tool goes back at least to Mozart, who composed a waltz which would now be described as a one-step Markov process: each measure was a state of the process, and the probability of another given measure occurring next depends on the current measure. The choice of which measure would actually follow a given measure in performance was to be made by rolling an appropriate (6-sided) die. This waltz of Mozart's can be used to introduce the concept of a mapping from state space to musical parameter space. The *state space* of a process is the set of all possible outcomes of that process. For example, the process which consists of repeated tosses of a coin outputs heads or tails, so its state space is the set { heads, tails }. For Mozart's waltz, the process (performance) outputs measures one at a time, hence the state space is the set of all possible measures. He composed and labeled these measures with a number from one to 92. For a Markov process, the set of all possible sequences of states and their relative probabilities is described by *transition probabilities*: the likelihood of moving from a given state to another. In Mozart's score it is shown that there are only 6 measures which are allowed to follow any given measure, and one out of these 6 measures is to be chosen randomly, that is, with equal chance of any of the six occurring. Thus the transition probability of going from measure A to measure B is zero, if B is *not* one of those 6 measures, and is 1/6 if it is.

Abstractly, we could describe this process by giving only these transition probabilities, and by saying we are dealing with a state space of 92 discrete elements. The performance could then be described by a *mapping*, or function, from this state space to *musical space*. In the waltz, the mapping associates a number between 1 and 92 with one measure of music, or a short sequence of pitches with their durations. Notice that this process, though random, does not produce a random sequence of pitches. All of the pitches are predetermined by the composer. In fact the ordering of pitches on a small scale, the pitches within one measure, is also predetermined. This is significant since the direct mapping of numbers to pitches, which is the naive approach to the audification of a mathematical process, should be considered as only one of many possibilities, and yet it is the most commonly heard. The application of mathematical structures in real-time, whether these structures are random or deterministic, can be applied at any or many of the levels in the musical hierarchy. Exploration of the range of possibilities is one of the goals of the MIMI project.

In our pieces, the visual and audio realizations of the mathematical processes are bound together by virtue of their common origin, but this connection could be either emphasized by synchronizing noticeable features of the sound and visuals, or it could be de-emphasized by using mappings which incorporate varying amounts of delay. Both extremes are displayed in the two examples, as well as a range of performer interaction and improvisation.

5. *The Pieces*

Morphic resonance

This piece is governed by the Brusselator, a two-dimensional lattice of oscillators introduced by Ilya Prigogine as an evolution of Alan Turing's 1952 model for chemical morphogenesis. An initial pattern chosen by performer (L) sets off an evolutionary sequence of images, computed in real time by the super-computer, subject to parameters chosen by performer (V).

This CD (cellular dynamaton) evolves relatively slowly, and it suggests slowly evolving sonic material. Although individual spots vibrate with swiftly changing colors, the overall image is made up of slowly spreading regions of color, sometimes made up of many colors, sometimes more or less monochrome. An attempt to represent these features sonically resulted in the use of an averaging over many samples rather than requiring a perceptual change with each numerical value.

Information-theoretic entropy is a measure of complexity which was adapted from information theory in the 1950s and applied to dynamical systems. Roughly speaking, it measures the average amount of information required to specify the next observation. If the process is completely predictable, no information is required at all, since it is known ahead of time what will happen next. Hence, *predictable* processes have zero entropy. Since this entropy is determined by the infinite future, it is impossible to actually compute it on the fly from observations of the output of a given process. However, an estimate can be made by counting the output of different sequences of digits appearing in a string of a fixed length and divided by the logarithm of this number and by the length of the string:

$$H_N(P) = \log \text{ (the number of strings of length } N\text{) / N}$$

The higher the entropy, the more complex the stream of numbers.

The MAX patch for this piece estimates the entropy of the process by looking at sequences of length 127. This number, which we refer to as the *frame entropy*, is then fed to another subroutine which creates chords. The higher the frame entropy, the more dissonant the chord will be. This is accomplished by adding to the chord pitches which appear later in a specified harmonic sequence. As soon as one frame entropy is computed, the next series of 127 numbers is fed in, and a new frame entropy is output to the main patch. In MAX, this computation does take some time, and there is some lag between "what you see" and "what you hear".

The overall harmonic progression is predetermined, but the rate at which it progresses is also affected by the complexity of the incoming numbers through the main patch. The timbres are singing voices, and they provide an accompaniment to an obbligato cello line which follows the evolving harmonies.

Fruit fly fandango

The second selection in the video provides an example of audification on a larger scale: this cellular dynamaton is distinguished by abrupt, almost periodic changes in the time-series of a given lattice point. In order to hear this aspect of the evolution of the system, amplitude was chosen as the dominant perceptual musical parameter. The underlying process is a two-dimensional array of logistic functions connected by Laplacean coupling on the torus.

Performer (L) again selects two time-series for transmission to the Macintosh. Each of these time-series is visualized by mapping one variable to a color spectrum. The same variable, which we'll denote by θ, is mapped to one of four amplitudes by rounding it off to the nearest quarter, and using the map:

$$P: \theta \rightarrow \{\text{rest, p, mf, f}\}$$

where

$$0.0 \rightarrow \text{rest}$$
$$.25 \rightarrow p$$
$$.50 \rightarrow \text{mf}$$
$$.75 \rightarrow f$$

The second variable is mapped to a pitch set which is selected by choosing one of five scales. A large jump between successive values causes a change in instrumental timbre. The rapidity of the evolution of the system, along with the abrupt numerical changes are seen as vibrating colors, and heard as rhythms which often seem to repeat but eventually evolve on a larger time-scale. When a new initial condition is selected by performer (V) it is obvious in the visualization as a discontinuity: the appearance of a new and unrelated image. One hears this discontinuity as an abrupt change in the melodic patterns.

6. Summary

These examples illustrate a few of the possibilities in the audification of cellular dynamata. The choice of mappings from state space to musical parameter space is made according to the process which is running, and to the region of interest in parameter space. The mapping can involve an averaging of information, to capture the complexity of the process, rather than individual trajectories. On the other hand, when one or two trajectories are of particular interest, a mapping whose domain allows aural distinction between a wide range of numerical values, such as pitch or timbre, is preferable. Since the ear easily places pitches in a linear ordering, this is a simple way to audify a relatively slowly changing, linearly ordered sequence of numbers. If it is only the distinction between different values that needs to be emphasized, then a subspace of timbre space can be used effectively: different instruments from some "orchestra" or different values of timbre modulation, for example. For widely and rapidly varying processes, using pitch or timbre as the range of the mapping results in a jarring, confusing sonic representation. Using amplitude as the target space instead allows the ear to hear longer sequences as units, and to use rhythmic comparisons to pick out patterns in the evolution of the structure in terms of these longer units.

These are but a few of the possibilities, and these examples should be viewed as preliminary experiments. The use of continuous controllers which allow navigation through parameter space in real time encourages exploration with a variety of mappings even for one system. When particularly beautiful areas of parameter space are discovered, and when appropriate audification mappings have been determined, a score can be written with whatever performer interaction is desired, be it as repeated initialization of values, movement in parameter space, control of the mappings themselves, or the addition of other musical lines. The rich structures of endomorphisms and cellular dynamata, most of which are based on models of real biological or chemical systems, can then be enjoyed by audiences without the abstraction and special vocabulary of mathematical formulae.

Acknowledgment

It is a pleasure to acknowledge the generosity of William Irwin Thompson and the Lindisfarne Association, James Morton and the Cathedral Church of Saint John the Divine, and Silicon Graphics Inc. for their support of the October 17th event. Also, we are grateful to John Dorband for a video of his endo, and to Jack Corliss for introducing us to the two CDs: the toral logistic lattice and the brusselator.

Notes

1 (See R. M. Schaefer *The Art of Sound*)

Chapter 14
The Electronic Rose Window

Abstract

Previously, we have described a project to build an electronic stained glass window in the south transept of the Cathedral Church of Saint John the Divine in New York City, the largest Gothic Cathedral in the world. Here, we sketch the historical background and motivation of this project.

Dedicated to: Father Louis Bertrand Castel, 1688-1757

Publication

Ms #80, written July 22, 1993 . Submitted to *Annals of Earth*, August 8, 1993.

Contents

1. Introduction
2. Early Stained Glass
3. Gothic Cathedrals
4. Rose Windows
5. The Cathedral of Saint John the Divine
6. Conclusion
Acknowledgments

1. Introduction

The idea for an electronic stained glass window for the Cathedral of Saint John the Divine emerged in a talk by William Irwin Thompson before the Lindisfarne Association at the Cathedral a few years ago. The story of this fantasy has been recounted elsewhere.[1] The materialization of an actual window, as originally imagined, would be part of the completion of the South Transept of the Cathedral, which is also just a dream at this point. It would be a large, circular collage of transparent computer screens, that is, an electronic rose window. Some possibilities for the computer graphic animations to be projected by the proposed window were demonstrated by a concert of visual mathematics and music in the Cathedral Church, entitled Cathedral Dreams, on October 17, 1992. This was part of another Lindisfarne Association meeting, during which we attempted to motivate the window project, in the context of the plan to complete the entire Cathedral, including the Cathedral Bioshelter and the South Transept, within the Green Cathedral concept. Here, based on that presentation to the Lindisfarne Fellows at the Cathedral, is the historical matrix for electronic stained glass in the rose window of the future.

2. Early Stained Glass

We are all familiar with stained glass windows, abundant in secular and religious buildings all over the world. Always uplifting, it seems natural that they should be a standard feature in places of worship, from caves to cathedrals. And yet, the manufacture of stained glass plates is sufficiently recent that we may trace the entire life of this phenomenon in a short space. Colored glass was known in ancient Egypt, and clear glass plate windows were used by the Romans since 100 AD.[2] By the year 400, the Christian churches of Constantinople were extensively decorated with small windows of colored glass, probably abstract mosaics.[3] These small, Byzantine, stained glass windows reached Ravenna by 540, where they appeared with painting added to the glass.[4] They arrived in England by the year 1000.[5] But in Early Christian and Byzantine churches, windows were small and few, to preserve the maximum wall area for mosaic pictures. The small, round, stained and painted glass windows of the Romanesque achieved the quality of jewels of light.[6]

3. Gothic Cathedrals

The name Gothic was coined in the sixteenth century by Giorgio Vasari as a perjorative for Medieval architecture. It denotes the style between Romanesque and Renaissance, characterized by pointed arches, extended door and window space, structural complexity, immense size, and (especially in northern Europe) by large stained glass windows and sculptured doorways. As the style evolved, door and window sizes grew, and the masonry was reduced to webs of ribs, pillars and arches. The early exemplars in the north of France were the churches of Saint Denis (1144), Chartres (1150), Laon (1160), Paris Notre Dame (1163), Reims (1211), and Amiens (1220). All are graced by spectacular stained glass windows, some of circular form, the inspiring rose windows. The Gothic cathedrals of Chartres, Reims, and Amiens are regarded as the classic examples of High Gothic architecture extant today. Indeed, the stained glass of Chartres provides our best knowledge of the Gothic stained glass art, with 152 original windows still intact.[7] The main period of creation of the Chartres windows began with the cathedral reconstruction of 1194. The three great rose windows were made around 1200, and most of the 160 windows were competed by 1240.[8]

Chartres is also important for the link it provides between the prehistoric Goddess tradition, antique Neoplatonic philosophy, and Gothic Christianity. This link is significant for the special appeal of the Gothic tradition to the spiritual revival and the Green movement, today. The structural revolution of the Gothic cathedral, with its supporting webs and ribs revealing the walls of their compressive function, enabled the spectacular expansion of glass which dominates these buildings from the interior perspective. The illuminationist motive for the expensive decorations in these transparent walls may be traced back to Dionysius, Boethius, and Saint Augustine.[9] The aspect of the luminescent scenes from within was slowly animated by the constantly changing light without.[10]

4. Rose Windows

Perhaps it is appropriate that the rose window tradition began at the Abbey of Saint-Denis. For Saint-Denis, the patron saint of France, is none other than Dionysius the Areopagite, the author of the Early Christian Celestial Hierarchy, which first described the Illuminationist doctrine of the nine choirs of angels, and inspired Saint Augustine.[11] In any case it was there, in 1144, that Abbe Suger envisioned the first Gothic building, illumined by enormous, jewel-like, stained glass windows. By 1200, his inspiration had spread to numerous churches around Paris. The giant rose windows appeared along the way, and a trinity of them adorned each of the three early large cathedrals of Chartres, Reims, and Amiens. At Chartres, in particular, the three rose windows, facing north, south, and west, were devoted to the past, the present, and the future, respectively. Thus, the whole of human history was stretched over the plan of the building. The north (past) symbolizes the Old Testament, the south (present) the New Testament, and the west (future) the Last Judgment and the New Jerusalem. Also, Christ appears at the center of each rose: as the child in the north, resurrected in the south, and in judgment in the west. The integrity of the entire stained glass environment at Chartres was based on the Logos of Philo Judeus and the Gospel of Saint John, embodying geometry, number, and light. All this sacred art, divine geometry, and Pythagorean philosophy was characteristic of the School of Chartres, which flourished at that time (a century after Bernard de Silvestris) under John of Salisbury and Chancellor Thierry.[12]

5. *The Cathedral of Saint John the Divine*

Originally conceived in the Romanesque style a century ago, and now the largest Gothic cathedral (and second largest church) in the world, this Anglican cathedral church is about two-thirds complete. The nave, oriented on an east-west axis, is complete and functions as a church. Its massive stonework is pierced by many splendid stained glass windows, including a magnificent rose window over the west entrance. Absent are the north and south transepts, along with their rose windows. Thus, among the plans for the completion of the building in the next century are the construction of two more great rose windows. Following the scheme of the School of Chartres, to the existing west rose (the future) would be added a north rose (the past) and a south rose (the present). The past and present, during the construction of the rose windows of Chartres (1200) were the Old and New Testaments, respectively. Today, they might be Christianity and Environmentalism.

In any case, the rose window to be constructed at the end of the north transept may be a traditional, static, stained glass window. But, we propose, the rose window for the end of the south transept, to represent the present, must be capable of animation, renewal, and environmental representation. For these reasons and many others, we have therefore envisioned electronic stained glass for this particular window.

6. Conclusion

In weighing the merits and costs of electronic stained glass in a religious setting, we must keep in mind that it already exists and is extensively used at sports events and rock concerts. The main cost of an electronic window (more for construction than materials) is not significantly more than that of a traditional window of stained glass. The merit, as in the case of the Gothic Renaissance stimulated by the School of Chartres, might be the inspiration of a major paradigm shift. Indeed, this is the destiny of the Cathedral of Saint John the Divine.

Acknowledgments

It is a pleasure to acknowledge the support of the Lindisfarne Association and the Cathedral of Saint John the Divine for their support, inspiration, and friendship over the years: material, emotional, and spiritual.

Notes

1. See our Chapter 13.
2. (Brisac, 1986; p. 7)
3. (Brown, 1991; p. 7)
4. See (Brisac, 1986; p. 7) and (Brown, 1991; p. 8).
5. (Eden, 1913; p. 25)
6. (Brisac, 1986; p. 13)
7. (Jantzen, 1984; p. 157)
8. (Brisac, 1986; p. 33)
9. (Brisac, 1986; p. 13)
10. (Brown, 1991; p. 8)
11. (Male, 1972; p. 8)
12. (Cowan, 1990; pp. 7-15)

Chapter 15
Vibrations:
Communication Through a Morphic Field

Abstract

This is a progress report on the computer simulation of a mathematical model for a morphic field. The model is a two-dimensional lattice of oscillators derived from the d'Alembertian wave equation by spatial discretization. The communication is between two clamped objects inserted into the field. A change of shape in one of them sets off a transient wave which perturbs the boundary field of the other one after a brief delay. Unlike radio propagation, this is a static monopole transmission.

Publication

Ms #86, written December 8, 1996. This was presented to the Second World Congress on the Synthesis of Science and Religion at the Bhaktivedanta Institute, Kolkata, 1997. Publication unknown.

Contents

1. Introduction
2. Vibrations and Morphogenesis
3. Reaction-Diffusion Models
4. Wave-Diffusion Models
5. Morphic Fields
6. Our Model
7. Simulation Results
8. Conclusion
Acknowledgments
Notes

1. Introduction

Morphogenesis is a branch of mathematics, of chaos theory actually, inspired by the problem of biological morphogenesis, the mystery of pattern formation in biological nature. For example, how did the leopard get its spots? How does an egg become a chicken? Today, most biologists believe that a leopard gets its spots from its mother leopard, and a chicken gets its internal organs through the information of DNA alone, in the process of embryogenesis.

But only a few decades ago, vitalists and organicists considered the idea that there are immaterial fields of intelligence which collaborate with DNA: *morphogenetic fields*. Around 1954, this idea was revived by the late theoretical biologist, Conrad Waddington. The renowned French mathematician René Thom, inspired by Waddington, provided mathematical models for Waddington's field theory of embryogenesis around 1966.[1] In the process, he introduced Waddington's teleological notion of *attractor* into the history of mathematics, a crucial contribution to dynamical systems theory (also known as *chaos theory*) and its applications.[2]

And more recently, it has been revised and extended by Rupert Sheldrake in a sequence of books.[3] *Morphic field* is the name given by Sheldrake, generically, to morphogenetic, mental, and social fields.[4] Lately, he proposed this field as the medium for telepathic communications observed between animals, for example, between people and their pets.[5] More importantly, one goal of his work is the depolarization of the conflict between the sciences and the major world religions which necessarily results from the mechanistic and materialistic paradigm rampant in the scientific community of today.[6]

In this paper we report on our recent computer simulation

of a mathematical model for this kind of communication.

2. Vibrations and Morphogenesis

In 1972, while visiting René Thom in France, I discovered the work of Hans Jenny of Basel. Under the influence of the esoteric Christian mystic Rudolph Steiner, Jenny had continued the research of Ernst Chladni, the founder of acoustics, upon the forms created in a field of acoustic vibration. Later that year, while staying at the ashram of Neem Karoli Baba at Kainchi, in the Himalayan foothills of North India, I abstracted the work of Chladni and Jenny into a mathematical model for morphogenesis, and applied it to neurobiology, that is, brain waves. This work was published on my return from India to the University of California, in 1975, as the paper, *Vibrations and the realization of form*. During this same period of time, Rupert Sheldrake was writing his first book on morphogenesis in the ashram of Dom Bede Griffiths, in Tamil Nadu, South India. Both of us were undoubtedly influenced by the Hindu theories of the *akasha*, that is, an infinite, vibrational field of intelligence. Naturally, when we met in 1982, we found we had much in common. Our friendship and discussions over the years are the basis of the work reported here.

3. Reaction-Diffusion Models

The evolution of mathematical models for morphogenesis began in 1924, with the work of Roland Fischer. This was the first example, to my knowledge, of a reaction-diffusion equation. This type of model combines a spatially distributed chemical reaction with a diffusion of the chemical reactants through the spatial substrate. After intuitive and theoretical discussions of this sort of model for embryogenesis (by Rashevsky, the founder of mathematical biology, in the 1930s) and for plant phyllotaxis (by Turing, in England, in the 1950s) the computer simulations began in the 1970s, in the group of Prigogine in Brussels. These simulations proved conclusively that the reaction-diffusion models were capable of morphogenesis, and many more studies have followed (see the books of Murray and Meinhardt in the Bibliography).

4. *Wave-Diffusion Models*

Following the success of reaction-diffusion models for chemical and biological morphogenesis, successive generalizations were reported in various works. The wave diffusion models were based on the foundational work of mathematical physics, the wave equation for the vibrating string of d'Alembert, published in 1749. An early model of this type was the one-dimensional lattice of oscillators of Fermi, Pasta, and Ulam, in which chaotic behavior was observed in the 1950s. A very general model of this type is the *cellular dynamical system* discussed in the 1970s, and reported in my book, *Complex Dynamical Systems*.

5. *Morphic Fields*

The physical fields of modern physics are recent inventions. They are cognitive strategies only: it is impossible to prove they exist. The first one, the gravitational field, was the invention of Isaac Newton, 300 years ago. The second one, the electromagnetic field, was invented about a century ago to represent the observations of Michael Faraday in the 1830s, and later, of Heinrich Hertz with his high voltage coil. Soon, this concept was embedded in a highly successful mathematical model by Clerk Maxwell, now known as the *Maxwell equations*. Just a few years later tensor analysis was developed by mathematicians, and applied to both the gravitational and electromagnetic fields. These two fields are called material fields, although they are not material themselves, because they are created and maintained by physical mass or electromagnetic properties, and they interact with matter. The morphic fields of Rupert Sheldrake may be called immaterial fields, in that their creation and maintenance may be outside the material universe, like the akasha. They are nevertheless amenable to mathematical models, which may improve our understanding of them.

6. Our Model

Our model for the tensorial morphic field (in this simple model, a scalar field) is derived from an electromagnetic field on a two-dimensional, flat torus, in which are placed two conductors. One, A, will be the receiver of a communication transmitted by the other, B. In imitation of the senses of sight, hearing, and smell, we imagine that B sends the message by a motion or change of shape, like ringing a bell. An oscillatory transient then propagates through the scalar field, a vibration like a sound wave. As the transient arrives at the boundary of the receiver, A, a *perception* occurs.

This is a boundary event, in which the morphic field external to A (which we visualize in our model as a small, hollow square) disturbs the equilibrium state on the square boundary, of A (think of an imperfectly grounded conductor in a field of radio waves). This disturbance crosses the boundary, by becoming a changing boundary condition for the tensorial state representing the inner psychological space (psychocosm) of A. This interior effect might also be modeled

Communication Through a Morphic Field

by a tensorial field, but we have not done so.[7] But if we did, the perception event might be modeled by a tensor field on the boundary of A.[8] Thus, we would have three tensor fields: the external morphic field, the boundary perception field, and the interior mental field.

Here, we simulate the perception by conductor A of a transient wave triggered by a sudden change of shape in

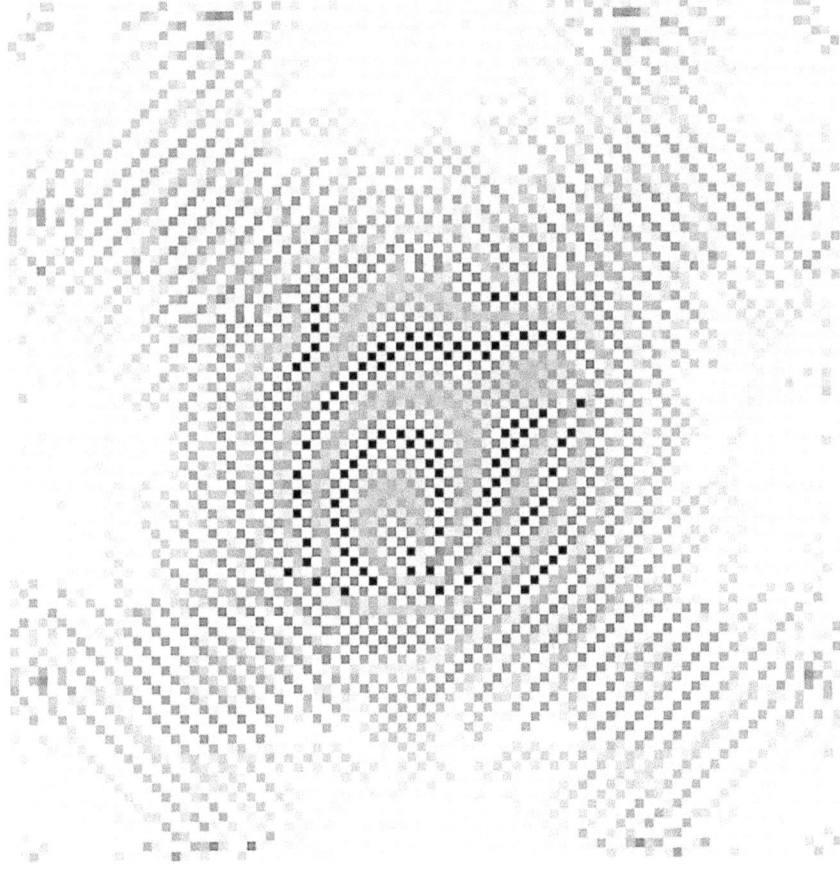

Figure. This image, a single frame from a video of our simulation, shows the magnitude of the morphic field as a shade of gray. A full color image of the same frame is shown on the front cover.

conductor B in a simpler scheme: we just image the waves arriving at the square boundary of A, as a retina. We visualize the morphic field restricted to the neighborhood of the square boundary. This mode of communication is monopolar. A change of shape is transmitted through the field, without oscillation of either conductor. A transient carries the information, and we regard this as a model for morphic resonance, as defined by Sheldrake.[9]

7. Simulation Results

The simulation was carried out by Peter Broadwell, using the software system MIMI (Mathematically Illuminated Musical Instrument) which we have developed, along with Ami Radunskaya, for our live performances of visual mathematics and music. A toral lattice of about 8,000 oscillators with Laplacean coupling (that is, the 88 x 88 cell discretization of a d'Alembertian wave equation on a two-dimensional rectangle with the opposite edges identified) was imaged by color coding the displacement (that is, the wave amplitude) on the computer screen. The simulation ran on a Silicon Graphics Iris Indigo computer, at about 10 iterations per second. The result is an animated color image on the screen, which is available in a ten-minute videotape, in which the communication potential of this kind of morphic field is clearly demonstrated.

8. Conclusion

In this first experiment, we have a convincing demonstration that communication of a semiotic (iconic) nature (analogous to radio broadcasting in the electromagnetic field) may be supported by an immaterial field such as the morphic fields of Rupert Sheldrake. We do not claim to establish the existence of such fields, nor the capacity of the brain to emit or receive them. However, the whole language and cognitive strategy of Sheldrake involving morphic fields and morphic resonance as the basis for physical, biological, and social morphogenesis, is strongly supported by our results.

Acknowledgments

We are grateful to René Thom, Hans Jenny, Neem Karoli Baba, Erich Jantsch, Terence McKenna, Rupert Sheldrake, and Peter Broadwell, for their contributions to this work, and to Prasun Roy for sharing his work with us, and for his invitation to present our work in Calcutta.

Notes

1 The main source is (Thom, 1972).
2 A basic text is (Abraham, 1992).
3 Especially (Sheldrake, 1981) and (Sheldrake, 1988).
4 See p.112 in (Sheldrake, 1988).
5 See (Sheldrake, 1994), especially pp. 88-89.
6 See the interview with Sheldrake in (Webber, 1986), as well as Ch. 9 in (Sheldrak.e, 1991).
7 But see Roy, 1996.
8 See Hoffman.
9 See pp. 95-86 in (Sheldrake, 1981).

Chapter 16
Vibrations:
Communication Through a Morphic Field
Part 2: Simulations, Results and Video

With: Peter Broadwell

Abstract

This is a further progress report on the computer simulation of a mathematical model for a morphic field. The model is a two-dimensional lattice of oscillators derived from the d'Alembertian wave equation by spatial discretization. The communication is between two clamped objects inserted into the field. A change of shape in one of them sets off a transient wave which perturbs the boundary field of the other one after a brief delay. Unlike radio propagation, this is a static monopole transmission. In this second simulation, we clamp the field at the edges of a rectangular region. This note is an explanation of the companion video, which is a record of the experiment. [http://www.ralph-abraham.org/articles/MS%2386.Video/]

Publication

Ms #86B, written December 8, 1996. Not previously published.

Contents

1. Introduction
2. The Model
3. Visual Representation
4. The Actors
5. The Play
6. The Retina
7. The Written Record
8. The Experiments
9. Conclusion
Acknowledgments

1. Introduction

This note is a supplement to our Ms #86, and is intended to explain the companion video. Its most obvious features are:

- the model, the mathematical object which rules the simulation,
- the field, a wildly vibrating color pattern in a square frame,
- actor H, a black square in the field,
- actor D, a black triangle in the field,
- the play, in which the actors play their roles,
- the retina, a broad vertical line alongside actor D,
- the retinal recording, a vertical column with a web-like pattern,
- the color bar, which indicates the mapping from numerical values to colors, and
- the time (iteration) counter, in the lower right corner of the screen.

We now describe these features, and the sequence of the companion video.

2. The Model

Our model for the morphic field is derived from an electromagnetic field in two dimensions. The field may be conceptualized as the vertical displacement of a horizontal drumhead on a square drum. However, there is no damping. Thus, once the membrane is struck, it vibrates endlessly. The displacement is restricted to a range of minus 1 to plus 1 unit, relative to the equilibrium (flat, horizontal) configuration, in our computer simulations. The bounding square is clamped at value 0. Further, the membrane is discretized as a square array of harmonic oscillators connected by springs, in the classical style of the Bernoulli and d'Alembert. We used an array of size 88 by 88. The coupling is Laplacean, as always, in the discretization of the wave equations of mathematical physics.

3. Visual Representation

The displacement is represented on the computer screen as a pattern of colors superimposed upon the square membrane. The range -5 to +5 units is represented by spectral hues from blue to red. With each discrete increment of time, typically 0.01 units, the displacement (and thus the color) at each point of the array is updated, creating a new pattern of color on the square array. These successive patterns are then recorded to videotape at the rate of 10 frames per second.

4. The Actors

We use this model to simulate the effect upon the field (membrane) due to two actors. One, D, will be the receiver of a communication transmitted by the other, H. In imitation of the senses of sight, hearing, and smell, we imagine that H sends the message by a motion or change of shape, like ringing a bell. An oscillatory transient then propagates through the scalar field, a vibration like a sound wave. As the transient arrives at the boundary of the receiver, D, a perception occurs. In this simulation, the actors are represented by grounded (that is, immovable) objects: D by a triangle, H by a square. These figures hold down the membrane, that is, they clamp the field or displacement at the zero value.

5. The Play

In these experiments, the actors are directed to play out a scenario of communication as follows. First, the stage (the square array or membrane) is empty. Then D takes his place on the stage, creating an excited state of the membrane. We wait a few minutes. This is a state of active silence or background noise. Then, H appears upon the stage. She effects the active silence as by a heavy weight upon a drum head. The entire vibrating field is effected. The effect near the receiver, D, is subtle, but perceptible.

6. The Retina

The receiver (D, triangle) is supposed to be sensitive to motion of the field nearby. We model this supposition by inserting a retina into the field near the receiver. This may be interpreted more as an organ of Corti, which senses the vibration of the basilar membrane in the perception of sound, or a sort of microphone. However, as we are representing the field visually as a pattern of spectral colors, we are going to think of the organ of perception as a (one-dimensional) retina. It sees, instant by instant, the row of colors written upon it by the membrane motion.

7. The Written Record

It is difficult to remember the moving patterns of color near the actors, so we create a written record of the retinal images by stacking up the rows of color into a two-dimensional pattern, a memory engram as it were. This is shown alongside the square array in the video. The rows of color are written from the bottom up. The upward gliding black line is the recording head. When it reaches the top of the screen, it reappears at the bottom, and writes over the previous records. These space-time patterns comprise our experimental results.

8. The Experiments

Two plays of three acts each are recorded on the video, which lasts about 20 minutes altogether. The two plays differ primarily in the stiffness of the membrane (a parameter in the model). The frequency of vibration is higher in the second simulation, and the wavelengths correspondingly shorter.

First play, act 1

At iteration 0, D appears alone on the stage, and sits still for five minutes (about 3574 iterations). This soon settles down to a steady vibration. Note the left-right symmetry in the retinal recording as it gradually develops.

Act 2

Then H is placed on the stage, and we watch for another five minutes. Notice a slowly increasing left-right asymmetry in the retinal recording, and a tightening of the web. The weight of H on the drumhead skews the vibrating field, and increases the frequency.

Act 3

Around iteration 7200, H is removed from the field. The retinal recording relaxes to its equilibrium state in Act 1, as the shadow of the square fades from the field by the end of play, iteration 14,000.

Second play

In the second play, we see the same scenario in three acts, with all the action accelerated, and completed in about 5000 iterations.

9. Conclusion

In these experiments, we clearly show that the space-time record of perception by actor D of the vibrating field is significantly changed by the sudden arrival of actor H on the stage . There is skewing and tightening of the web of excitation in the retinal recording of D's perception when H is in the field.

Acknowledgments

We are grateful to Rupert Sheldrake for his support of this work, and deeply in debt to the Mathematically Illuminated Musical Instrument Project for use of its software, MIMI.

Chapter 17
Vibrational Resonance and Cognitive Internalization

Dedicated to
Erich Jantsch (1929-1980)
Terence McKenna (1946-2000)

Abstract

Continuing in the spirit of earlier works, we propose a mathematical model for the process of internalization of ideas. This entire concept presupposes a paradigm of mind with internal and external regions, which we accept provisionally for the sake of discussion. In short, we envision a physical model comprising several excitable, continuous media in parallel planes, interconnected by a process of resonance of vibrations. The mathematical model for this physical analog is then discretized, and proposed verbatim as a computational model for the mental system. This model is typical of complex dynamical systems, as they have evolved during the last twenty years or so.

Publication

Ms #86B, written March 22, 2000 for the *Proceedings of Einstein Days in Visva Bharati University, Santiniketan, West Bengal, India, March 15-18, 2000: International Seminar on Cognitive Processes of Internalization in Humanities and Sciences.*

Contents

1. Introduction
2. An Exemplary Complex Dynamical System from Classical Physics
3. An Exemplary Complex Dynamical Model from Classical Mathematics
4. The Modern Computational Form of the Complex Dynamical Model
5. Application to Conscience
6. Conclusion
Acknowledgment
Notes

1. Introduction

In July, 1930, Einstein and Tagore met twice in Berlin. This excerpt is taken from the second conversation.[1]

> EINSTEIN: The problem begins, whether truth is independent of our consciousness.
>
> TAGORE: What we call truth lies in the rational harmony between the subjective and objective aspects of reality, both of which belong to the super-personal man.

In this short paper we construct a mathematical model for Tagore's idea of truth as the rational harmony of two aspects of reality. We translate aspect as field, and harmony as resonance. That is, reality is imaged as an immaterial, excitable field, capable of maintaining vibratory activity and space-time patterns. Our model of reality is derived from our earlier work on the morphic resonance concept of Rupert Sheldrake.[2] In fact, the views of both Tagore and Sheldrake are informed by ancient Indian roots. The objective aspect or field is the cognitive domain of science, nature, or external reality. The subjective aspect or field is the cognitive domain constructed by an individual being, or internal reality.

To Einstein, the external aspect was true reality. His use of the word *consciousness* above seems to mean individual (internal) consciousness or awareness, as opposed to the more literal meaning of shared (external) understanding, also known as *conscience*. To Tagore, the two aspects together comprised true reality: awareness and conscience in harmony. This fundamental disagreement was the topic of the conversation from which the quotation above is taken.

Naturally the question arises: Why, in this postmodern world, would we wish to add new mathematical models to a verbal discussion ongoing for thousands of years? The new mathematics we are now injecting into this long-ongoing dialogue — complex dynamics, chaos theory, fractals, and the like — belongs to both the internal and external aspects of reality. And being new, or newly discovered, it partakes of the evolutionary aspect of reality. It is because of this mathematical evolution, or more properly, the coevolution of mathematics and conscience, that new models are appropriate. New math, new shared understanding, new individual awareness, new math, etc. This hermeneutical cycle is basic to the evolution of conscience. In science, it is manifest in the concepts which are purely mathematical rather than actually physical, such as the gravitational field of Newton and the electromagnetic field of Maxwell.[3] The wave and heat equations of mathematical physics are derived from these field concepts, and these in turn are the tools of the modern theories of morphogenesis, such as the reaction-diffusion equations of biological morphogenesis, which is such a large part of mathematical biology, following from the works of Rashevsky, Kolmogorov-Piscunin-Pontriagin, and Turing.

Using these tools of mathematical morphogenesis, we go on now to develop a model for the internalization of a concept from the objective (external) aspect or field of conscience to the individual (internal) field of awareness, or vice versa, by a process of vibrational resonance or harmony. In other words, a model for Tagore's reality. The outline of our presentation is shown in Figure 1.1.

Vibrational Resonance and Cognitive Internalization 247

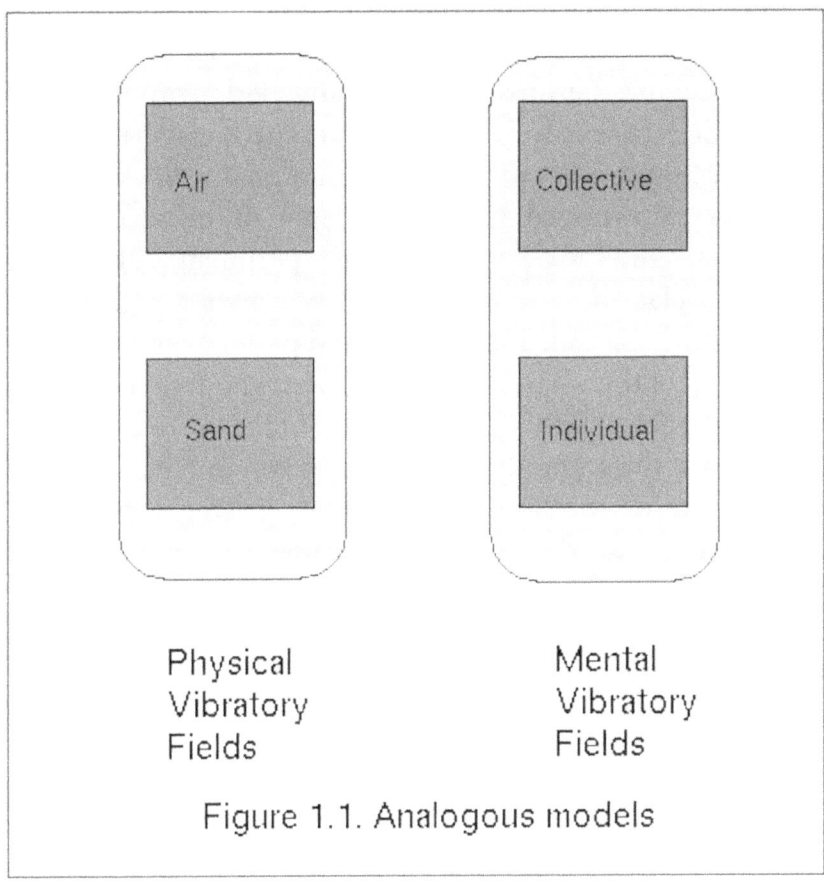

Figure 1.1. Analogous models

2. An Exemplary Complex Dynamical System from Classical Physics

Inspired by Benjamin Franklin's invention of the glass harmonium, Ernst Chladni studied the patterns of vibration in glass plates by observing the motion of sand sprinkled on the plate, maintaining its vibration by bowing the edge with a cello bow. With this project, around 1820, he founded acoustics, the branch of physics devoted to the production and transmission of sound.[4] A similar phenomenon was observed by Michael Faraday in a thin layer of liquid on a vibrating plate. He named these patterns *crispations*.[5]

Controversy regarding the mechanism producing these patterns led to experiments in a vacuum, and revealed that grex vortices in the air over the plate, excited by its vibrations, moved the sand. A *grex* is a toroidal motion, in which the fluid moves downward through the center of the torus and upwards around the outside. Further experiments using a light powder in place of sand gave further information regarding the vortices in the air. The heavier sand particles are moved by the bottom of the vortices, collecting at the nodes. The lighter powder particles are lifted over the top of the vortices and deposited at the antinodes. All this is shown in Figure 2.1.

More recent experiments by Hans Jenny using a mixture of black sand and white powder dramatically demonstrated this filtration by density in the vortices, with the sand moving to the nodes, and the powder to the antinodes. The pattern so produced is highly suggestive of biochemical pattern formations in embryogenesis, and other morphogenetic processes.[6] An experimental arrangement for the study of Faraday crispations is shown in Figure 2.2. An electrical wave delivered to a transducer (loudspeaker) creates a sound wave in the air beneath a plastic plate, inducing and maintaining a pattern of vibration. This in turn activates a related pattern of vibration in the thin layer of liquid resting on the plate, and thus a pattern of grex vortices in the layer of air over the plate. Air, plastic, liquid, air: four layers of coupled pattern formation processes.

3. An Exemplary Complex Dynamical Model from Classical Mathematics

We begin with a simple dynamical model for a single layer of a vibrating medium from classical mathematics. That is, a

Vibrational Resonance and Cognitive Internalization 249

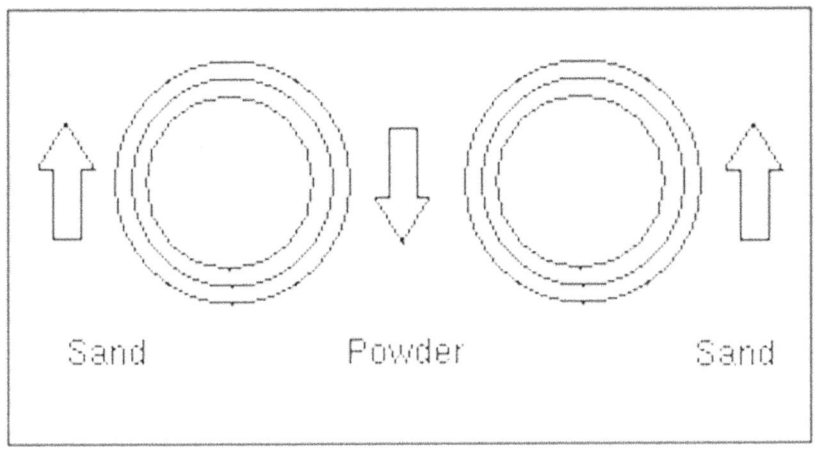

Fig. 2.1. Section of a grex

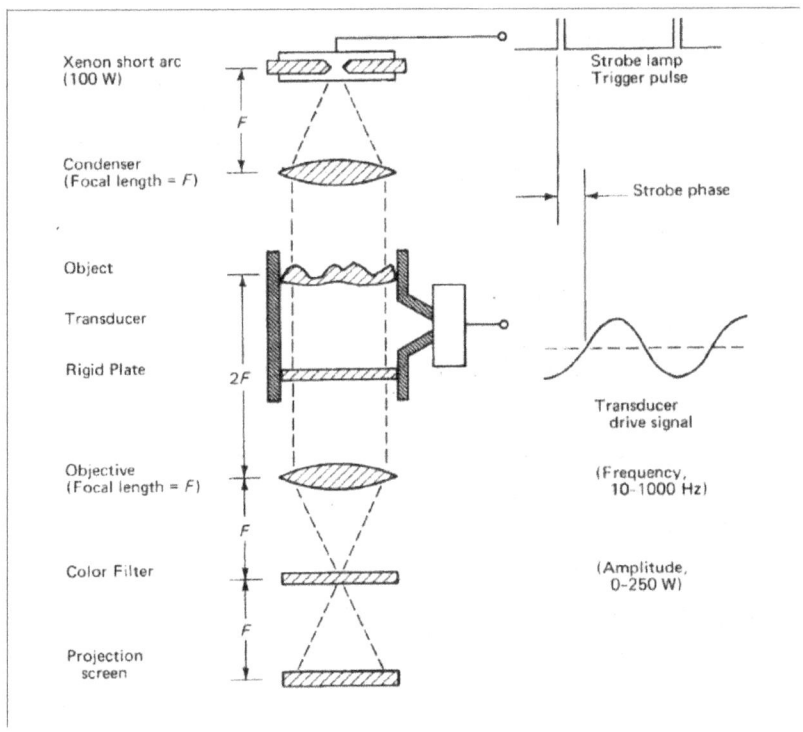

Fig. 2.2. The Jenny macroscope

partial differential equation of evolution type for a function which may be regarded as an abstract representation of the instantaneous state of the medium. For example, in the case of a wave equation, the function may represent the displacement of the two-or three-dimensional material from an equilibrium position. Or in the case of a reaction-diffusion equation, the function may represent the concentrations of several chemical reactants. Not wishing to ascend to the level of the symbolic notations of classical mathematics, we may think of the function as a point in an infinite-dimensional geometric space, and the equation of evolution as a vectorfield (or flow) in that space. Thus, our ordinary intuitions from dynamical systems theory — attractors, basins, bifurcations, and so on — may come into play. In short, our model for a single excited layer is a flow scheme, that is, a continuous dynamical system with control parameters, defined on an abstract space of functions representing the states of the medium — the state space. The meaning of this will be elaborated in a special context in the next section. For the moment, we may simply regard the model, a dynamical scheme, as a black box. A point in this box is a mathematical representation of an instantaneous vibratory state of the medium, another (very thin) box, a layer. The height of the point may be regarded as an index of the possible vibratory states, and the horizontal position an index of the control parameters of the model.

We next consider two layers of vibrating media. For example, a thin, horizontal layer of air, lying upon a thin layer of water. For each layer, we imagine constructed a mathematical model, a dynamical scheme. Visualizing each model as a black box, we thus have two boxes, one above the other. But we further suppose that the two layers are in contact. Thus the motion of the water influences the motion of the air, and vice versa. To represent these mutual influences in our mathematical models we must connect the two black boxes. First, the state of the water affects the control parameters of the air. In the theory of complex dynamical systems, this is called a serial coupling.[7] Next, the state of the air affects the control parameters of the water, another serial coupling. Taken together, the two links represent a serial bicoupling, in the language of complex dynamical systems theory.

Our physical experience of vibratory systems in contact, strings of a musical instrument for example, includes the phenomenon of resonance. In this phenomenon, the vibrations of each string encourages the vibration of the other, if the vibrations are harmoniously related. More generally, we may say that a space-time pattern in one vibratory medium induces a harmonious space-time pattern in another medium. This is, in fact, the situation with the experiments of Chladni and Faraday, in the 19th century, as described above. Specific dynamical schemes have been elaborated for the crispations of Faraday, in particular, and there is a growing literature regarding them in mathematical and scientific journals today. But we will be discussing only the computational form of these models, to which we now turn.

4. The Modern Computational Form of the Complex Dynamical Model

The study of the space-time patterns determined by equations of evolution — such as those of mathematical physics, chemistry, and biology described above — were initially carried out with the methods of classical analysis, the only mathematics known to the early pioneers in this field: Euler, d'Alembert, Fourier, and so on. These methods were very limited, and yielded results only in the hands of the most gifted analysts. They conceived of computational methods also, in which extensive arithmetic done laboriously with paper and pencil gradually revealed some faint image.

A dramatic example of the computational approach, before the advent of computing machines, was provided by Richard Southwell. As part of the war effort in Great Britain during the Second World War, Southwell commanded a troop of arithmetically gifted youth, drafted from universities for this purpose. Following a computational method of his own devising, still used today, Southwell directed the clever kids, scampering in stocking feet over huge paper carpets, from atop a tall step ladder. Doing arithmetic upon numbers they read from the paper at their feet on small scratch pads in their hands, they would stoop from time to time to write a new result on the large paper carpet, crossing out the previous result.

The computer revolution tipped the scales, giving great advantage to computational methods over the analytical techniques. Not only faster and more general, these new methods could be applied by any computer-literate person. This is the dominant style of applied mathematics today. Applied to our problem of the space-time pattern of vibration maintained by an external force acting on an excitable medium, such as an elastic membrane, the Southwell method reduces the membrane to a two-dimensional lattice of identical cells, each described by a small oscillator — for example, a simple pendulum, or a weight hanging from a coil spring. Each such cell is coupled somehow to its four nearest neighbors. Such a mathematical object is called a cellular dynamical system, or cellular dynamaton, or CD for short.

The CD for one membrane, or layer, is visualized on the computer monitor as an apparently continuous image of changing colors. Each pixel (point on the screen) is given a

Vibrational Resonance and Cognitive Internalization 253

color which is a code for a number. For example, red might denote the displacement of a pendulum to the left by one inch, while blue indicates displacement to the right by one inch. Colors in between may be coded for intermediate positions of the pendulum. One starts with any convenient pattern of colors on the screen. The equation of evolution for the vibrating state of the membrane, interpreted by the Southwell method, then determines, from this initial pattern, a new one. And repeated application of this method with the new pattern yields still another, and so on. Thus, a moving image is seen on the screen, and after a few iterations of the computational method of Southwell (if all is going according to Hoyle) we are viewing the space-time pattern determined by the equation of evolution chosen at the start of the process.

Finally, this strategy may be applied to the complex system

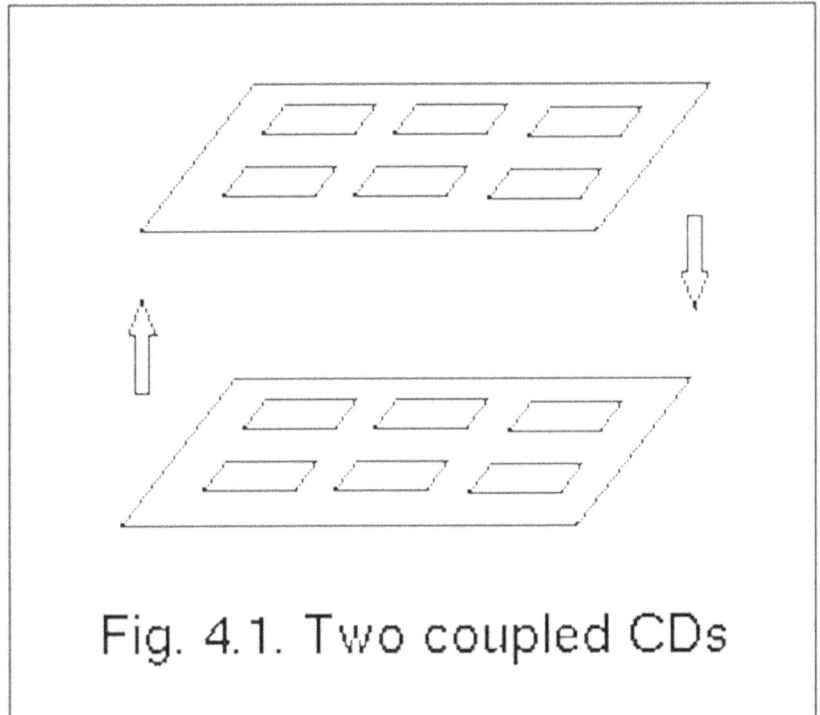

Fig. 4.1. Two coupled CDs

of two coupled membranes. Each membrane is modeled by a CD, and the two CDs are coupled to each other, cell-by-cell, as shown in Figure 4.1.

5. *Application to Conscience*

Consciousness is among the vaguest and most important of words, but the conventional meanings fall into two main groups. On the one hand, the Einstein view, it is taken to mean individual awareness — the conscious, inner self. And on the other hand, in the Tagore view, it means an emergent, collective property of whole communities of individuals — schools of fish, herds of cattle, flocks of birds, cultures of humans. Here we mean this latter, literal meaning: shared understanding. This is also called conscience. With this agreed, "I am conscious" would mean that I have an open channel of communication between my individual, internal awareness, and the collective mental field of consciousness, or conscience, of my culture.

Just as the early cartographers made maps of the world by gluing together individual charts brought back by pioneering navigators, shared understanding may have been constructed by convergence, or emergence, of individual understandings. This map of the intellectual world, constantly evolving, becomes stored in libraries and perhaps in an immaterial or mental field of living, collective memory. New individuals — infants, children, young adults, immigrants — are brought into this collective field, or acquire conscience, through an educational process commencing perhaps in conversation with family members or neighbors. There is also evidence that some sort of telepathy, such as morphic resonance, contributes to this induction process.[8] Such a resonance process of mental fields, individual and collective, is consistent with the Sanskrit heritage which informed Tagore and Sheldrake. In the Kashmiri Shaivite tradition, a divine oscillation (*spanda*) is the driving force which maintains an excited state of vibration in the collective field.[9] The existence of such fields is, of course, controversial. Even assuming their existence, the idea that information is encoded into the field as a vibratory space-time pattern — like a radio broadcast into the electromagnetic field — is a further flight of fantasy. And yet, this vibration image has been a part of our conscience for thousands of years, due to prophesy, sacred texts, gnostic experiences, and the like. Finally, accepting all this for the sake of discussion, there is the further question: Is the vibrating field evolving, or eternal? We summarize all views in one image in Figure 5.1.

And in Figure 5.2 we see, side-by-side,
- the physical experiment of Chladni, Faraday, Jenny, myself, and others, and
- the vibratory model of conscience which is the justification for our common mathematical model, based on complex dynamata, for both.

6. Conclusion

How is information, such as Euclid's geometry, encoded into a vibratory field? We have not gone into this question. What we have done is to describe a complex dynamical model for the resonance of two vibrating membranes. What is the use of this? We suggest (based upon extensive personal experience) that experiments with this model, performed with a personal computer, will be highly educational as well as artistically beautiful. One may gain thus an intuitive understanding of intuitive understanding itself, an interesting self-reflection.

Acknowledgment.

Many thanks to Prof. Prasun K, Roy for instigating this article.

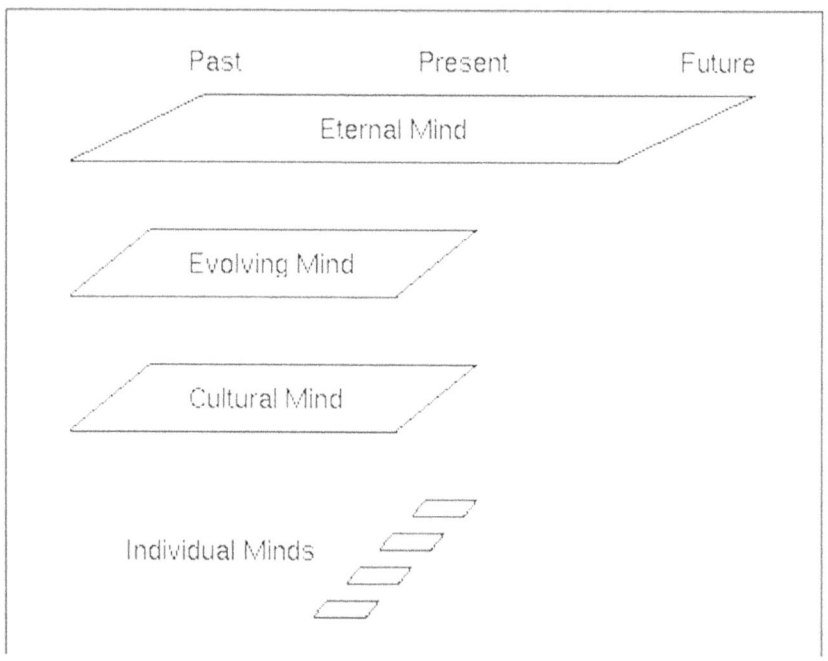

Fig 5.1. All views combined.

Driver	Eternal mind
Plate	Evolving mind
Air	Cultural mind
Sand	Individual minds

Fig. 5.2. Two systems, side-by-side

Notes

1. (Tagore, 1931, p. 224); (Chakravarty, 1961, p. 112)
2. (Sheldrake, 1981)
3. (Kline, 1985)
4. (Abraham, 1988)
5. (Abraham, 1976)
6. (Jenny, 1967)
7. (Abraham, 1993b)
8. (Sheldrake, 1981); (Radin, 1997)
9. (Dyczkowski, 1992)

Chapter 18
A Two-Worlds Model for Consciousness

Dedicated to
John William Dunne (1875-1949)

Abstract

A model is proposed in which communication and action are extended both into the past and into the future. The chief feature of this model is its duality, manifest in a pair of parallel space-time worlds. Interaction between these worlds — consciousness — is effected by a moving window, through which influences pass by a process of resonance.

Publication

Ms #106, written June 1, 2000. Not previously published.

Contents

1. Introduction
2. The Step-Time World
3. The Slope-Time World
4. Interaction Between Worlds
5. Conclusion
Notes

1. Introduction

A number of simultaneous paranormal or psi phenomena have been explained, or understood perhaps, through the medium of a hypothetical field, or immaterial force.[1] Indeed, even some normal phenomena have received hypothetical explanations of this sort.[2] Quantum mechanics is frequently mentioned in these contexts.[3]

These constructions are helpful for psi phenomena such as telepathy, which do not involve a dislocation in time. But precognition remains a challenge in the psi-field context, and additional constructs have been proposed, such as serial worlds[4] or two-dimensional time. The phenomena involving revision of the past, such as influencing a tape-recording of a random number generator, is even more of a challenge.[5]

In this brief paper, we are going to meet this challenge by proposing a minimal extension of the world-view of conventional science, namely, by the addition of a second space-time world, parallel to the ordinary one. This is partly inspired by the serial worlds model of Dunne,[6] and partly by the morphic resonance idea of Sheldrake.[7] We are aiming here at a *chaontic* world-model that can accommodate the data of transtemporal psi research.

Note: By *world*, we mean a four-dimensional, space-time universe. By *model*, we mean a mathematical model (geometry plus dynamics, in the spirit of chaos theory) intended as a cognitive strategy. *Chaontic*: from *chaontology*, meaning ontology informed by chaos theory.

2. The Step-Time World

By the step-time world we mean all of the space-time world of ordinary reality, as modeled by conventional modern science, including the whole universe of material particles, waves, fields, forces, and all of the biospheric miracles of life, societies, and individual and collective consciousness.

The chief feature of this familiar world, or more precisely, the way it is seen in our present world-view, is the discreteness of its time. That is, time is seen as cut by a moving, spatial, three-dimensional hyperplane. Behind it, everything is determined, and cannot be changed. And ahead, everything is — to some degree — undetermined, inchoate, unknowable. In other words, the definiteness of the world follows this moving hyperplane, changing as it passes from nothing to all, from zero to one, like a Heavyside (step) function (see Figure 1).

This assumption, hidden so deeply within our world-view that it does not even have a name, is among the primary reasons that the results of well-done parapsychological research are rejected by our scientific establishment, and to some degree, by most people.

So, to give this nameless assumption a name, we may refer to it as *the hypothesis of step-time*. And hence, we call this world *the step-time world*.

3. The Slope-Time World

By the *slope-time world* we mean a new construct, which is nearly identical to the step-time world, and parallel to it. We may even think of two parallel hyperplanes in euclidean five-dimensional space, rather close together. It does no harm for our present, informal purposes, to think of them each as a flat three-dimensional space, extended by a flat one-dimensional time. Both worlds have physics, chemistry, planets, people, history, and so on. But there is one hypothetical feature of the slope-time world by which it differs substantially from our familiar step-time world. And that relates to its time. It

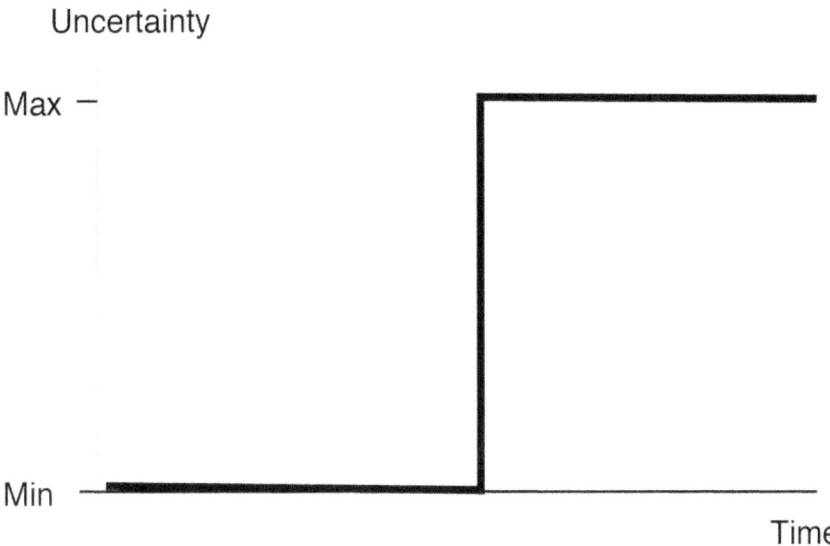

Figure 1. Heavyside step function.

lacks step-time. Instead, it has *slope-time*. By this we mean, roughly, that instead of the instant passage of the knife of the present, cutting known space away from the unknown, we have a window, the *extended-now window*, in which the future gradually freezes into the past.

The *width* of the extended-now window is a parameter of the slope-time model which we have not specified. Appropriate width values might best be obtained experimentally, from transtemporal psi experiments. Also, the *shape* of the extended-now window might be determined by experiments. A few shapes are shown in Figures 2, 3, and 4. For the *alignment* between the extended-now window of the slope-time world and the *instantaneous-now* of the step-time world, we propose to locate the now instant of the step-time model in the center of the extended-now window of the slope-time model, and they move together. But this alignment also might be determined experimentally.

We know well how to conceptualize the knife of step-time. But how can we conceive of this moving window? We suggest thinking of the whole slope-time world as a vibration in an immaterial field. The vibration stretches along the direction of time as a moving soliton, like a solitary wave in the sea. A tsunami, perhaps. And where its crest passes, the illusion of a present moment is the greatest. Were this soliton to be a delta function — that is, the width of the wave shrunk to zero — we would then have step-time.

Another conceptual strategy is provided by the image of a rolling pin, rolling down the thickness of a pad of pizza dough. Or, the steam-roller of fate, speeding down the highway of time, crushing possibilities down to certainties. The larger the roller, the wider the window.

4. Interaction Between Worlds

So now we have two models. One is the usual world, in which the present lasts only a moment. The other is very similar, but the present lasts for awhile. Why have two model worlds? Could we not just swap the old one for the new?

Well yes, in principle, we could. However, the present instant of the step-time world has become ingrained in our world-view because that is how we experience time. It appears as an experimental law of consciousness. Perhaps that is an artifact of our neurophysiology. But in any case, it behooves us to keep the old model alongside the new. At least, that is the strategy of this paper.

So let us regard the old, step-time world as a low-resolution model, convenient and traditional for ordinary mortals, and the new model as a high-resolution supermodel, useful for kings, philosophers, and parapsychologists.

Then we may regard conscious perceptions, as well as scientific observations, as communications between worlds. Precognitions are communications from the early part of the moving window of the slope-time world to the knife-edge of the step-time world. And psychokineses into the past are communications from the sharp present of the step-time world into the latter part of the window into the slope-time world.

Besides providing more room for our conceptualization of transtemporal effects, the two-worlds model may offer a context for a new wave mechanics, in which the Schrödinger equation is replaced by nonlinear dynamics, wave functions are not collapsed by observations, nonlocality is normal, and so on.

5. Conclusion

We set out to provide a minimalist extension of our worldview in which transtemporal phenomena may be fit. And we end up, perhaps, with rather more. In the two-worlds model, we may interpret perceptions, and individual conscious awareness. In the future, we have in mind to combine this model with our earlier models for telepathy via vibrational resonance in the morphic field.[8] In these models we placed individual conscious agents, and effected semaphoric messaging between them.[9] This style of communication is best understood by computer graphic simulation.[10]

Thus we may envision our two parallel four-dimensional worlds, placed in parallel within a five-dimensional geometry, and embraced by an immaterial vibrating field which is a medium of communication. Collective consciousness among an ensemble of individual minds might be modeled in this way.

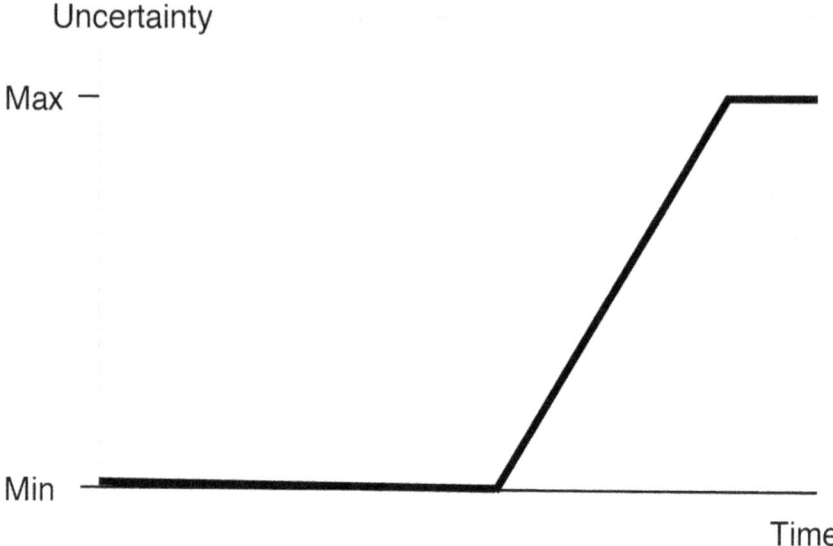

Figure 2. Piecewise-linear sigmoid function.

Figure 3. Smooth sigmoid function.

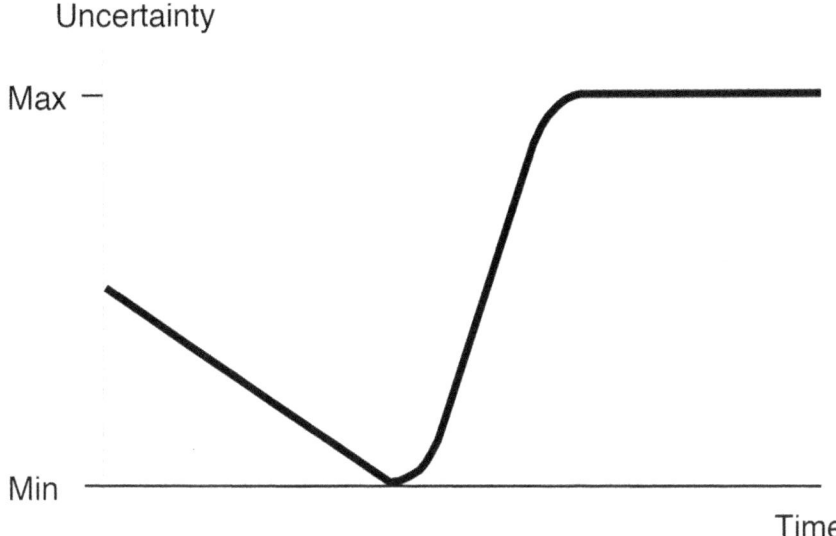

Figure 4. Smooth sigmoid function with forgetful past.

Notes

1 (Laszlo, 1996)
2 (Sheldrake, 1981)
3 (Herbert, 1987, 1985), (Laszlo, 1996), (Penrose, 1989), (Walker, 2000)
4 (Dunne, 1927)
5 (Radin, 1997)
6 (Dunne, 1927)
7 (Sheldrake, 1981)
8 Abraham (1976; pp. 134-149), (1981; pp. 153-168), (1985; pp. 13-26), (1987; pp. 13-19), (1993a), (1993b; pp. 75-79), (1995; pp. 80-85)
9 (Abraham, 1996)
10 (Abraham, 1997)

Chapter 19
Vibrations and Forms

Abstract

Based upon a presentation to the third Conference on Science and Consciousness, Ramakrishna Mission Institute of Culture, Gol Park, Kolkata, West Bengal (India) on 14 January, 2006.

Publication

Ms #118, written January 14, 2006. Published in *Consciousness: A Deeper Scientific Search. Proceedings of the 3rd Int'l. Conf. on Science and Consciousness. Ramakrishna Mission Institute of Culture, Golpark, Kolkata, India, 13-15 January, 2006.* J. Shear and S.P. Mukherjee, eds.

Contents

1. Introduction
2. Personal Experiences of Vibrations and Forms in Actual Consciousness, 1967-1972
3. My Miracle Year, 1972
    3a. Winter 1972, Paris
    3b. Summer and Fall 1972, Nainital
4. The Vibration Metaphor for Levels of Consciousness
    4a. My Experience
    4b. The Greek Tradition
    4c. The Jewish Tradition
    4d. The Indian Tradition
5. Beyond Maps of Consciousness: Communication Between Levels
6. Personal Experiences of Vibrations and Forms in Artificial Consciousness, 1974-1996
7. Conclusion
Notes

1. Introduction

My main goal in this paper is to give an idea, especially a visual idea, of my experiments with vibrations and forms in consciousness, over the past thirty years. The visual representations, computer graphic animations, may be best understood in the context of my personal experiences in actual consciousness exploration during the years 1967 to 1972, which motivated the work, and the philosophical frames, or maps of consciousness, in which I am trying to understand my experiences. These maps are based jointly on my own experiences, and on the philosophies of Greek, Jewish, and Indian origin. I must thank Dr. Paul Lee for his tutelage on the Platonic and Neoplatonic philosophies of the Greek tradition, Dr. SenSharma for his explanations of the Kashmiri Shaivite or Trika philosophy and other features of the Indian tradition, and Swami Prabhananda and the Ramakrishna Mission Institute of Culture for extraordinary hospitality during my month in Calcutta, and the privilege of attending this fascinating meeting.

2. Personal Experiences of Vibrations and Forms in Actual Consciousness, 1967-1972

My story begins in 1967, when I was a professor of mathematics at Princeton University. This is a wonderful university, especially for mathematics, and I was privileged to have colleagues and undergraduate and graduate students, whom I remember fondly to this day. Also, the 1960s was the time of student political unrest, and concomitantly, the time of the Beatles, and the Hip Subculture, or "sex, drugs, and rock and roll", as they used to say. My wonderful students were involved in both of these popular movements, and through them, I also became involved.

In 1967, the three notorious and defrocked psychology professors of Harvard University — Timothy Leary, Richard Alpert (later aka Baba Ram Dass), and Ralph Metzner — were barnstorming about the USA plumping the powers of LSD as an agent of spiritual growth. Leary, under the influence of Vedanta and Gayatri Devi of Los Angeles, used to affect Indian dress, and hold forth on Eastern philosophies. I heard their performance in the Lower East Side of New York City, and decided to try LSD and see for myself. One of my undergraduate students helped me onto the path, and my first experience was an epiphany indeed.

Through this epiphany, I became fascinated with the exploration of consciousness, as we called this path, and continued the work in irregular episodes as I followed my career to the University of California at Santa Cruz in 1968, and subsequently to Amsterdam, to Paris, and to Nainital in the Himalayan foothills. In 1973, I returned to Santa Cruz, and migrated from personal explorations back to academic research on consciousness, chaos theory, and other concerns. My walkabout of five years was over, but was to have a lasting effect on all aspects of my life. I had had hundreds of meditations of the sort practiced in Yoga Nidra, that is, lying prone through the night, in the so-called fourth state of consciousness, and amplified by small doses (eg, 25 mg) of LSD.[1] Like Yoga Nidra meditation, the LSD experience provides a trip to the fourth state lasting typically about eight hours, during which sleep is held at bay. These sessions were usually done alone, but sometimes in teams of from two up to a dozen or so others, flying, so we thought, in group formation like a flock of birds. Marijuana use was ubiquitous during this period, but in my experience it made no important contribution to my research, and, generally, I avoided it.

At one time, around 1969, we used large doses of DMT, and this period was crucially important to the whole evolution of my mathematical understanding of consciousness, based on geometry, topology, nonlinear dynamics, and the theory of vibrating waves. For in these experiments, although lasting only a few minutes, the reciprocal processes of vibrations producing forms and forms producing vibrations were clearly perceived in abstract visual fields.

Our perspective during this time and later, was gnostic. That is, we rejected teachers and teachings, and sought to discover cosmology for ourselves. Throughout this period, most of us in the Hip Subculture were apprenticing ourselves to teachers of ancient traditions from East, Mideast, and the West, sharing our experiences, traveling to faraway lands to find teachings, and so on. Teachers traveled through California, and we circled the globe in search of them. Personally I experienced yoga, martial arts (judo and aikido), prehistoric moon rituals, musical meditations, fasting and strict diets (eg, macrobiotics), and Native American ceremonies. This was the background of my interest in vibrations and forms in the field of consciousness.

3. *My Miracle Year, 1972*

This final year of my walkabout was blessed with two special learning experiences, one in Paris at the beginning of the year, the other in the Himalayan foothills, in the Summer and Fall.

3a. Winter 1972, Paris

This was the final year of my walkabout, following which I returned to ordinary reality and my post at the University of

California at Santa Cruz, an arduous process taking about a year. I began 1972 as a visiting professor at the University of Amsterdam, teaching catastrophe theory. At the same time, I had a visiting position at the Institut des Hautes Etudes Scientifiques (IHES) at Bures-sur-Yvette outside Paris. I used to commute weekly on the train, which I loved. At this time, IHES was newly formed, and had only two permanent professors, David Ruelle and René Thom, both of whom were superb. Thom was one of the great mathematicians of the 20th century, and had received the Fields Medal at the International Congress of Mathematics in 1956 for his work in differential topology. I had met him in 1960 in Berkeley, where we began working together on the foundations of catastrophe theory. During 1966, I had written my first books, *Foundations of Mechanics*, *Transversal Mappings and Flows*, and *Linear and Multilinear Algebra*, while René had written his foundational work on catastrophe theory, *Structural Stability and Morphogenesis*, which I arranged to have published by my publisher, Bill Benjamin.

Early in 1972, René and I were both stymied in our work and were browsing the borderlines of science looking for clues. I had been reading Kurt Lewin on topological psychology, and on arriving at IHES one day, I asked René what he was working on. He pulled a book from his desk and began showing me photo after photo of familiar forms from nature: spiral galaxies, cell mitosis, sand dunes, and so on. These forms, he said, had been photographed in vibrating water. The book was *Kymatik*, by Hans Jenny, a medical doctor from Dornach, a suburb of Basel, Switzerland. I was thunderstruck to see images from my meditations on the pages of a book, especially in support of the vibration metaphor of the Pythagoreans.

I immediately called Jenny in Dornach, and he agreed

to meet me. I took the train to Basel, and was met at the station by Jenny's son-in-law, Christian Stutten, who drove me to Dornach. Along the way I learned that Dornach was the world headquarters of the Anthroposophy movement founded by Rudolf Steiner, the esoteric Christian follower of Madame Blavatsky's *Secret Doctrine*, around 1900. Jenny was a follower of Steiner, and lived in Dornach along with many other Anthropops. Jenny greeted me in his home, showed me part of his lab, and an animated film of some experiments in progress. I collected his papers and books and went home to Paris and Amsterdam inspired.

As the winter progressed, I thought much about morphogenesis and the mathematics of coupled systems of vibrating membranes and fluids, while continuing to teach catastrophe theory in Amsterdam, and giving many lectures on these subjects at universities all over Europe. Also, my chemically assisted meditations continued, and in them, I pursued the vibration metaphor in conceptual space, and simultaneously, in experiential space.

These experiences were dominated by rapidly vibrating patterns of brightly colored abstract forms, somewhat like the video art and rock concert light shows of the 1960s. The scintillating light caustics projected by the bright sun on the bottom of a swimming pool also give an intimation of the visual aspect of these meditations. An excellent computer simulation has been achieved by Scott Draves in his art works called *Electric Sheep*, and may be seen on his website.[2]

3b. Summer and Fall 1972, Nainital

Suddenly, the spring semester in Amsterdam was over, grades were recorded, and I had a small savings account. It occurred to me to pay India a brief visit before school began again in the Fall of 1972. Here I was influenced by the ambiance of Amsterdam culture, in which I met so many people who had just returned from, or were about to go again to, India. One young man just returned told me how he organized his explorations of the Himalaya: just sit in a tea shop until somebody offers you an experience, then accept it, he said. Just go with the flow. This was my plan. One day at the Kosmos, a psychedelic and meditation hall run by the Dutch government (bless it), I looked up and saw my old friend Baba Ram Dass. The former Richard Alpert, he was among the Harvard trio of professors who had encouraged my decision to experiment with LSD in 1967. Then he had lived briefly in my house in Santa Cruz, California. He had stayed for a time in Nainital, near the western border of Nepal in the Himalayan foothills, where he became attached to a guru called Neem Karoli Baba. I told Baba Ram Dass about my plan to visit India and he gave me instructions for connecting with Neem Karoli Baba. Find your way to Nainital, he said, then hang out at this particular hotel, and if I was supposed to meet Neem Karoli Baba, somebody would approach me and take me to the ashram outside Kainchi, a small village.

And so, late in June, 1972, it came to pass. I went to the ashram with a group of western devotees in a taxi. But on arrival I felt a bit disappointed by the amplified music and carnival atmosphere. I saw the devotees sitting in darshan formation in front of Neem Karoli Baba on his tucket, all in silence. Something seemed to be going on but I was blind to it. Someone would give him prasad, a fruit for example, and he would immediately toss it to someone else. I went back to the hotel in Nainital determined to go on with whomever next approached me.

This process took no time at all. Once back at the hotel, I met a young barefoot Canadian dressed in a simple smock.

He introduced himself as Shambu. As I had been on the road for a long while with a highly evolved travel kit that fit into a small shoulder bag, I was greatly impressed by his kit, which required not even a bag. Shambu explained that he had been living in a cave in the jungle for several months with two other saddhus. There were three small caves by a stream in the jungle, two miles from the nearest town. One of the saddhus had just left, and the village had dispatched Shambu to find a replacement. Apparently the villagers felt their prosperity was only possible with all three caves occupied by appropriate persons engaged in full-time spiritual practice. Smoking ganja apparently counted as spiritual practice, worship of Shiva it seems. Shambu was sure that he had been guided to me as I was the chosen person.

Shambu put me on a bus with the usual sort of instruction: ride the bus to the end of the line at Almora, from there I would be guided somehow. This was monsoon season, and there had been heavy rain. After a short while the bus was firmly halted by a major road washout. Everyone climbed out of the bus. Looking down the slope, I was surprised to see Neem Karoli Baba's ashram for the second time. What a coincidence! Then someone came out to say I should come in at once, as Neem Karoli Baba was asking for me. Was this really happening, or was there some mistake? Neem Karoli Baba gave me a bag of breakfast cereal. He said I was going to need it in the jungle. Two young Indian devotees were told to guide me on a trek through the jungle around the washout, and put me on a bus for Almora on the other side. By this time I was losing my Western mind, and all this seemed more like paranormal phenomena than conspiracy theory.

It was midnight when finally the second bus arrived in Almora. The village was dark, but moonlight through a clearing in the clouds showed the shops in silhouette. A man descended from the bus after me. He had a bearer with a long box balanced on his head. I asked him where he was going, hoping for a clue for my next steps. He said that he was a student of Jim Corbett, the famous hunter of man eating tigers. I had just read Corbett's book, *Maneaters of the Kumoan*. Actually, we were now in the Kumoan Hills. The man said the long package was his rifle. There was a maneating panther on the loose nearby, and he was about to spend the night in a tree overlooking a fresh human kill, hoping to shoot the panther. This was his job, he had been sent by the government. I decided not to follow him into the jungle.

I followed some other people who descended from the bus. They seemed to know where they were going, on a footpath into the jungle. One by one they vanished into side paths, and then I was walking alone into the dark unknown, following this single-track footpath. I could not stop to sleep, for fear of the panther. As long as the path continued, and looked like it was used by humans, I would continue, until I found where it went. Another village or whatever. Seemed like a plan, for an hour or so, until there was a fork in the path. In the dark I could see no indication which way to go. Just then I was startled by a rustle very close by. I could see only grey on grey in the darkness. Then a voice said in clear English, "Good evening saheb, I am from the Wisdom Garden School. I have been waiting for you. You are to go this way." Then he pointed to the left fork, and vanished. So on I went, until I heard voices. Following the sound, I came upon a group of Western hippies in a house, who offered me a place to sleep. Apparently this was the Kasa Devi Ridge, where the German Lama Govinda had established himself some years ago, after going totally native in the Himalaya. In the morning they showed me the way to a village nearby, which was Dinapani, my destination. The headman interviewed me in his chai shop, approved me for cave service, and asked his young son to guide me into the jungle to the cave.

Indeed there were three caves and two jungle babas, who were muni, that is, they did not speak. Not out loud at least. But voices in my head made me welcome, and spelled out the rules. I must keep a fire going in my cave every night, or a panther would come to claim the space. I must go to the stream every morning to wash, and worship Shiva in an underwater grotto that has been used for centuries and has a polished lingam. The dhuni (small ritual fire) must be kept going. Food would be brought by villagers every morning on their way into the forest to tap turpentine trees.

All went well for a week or so. I thought of writing my mother to say I had found a place where I should stay for a few months to further my education, but I could not manage to write. Every night I practiced my yoga nidra, and explored further the vibrational realms. There seemed to be instruction regarding the use of "tools of light" for self-defense and self-maintenance. I practiced, according to these instructions, during the day, while sitting meditation by the dhuni after my bath with Shiva and the daily meal of dhalbhat (rice and lentils), gor (raw sugar), and the mandatory chillum (straight pipe) of hashish.

Then the trouble began. I had some unwelcome orders during the night. I was to leave this place immediately. I resisted. Then the orders were repeated with physical discomforts, which would go away as soon as I agreed to leave in the morning. But in the morning I changed my mind. And so on, in a cycle.

Until one day, around my 36th birthday, July 4, while the other two yogis were away on mysterious missions and I was hard at work meditating by the dhuni, I saw a person approaching, far down the jungle path. This figure got larger and larger, and eventually resolved into a vision from hell, a wild man with a spear, clothed primarily in ashes. He sat down by the fire and accepted a toke from my fully loaded chillum. My paranoia subsided, as apparently he meant no harm. After an hour or so staring into the distance, he turned to me and spoke in unaccented American, "Don't you understand, you are supposed to leave here. I am going to get up and leave now, and you are to follow me". Which he did. And I did, after collecting my small bag from the cave. After a walk of a mile or so down a path I had not seen before, he said, "I am going this way, you go that way", and disappeared around a bend. I followed the indicated jungle path, I am not sure how far, and it led directly to Neem Karoli Baba's ashram. Again, the old fellow was apparently expecting me, bellowing, "Where is that professor from California? Bring him here." And so, reluctantly, began my relationship with Neem Karoli Baba.

I was setup with a house, a library of Sanskrit classics in English translation, and a few devotees for company — including one with Sanskrit skills, Kedarnath, his partner, Uma, and their baby, Ganesh, born during one of our meditations. I was informed by Neem Karoli Baba that I had a mission to relate my meditation experiences to the Sanskrit classics, and transmit the understanding somehow to my colleagues in the USA. These sources included the Vedas, a few Upanishads, works by Sri Auribindo, and the *Yoga Vasistha*, a primary text for the Trika philosophy of Kashmiri Shaivism.

I became known at Veda Vyaasa. I remained in this setup for six months, most of the time with Ray Gwyn Smith, now my wife, who had arrived from California in the meanwhile. The night meditations amplified by microdoses of LSD continued, as I had brought a supply with me from Holland right from the start. Yoga Vasistha was a great inspiration and support for my ideas of vibrations and maps of consciousness. For example:

VASISTHA replied:

> There does exist, O Rama, the power or energy of the infinite consciousness, which is in motion all the time; that alone is the reality of all inevitable futuristic events. For it penetrates all the epochs in time. It is by that power that the nature of every object in the universe is ordained. That power (cit sakti) is also known as Mahasatta (the great existence), Mahaciti (the great intelligence), Mahasakti (the great power), Mahadrsti (the great vision), Mahakriya (the great doer or doing), Mahadbhava (the great becoming), Mahaspanda (the great vibration). It is this power that endows everything with its characteristic quality.[3]

Neem Karoli Baba and the entire satsang departed for warmer climes to the south, after the thermometer in Nainital dropped below freezing in October. Ray and I departed in December for a Himalayan trek in Nepal, where I donated my library to a local university. We walked about 400 miles and returned to California early in 1973. And thus ended my miracle year, 1972, and also the five-year period of one-point focus on spiritual exploration. After returning to Santa Cruz and my job as math professor at UCSC, I reinterpreted the mission given me by Neem Karoli Baba as a program of academic research on vibrations and forms in mathematical models, and in physical fluids as well.

What I learned about cosmos and consciousness during this final year of the five-year project cannot be said in words, perhaps mathematics will be helpful. I imagined this as my task intended by Neem Karoli Baba. But I had to go on alone, as both Neem Karoli Baba and Hans Jenny died at this time.

4. The Vibration Metaphor for Levels of Consciousness

All my experiences in inner research conformed to the conceptual framework of levels. These levels of consciousness are alternate realities, that may be experienced only one at a time. In the meditation experience, they are transited, in a sequence, from ordinary reality to more abstract levels. This framework is well known from the Greek, Jewish, and Indian traditions, as we describe below.

4a. My Experience

The same levels of consciousness always appeared in the same order of increasing abstraction, and were recognizable as forms of reality. They seemed as real as ordinary reality. With successive visits, they always had the same recognizable characteristics: visual aspects, colors, speeds of vibration, typical forms. I thought of these levels, each having its own spatial and temporal dimensions, as being stacked up in another dimension, like horizontal planes stacked vertically, with the more abstract levels "higher." In fact, we spoke of these meditations as "getting high." We spoke of the ascent to higher consciousness. At the end of a meditation, we would descend through these levels in the reverse order of the ascent. This was commonly called "coming down." The whole meditation was called a "trip," like a stairway to heaven and back.

The lowest level, ordinary reality, as we all experience it in everyday perception, is matter-like. It is the world of matter and energy, spatially localized, ego-centered, and so on. Things are objects. Philosophers may speak of vibrations or vital forces, but we do not normally observe them.

On the next level, ordinary objects appear the ordinary way, but are seen to have "vibratory fields" or "auras" around them, They are surrounded for a short distance by these shimmering auras. In this level of reality or consciousness, we may interact with objects in the ordinary way; for example, by touching, and observing the ordinary response, and also by a reaction of the objects' auras.

What do I mean by "vibratory fields?" This can be best answered by computer graphic animations that simulate my visions quite well, and that is one reason for my research with analog and digital simulations of artificial consciousness over these past thirty years, which I discuss below. Meanwhile, you might just think of the patterns of light caustics on the bottom of a swimming pool, from the bright sun overhead, as you paddle about on the surface of the water, looking down. That kind of moving image, in brilliant colors, changing with great rapidity — all the time appearing meaningful in a mysterious way, as abstract visual music seems familiar as deja vu — is exemplary of my idea of a vibration: visual music in air, light through water, waves on the ocean, and so on. The "field" is the unknown medium that supports the vibration in consciousness, as water supports the waves on the ocean.[4]

In the next level up, the object aspect is greatly reduced, and auras predominate. And higher yet, objects vanish, and the auras join together into a single cosmic vibrating field. Parts of the field seem to behave like objects or beings or disembodied entities. It is possible to navigate and move about the field in some sense, or rather, to move the focus of attention by an exertion of will. Attention replaces the self, in that the self seems everywhere, but attention can be stopped-down, focused, panned, and zoomed-in, as it were. One is everywhere, but there is still a personal center of awareness. Yet above, there is nothing but the field, and that is as far as I have gone. But I do not think that the "pure consciousness" experience of no thought is the end of the line.

This is the essence of my recollection of these indelible experiences of long ago, up to 1972. I have maintained them to some extent by less extreme forms of meditation over the years, but much detail has been lost. If my description sounds like every other description of mystical experience, that is most likely due to a universality of the experience. I always had the conviction that the experience is universal, but the translations into words vary.

After my return to academia in 1974, a decade was to pass in mathematical research and teaching before I could resume my study of the philosophical and cosmological traditions that might shed light on my experiences from 1967 to 1972. My first focus was the Ancient Greek and Western Esoteric Traditions. Later I turned to early Jewish mysticism, and more recently, I resumed my search of the Indian literature.

4b. The Greek Tradition

The maps of consciousness from Ancient Greece have various levels, beginning with the ideas and forms of Pythagoras (570-500 BC), and formalized as a stack of levels by Plato (429-347 BC). Around 360 BC we find four levels described in Plato's *Republic*. From the top down, these are: Forms, Intellect, Nature, and Shadows.[5] Later authors usually refer to the four Platonic levels, described in the later dialogues, as the Good, the Intellect (*nous*), the Soul (*psyche*), and Nature (*physis*). The lore of the soul was extended in the *Chaldean Oracles of Julianus* (ca 200 AD).[6] The Greek map further evolved then in the Neoplatonic sources from Plotinus (205-270 AD) to Ficino (1433-1499).[7]

With Plotinus, Porphyry (232-304), and Iamblichus (250-326), we have the addition to Plato's scheme of the Spirit (*pneuma*). Also known as the Vehicle of the Soul (*okema*), this was part of the Neoplatonic theory of incarnation of the individual soul, in which a soul descended through layers of increasing density, being wrapped in Spirit (emanated from stars and planets) en route to incarnation and birth.[8] The Spirit mediated between the incorporeal soul and the corporeal body, and supported the functions of sense perception and imagination.[9] Later, especially in the theology of Proclus (409-487) and Ficino, the Spirit provided the basis of astrological influence: the ongoing astrological contact between the soul and the planets.[10] This theory of astrological influence survived in the works of Kepler (1571-1630).[11]

Relating all this to my direct experience, I identified my matrix (intermediating vibrationally between all adjacent levels, described below) with the Neoplatonic Spirit. But as far as the vibration metaphor is concerned, we have from the Greek tradition, as far as I know, only the harmony of the spheres concept from Pythagoras, Ptolemy, and Kepler. These sources offer abstract concepts, but there is no record of experiences obtained by meditation. Also, the harmony envisioned in the Greek tradition is only that of harmonious sounding dyads (pairs of musical tones), and not the vibration/form duality of my experience. For this, we know of no antecedent before Ernst Chladni (1756-1827), who founded acoustic physics around 1800, and inspired Hans Jenny.

This is a subtle yet important distinction: the vibration of Pythagoras, Ptolemy, and Kepler is one-dimensional, the musical vibration of a plucked string. Harmony for them is the musical consonance of two plucked strings, the tones related by the ratio of the lengths of the two strings. But the vibration of Chladni, Jenny, and myself is two-dimensional, the musical vibration of a struck flexible membrane or plate. Harmony for us is a matter of the forms created by a vibration of dimension two or more — as the forms seen in meditation, in the higher levels of consciousness, for example.

4c. The Jewish Tradition

Early Jewish esotericism and mysticism derived from Philo Judeus, Greek Gnosticsm, and Eastern sources in the early Christian era, especially in Alexandria.[12] The Merkabah tradition, it seems to me, is a coded story of early explorers of my own path. These pioneers would go down to the basement to spend the night in meditations guided by concentration on visual images, and amplified by breathing exercises. The path desired was an ascent through seven levels of increasing abstraction, each identified by visual features of abstract animations.[13]

4d. The Indian Tradition

The Indian tradition provides a number of different schemes or levels of consciousness, including the five koshas, seven chakras, 36 tattvas, and so on. The closest scheme to that of my own experience is that of the five koshas. These are, from the top down: the bliss body (anandamaya kosha), astral body (vijnanamaya kosha), mental body (manomaya kosha), pranic body (pranamaya kosha), and the food body (annamaya kosha). These subtle bodies, or levels, may be ascended by prolonged practice of yoga nidra, or other meditations, ultimately reaching the bliss body. The bliss body is described as an experience of total transcendence, where only the fundamental vibration of the unconscious system remains.¹⁴

The vibration metaphor that I encountered in the Yoga Vasistha explicitly entered the Indian literature in the Spanda (vibration), Urmi (wave), and Prana (life-force) concepts of Trika philosophy (Kashmiri Shaivism) due to Vasugupta, his disciple, Kallata, and his student in turn, Abhinava Gupta, tenth century AD. I am a beginning student of this tradition, and I am grateful to Prof. D. SenSharma of Calcutta for leading me to this historical information.¹⁵

Pythagoras may have visited India. And it is known that there were yogis in Ancient Greece; they were called gymnosophists. So vibration metaphors might have diffused either way. The origin of the vehicle of the soul has been traced to Babylonia.¹⁶

5. Beyond Maps of Consciousness: Communication Between Levels

In a preceding section, My Experience, I have set out the cosmographic (map of consciousness) that I had obtained before 1972, with the levels of consciousness stacked up, with ordinary reality and the individual soul or microcosmic levels at the bottom, the cosmic or macrocosmic levels above, and the mesocosmic levels interpolating in between. This personal cartography, although supported by received literature of all traditions, was lacking any model for the interaction or communication between levels. It was in 1972, especially in the cave near Almora, that this part of the picture was filled in. I can express this best in the mathematics of chaos theory, but here I will try in words.

First of all, we see in Hans Jenny's books — and in my

continuation of his work in my fluid dynamical vibration laboratory at UCSC in the years 1974 to 1980 — how a vibration creates a form. Similarly, a form impressed upon a spontaneously vibrating field modifies that vibration field, and results in a new vibration that encodes the form. Vibrations to forms, forms to vibrations, somewhat like the particle-wave duality of modern atomic physics. Okay, lets use this idea to connect levels of consciousness.

Consider just two of the levels, that are adjacent in the traditional cosmographic map described above, and each in a state of vibration, as we experience them separately in our meditations. In meditation, we experience a sort of quantum leap ascending, and also descending, between levels. We cannot directly perceive any connection or semaphoric transmissions in the space between levels. For this we are grateful for suggestions from the received literature of the rishis of East and West, who show us how to observe these hidden communications. The suggestions I found useful in 1972 were found in Yoga Vasistha, and I am grateful to Neem Karoli Baba for that. Subsequently, I discovered the Spanda literature of the Trika or Kashmiri Shaivite philosophical tradition, thanks to Professor D. SenSharma of the Research Department of the Ramakrishna Mission Institute of Culture, Gol Park, Kolkata.

This is the idea. In the space between levels there is yet another, finer, vibratory field, that I will call the matrix. This resembles the diffusion of neurotransmitters in the extracellular space between neurons in the mammalian brain. The vibration in level A creates a form in level A, this is impressed in the intermediate matrix field, modulating the ongoing vibration there, which carries a vibratory signal to level B, where it impresses a form on level B, and that creates a vibration in level B. This semiotic process, mediated by the matrix field, is hard to grasp in words. However, I have created (with help of Peter Broadwell) a computer graphic simulation, which is easily grasped. But this was not possible until the 1990s.[17]

6. Personal Experiences of Vibrations and Forms in Artificial Consciousness, 1974-1996

My experiments of vibrations and forms in actual consciousness of 1972 morphed, after my return to academic life in 1974, into a program of laboratory science modeled on the work of Hans Jenny. I like to think of this as research in artificial consciousness, but of course it was more practical to call it fluid dynamics.

The apparatus — I called it a macroscope — consisted of a coupled system of vibrations in various levels. At bottom was an electronic oscillator capable of producing sine waves, square waves, sawtooth waves, and so on, with control knobs for frequency and amplitude. This source was converted into up-down mechanical vibrations by a horizontal high-fidelity loudspeaker, that in turn vibrated a column of air above the speaker cone. And this moved a transparent membrane, and above that, a thin layer of water, in which was activated a pattern of thin water waves. These waves were imaged on a translucent screen by an optical system containing two telescope mirrors and a point source of light.

These layers could be regarded as a crude model for levels of consciousness, in that the vibrations of one level created forms on another level, and vice versa. Video recordings of the moving patterns of light on the screen were very reminiscent of the visual experiences seen in my meditations. Some of this work was reported during the 1970s.[18]

After 1975 or so, mathematical models and computer

simulations gradually replaced the analog simulations with the macroscope, and computer graphic video recordings have provided some moving patterns that are highly suggestive of the visual component of my meditation experiences.[19]

In particular, the papers Ms #86 and 86B describe a simulation of an experiment by Rupert Sheldrake on telepathy from a person to her dog. In our model, a vibrating two-dimensional field was modulated by the introduction of a geometrical form representing the person's thought to come home, and this modulation was recorded as a memory engram of the patterns perceived over time on a one-dimensional "retina" in the dog's mind. This clearly shows the role of memory in consciousness, as described by Henri Bergson and in Kashmiri Shaivism.[20]

7. Conclusion

A personal odyssey through the spiritual practices of several traditions, begun in 1967 and still ongoing, has motivated a research program in chaos theory and computational mathematics. The products of this mathematical program, unlike the subjective experiences of meditation, are open to the scientific paradigm of publication, replication, and the hermeneutical circle of theoretical and experimental synergy. This program belongs to the category of mathematics of consciousness begun by Pythagoras, Plato, and the Sanskrit classics, rather than that of science and consciousness, but may have some implications for science in the long run.

Figure. Vibration in an experiment of artificial consciousness: simulation of the Sheldrake experiment. From joint work with Peter Broadwell, Palo Alto, California, USA. The strength of the morphic field is shown as a shade of gray. A full color image is shown on the front cover.

Notes

1. (Saraswati, 1998)
2. (www.draves.com)
3. (Venkatesananda, 1993; p. 89)
4. (Hesse, 1961)
5. (Shear, 1990; p. 12)
6. (Julianus, 1989) (Lewy, 1956)
7. (Abraham, Ms #116)
8. (Walker, 2000; p. 38)
9. (Finamore, 1985; p. 1-2)
10. (Moore, 1982; p. 53)
11. (Rabin, 1987; Ch. 3) (Kepler, 1997; bk. 4)
12. (Scholem, 1978: pp. 8-21)
13. (Blumenthal, 1978; Ch. 5)
14. (Saraswati, 1998; p. 54)
15. (SenSharma, 2003, 2004; Dyczkowski, 1992; Singh, 1980.)
16. (Lewy, 1978; p. 413)
17. (Abraham, Ms #86, 86B)
18. (Abraham, Ms #14-20)
19. (Abraham, Ms #25-86)
20. (Chakrabarti, 2004)

PART 3
ATOMIC MODELS
2005-2011

Chapter 20
A Digital Solution to the Mind/Body Problem

with Sisir Roy[1]

Abstract

We have applied the concepts from the mathematical theory of cellular automata — as developed to understand the emergence of spacetime at Planck scale — to consciousness. This gives rise to a digital, spacetime solution to the mind/body problem.

Publication

Ms #122, written January 24, 2007. Published in *Integral Biomathics: Tracing the Road to Reality.* Plamen L. Simeonov, Leslie S. Smith, and Andree C. Ehresmann, eds. (2012). Heidelberg: Springer; pp. 213-225.

Contents

1. Introduction
2. The Mind/Body Problem
    2.1. Plato, 370 BC
    2.2. Kashmiri Shaivism, 1000 CE
    2.3. Descartes, 1649
3. Atomism
    3.1. Parmenides, 450 BC
    3.2. Democritus, 400 BC
    3.3. Dharmakirti, 650 AD
    3.4. Galileo, 1623
    3.5. Quantum theory, 1900
    3.6. Fredkin, 2000
4. The RRA Model
5. The Time Dimensions
6. The Mind/Body Problem Resolved
7. Descartes Reconsidered
8. Conclusion
Appendix. Summary of the RRA process
Notes

1. Introduction

Dualist-interconnectionist models for consciousness, from Ancient Greece to Descartes, have disjoint parts connected by a mysterious communication process. Usually no explanation is proposed for this communication process, although the resonance metaphor is sometimes mentioned. In this paper we consider this problem in the context of the mind/body model of Descartes. The intractability of this mind/body problem has been discussed by everyone from Plato on. We are going to apply to it an atomistic mechanism deriving from the theory of the quantum vacuum in modern physics.

We thus bring together the mind/body problem of Descartes and the digital philosophy of Fredkin and others[2] into a joint picture first described by Democritus.[3] Our starting point is a cellular dynamical model of the quantum vacuum due to Requardt and Roy (2001) and extended by Abraham and Roy (2007). This is a process, the RRA process, by which the illusion of analog spacetime self-organizes from a digital substructure — a submicroscopic, corpuscular, cellular dynamical system — a sort of finite point set on steroids. In this paper we further extend the RRA process from space to spacetime in the domain of terrestrial physics, and then jump up to the mental realm, where the constraints of physics no longer apply.

We apply the process twice, once to the mind, and again to the body, to obtain our resolution of the mind/body problem. In our final, composite picture, there is one enormous point set, its size estimated by Wheeler as 10 to the power 88,[4] operating beneath the perceived realities of macroscopic mind, body, and also quantum reality. We are grateful to Dr. Paul A. Lee for his guidance regarding the Ancient Greek tradition.

2. The Mind/Body Problem

The mind/body problem is a perennial thread in philosophy, East and West, so there are many illustrious names in its chronology. We will concentrate on just a few of these, to establish the main milestones of our story, and briefly describe their contributions. For the earliest history, beginning with Homer, see Jaspers (1998, Essay 8).

2.1. Plato, 370 BC

Plato expanded the teaching of Socrates on the perfection of the soul into a complete system. In this system, morals and justice were based on absolute ideas. Wisdom consists of knowledge of these ideas, and philosophy is the search for wisdom. In fourteen more dialogues, Plato elaborated this unified system.

Plato's theory of soul is set out primarily in six of the dialogues: *Phaedo*, *Republic II*, and *Phaedrus* (of the middle group of dialogues, 387-367 BCE), *Timaeus* (around 365 BCE, which divides the middle and last groups, and *Philebus* and *Laws*) of the last group (365-347 BCE). The development of the individual soul is given in the three middle dialogues.

The *Phaedo* is a long and detailed examination of the individual soul, its immortality and reincarnation, given by Socrates on the day of his death sentence.

The *Republic* describes Plato's mathematical curriculum for the Academy: arithmetic, plane geometry, solid geometry, astronomy, and music. At the end [10.614b] is the Tale of Er, which details the reincarnation process of the individual soul, as told by an eyewitness.[5]

In the *Phaedrus*, Socrates and Phaedrus discourse on love and rhetoric. To understand divine madness, one must learn the nature of the soul. [245c] Soul is always in motion, and is self-moving, and therefore is deathless. [245c, d, e] Then begins the important metaphor of the chariot: two winged horses and a charioteer. [246a-248a] This metaphor of the soul is then used to explain divine madness, and the dynamics of reincarnation.

The world soul is developed in the later three dialogues. Regarding the individual soul, the *Timeaus* explains that as a person becomes a rational creature through education, his human soul moves in a circle in the head (a sphere) of his mortal body. [44] In the *Philebus*, Socrates introduces the world soul as the source of individual souls. [30a]

In sum, we have from Plato a four-level, hierarchical cosmology, including (from the top):

1. The Good, an integral principle with no spatial extent.
2. The Intellect, or nous, including the Ideas or Forms (pl. eide, sing. eidos).
3. The World Soul (including individual human souls).
4. The Terrestrial Sphere of matter and energy.

Forms exist in the Intellect, and are outside of space and time. Terrestrial objects are instances, or particulars, of Forms. Individual souls are pieces of the World Soul which have instantiated, or incarnated, a Form. When people die, their individual souls reunite with their Forms.

To this Theory of Forms, Plato himself raised an objection in his dialogue, *Parmenides*. This problem, later called the third man argument, or TMA, has been the subject of much discussion over the past fifty years. It is somewhat like the Russell paradox of mathematical set theory. That is, if a Form (a class of objects) contains itself as a member, then an unwelcome infinite regress is set up, toward larger and larger collections.

Some have interpreted this objection another way, which we shall call TMA2. This applies when we have two categories which are disjoint — such as two parallel universes — and yet which exchange information. A matrix between the two categories — such as the air between two resonant guitar strings — must be interpolated, to carry the resonance or intercommunication. For example, in Plato's cosmology, the World Soul intervenes between the Intellect and the Terrestrial Sphere. Or on the individual level, Ficino's Spirit intervenes between the individual soul and the body.

2.2. Kashmiri Shaivism, 1000 CE

The Indian tradition provides a number of different schemes for levels of consciousness, including five koshas, seven chakras, 36 tattvas, and so on. The five koshas are, from the top down: the bliss body (anandamaya kosha), astral body (vijnanamaya kosha), mental body (manomaya kosha), pranic body (pranamaya kosha), and the food body (annamaya kosha). The bliss body is described as an experience of total transcendence, where only the fundamental vibration of the unconscious system remains.[6]

The TMA2 problem may be the ultimate cause of the profusion of levels in the Sanskrit literature on consciousness. No matter how many levels, the mystery of the communication between adjacent levels in the hierarchy remains. The vibration metaphor addresses this mystery, but still begs an encompassing matrix or medium to carry information from level to level. The vibration metaphor entered the Indian literature in the Spanda (vibration), Urmi (wave), and Prana (life-force) concepts of the Trika philosophy (Kashmiri Shaivism) due to Vasugupta, his disciple, Kallata, and his student in turn, Abhinava Gupta, tenth century CE.[7]

We may regard the mind/body problem as just the bottom level of a stack of similar problems. We intend that our attack on the M/B problem should eventually be applied throughout the koshas, chakras, or tattvas of a full model of collective consciousness and unconsciousness.

2.3. Descartes, 1649

Descartes was a dualist, to whom the world consisted of two original substances — body and mind — between which there was an enormous gulf. Man consists of body and mind, which interact through the pineal gland. His dualist theory, and his mechanical view of nature, dominated philosophy for centuries. His method of thought and his theories have been subjected to devastating criticism, for example, Jaspers (1964). For many historians, the mind/body problem in Western philosophy began with Descartes. We will reconsider this tradition later.

3. *Atomism*

Like the mind/body problem, atomism is a perennial thread in philosophy, East and West, with many illustrious names on its chronology. For us, atomism provides an especially important backdrop, as our mathematical model for the mind/body system is discrete. Again, we will concentrate on just a few of the key players.

3.1. Parmenides, 450 BC

According to Popper (1998), Parmenides — an important if little known presocratic philosopher of early 5th century

BC Greece — was the creator of atomism (atomos, Greek for indivisible). First of all, he is known for his Two Ways: the Way of True Knowledge (aletheia) and the Way of Human Conjecture (doxa), revealed to him by a goddess and described in his only work, *On nature*. The Way of True Knowledge includes the idea that behind the false and illusory world of change perceived by the senses there is an absolute reality that is totally static, a dark sphere of continuous dense matter, called the Being. In our sensory perceptions, we experience a dual world of atoms moving in the void, hence the Way of Human Conjecture.

3.2. Democritus, 400 BC

Democritus, a student of Parmenides, is widely regarded as the founder of atomism. And it is said that Democritus' ideas were formed to contradict Parmenides. Democritus wrote on math, astronomy, and ethics, and had a great influence on later Greek philosophy, especially Aristotle, and hence, on the whole of the Western Tradition.

Regarding atoms, he believed that material bodies were formed as temporary composites of eternal atoms, like flocks of birds. Atoms are variously shaped and sized. The primary qualities of a material body — its shape, size, and weight — and its secondary aspects — smell, taste, etc — all derive from the size and shape of its atoms. Atoms move in a "void" which is empty, and yet is not nothing. The soul is made of soul-atoms, which are very small and spherical, and can pass through solid material bodies, like neutrinos.

3.3. Dharmakirti, 650 AD

It is always a pleasure to follow a thread from Ancient

Greece, through trade routes to India, then circuitously to Early Islam, and thence to Europe. In this case we are just guessing. There is a long history of atomism in India. One of the ancient Hindu philosophers, Kanad, discussed the existence of atoms. In fact, the word Kanad is derived from the word Kana, which means atom. Among Buddhist traditions, Vasubandhu and Dharmakirti particularly discussed the existence of atoms. Dharmakirti was a student of Dignaga, a Buddhist logician and professor at the famed Nalanda University. Dharmakirti introduced into this thread a wondrous novelty, namely, that atoms are not eternal, but rather, flash into and out of existence as points of energy. This seemed somewhat outré until very recently, when the quantum vacuum emerged into physics, as we discuss in this paper.

3.4. Galileo, 1623

Galileo was famously condemned by the Vatican in 1633, overtly because of supporting Copernicus (that the earth moves) in his book, *Dialogues concerning the two chief world systems*, published in 1632. However, there is a competing (and controversial) theory, according to which his real offense was his earlier book, *The Assayer*, of 1623.[8] This work advocated an atomic theory, according to which (rather like Democritus) the secondary qualities of matter (taste, smell, etc.) were determined by the primary qualities (the shapes of atoms comprising the matter). This was of huge concern to the Vatican in that Transubstantiation — the official dogma of the Church since the Council of Trent (1545-1563) regarding the consecration in the Mass of the Sacraments (turning the bread and wine into the body and blood) — depended on secondary qualities being independent of primary qualities.[9]

3.5. Quantum theory, 1900

Shortly following the death of Descartes, atomism faded into the background, where it remained for two hundred years. Then it rose from the ashes in a sequence of developments, collectively known as the quantum revolution. Here is a chronology of some of these developments.

1808, John Dalton posed a unique atom for each element.
1897, J. J. Thompson discovered the electron (Nobel prize in 1906).
1900, Max Planck proposed energy quanta, founded quantum theory.
1905, Albert Einstein introduced the photon as a corpuscle.
1927, Dirac, Pauli, Weisskopf, Jordan, Quantum field theory.
1940, Feynman, Schwinger, Tomonaga, Quantum Electrodynamics (QED).
1966, H. Yukawa, Non-local Field Theory and Quantum Vacuum (QV).

At this point, following QED, we have the theories of the QV and the zero-point fluctuation (ZPF) which are basic to the RR model of Requardt and Roy (2001). This view of nature has the vacuum full of activity, in which particles jump out from, and then back into, the vacuum in pairs. In QED, as one calculates the transition amplitudes with respect to the vacuum state, the vacuum as such does not contribute in the calculations. However, Yukawa proposed the concept of non-local field theory where the seat of particles is considered as an extended region or domain in contrast to QED. Now if we take these domains to be quantum theoretical objects, then they are probabilistically connected, and there is no distinction between empty and occupied seats. Effectively, Yukawa introduced a new version of quantum theory of the aether with globular structure.

3.6. Fredkin, 2000

The cellular automaton (CA) ideas of Stan Ulam and John von Neumann in the 1950s rested in obscurity until the appearance of John Conways' *Game of Life,* in the 1970s. Then CA models of nature became a fad, and many successful models for macroscopic physical systems were made, especially in the circle around Feynman in the 1980s.[10] However, computer science models of the individual soul, such as we seek, are rare. In this connection we must mention the work of Ed Fredkin, one of the pioneers of the digital philosophy, and the mainstay of the website www.digitalphilosophy.org which explains:

> *Digital Philosophy (DP) is a new way of thinking about the fundamental workings of processes in nature. DP is an atomic theory carried to a logical extreme where all quantities in nature are finite and discrete. This means that, theoretically, any quantity can be represented exactly by an integer. Further, DP implies that nature harbors no infinities, infinitesimals, continuities, or locally determined random variables.*

In *On the Soul*[11], Fredkin proposed a computer science definition of the soul, concluding: "The *soul* is an informational entity, which is constructed out of the states and the arrangements of material things."

All these recent developments, which we subsume

under the classical heading *atomism*, support the idea that underlying our illusion of continuous space, time, matter, energy, etc (the analog part of the analog/digital dichotomy, and the wave part of the wave/particle duality) is a fundamental layer that is finite, discrete, and intelligent (that is, law-abiding). Sometimes, all this is called the *finite nature assumption*.[12] This is close to the view of Parmenides described above.

4. The RRA Model

In this section we recall the RRA process, as defined by Abraham and Roy in 2007. In the next section, we extend it from space to spacetime, and finally, we apply the process to the mind/body problem.

The RRA model is a two-level system. The microscopic level, QX, is a dynamical cellular network of nodes and bonds. Inspired by the cellular automata of Ulam and von Neumann, a dynamical cellular network is a directed graph with connections (directed links) which appear, disappear, and change direction, according to dynamical rules.

The macroscopic level, ST, that self-organizes from QX, is an another dynamical cellular network, in which the nodes are the cliques (that is, maximal fully connected subgraphs) of a graph, G, of the QX level, bound in a network by superbonds.

The system of RR ends with a metric space. But in a sequel paper[13] we have developed a neural network approach which imbeds the ST level into Euclidean spacetime, EST. Thus the ambient space of nature, according to consensual reality, is actually an epiphenomenon of the atomistic and finite QX network, according to the scheme: QX → ST → EST. This is the full RA process, which we call *condensation*. More details may be found in the Appendix.

5. The Time Dimensions

The discrete, microscopic time parameter, t, used above, does not represent macroscopic time. Rather, we propose to obtain macroscopic spacetime through our process of condensation. Macroscopic time, T, exists locally as a function on spacetime, but we may pretend that there is a cosmic time function, to simplify the exposition. We propose now to obtain macroscopic spacetime from the condensation process applied repeatedly to the entire, t-dependent QX object.

The condensation process is regarded as being accomplished in a single instant, and it determines instantaneous states for the macrocosmic system in which space appears to be a continuum. Even so, the network QX is changing rapidly by a time-discrete process, with time t. We are going to regard the stepwise increasing network time as an internal process variable, microscopic time, that is distinct from the continuous physical time aspect of the spacetime of general relativity, cosmic time. Thus, we envision two dimensions of time.

We adopt the Cauchy perspective of general relativity, in which the Einstein equation is regarded as a system of quasi-linear, second-order partial differential equations. The present is represented by a three-dimensional space-like hypersurface in the four-dimensional spacetime continuum, dividing it into past and future portions. The Cauchy initial value problem for this system regards the values of the metric tensor as known in the past and present, their future to be determined by integration of the system of equations along special (so-called characteristic) curves that radiate forward from the present into the future. The topology of spacetime, along with its geometry (that is, the metric tensor) and the physical parameters (energy, mass, electromagnetic fields, etc.)

must evolve according to this Einstein equation. Wormholes and black holes may evolve as caustics (eg, focal points) of the characteristic curves.

Alternatively, for a mathematically less-challenging exposition, we may suppose, like Einstein, that spacetime is created as a finished system, a complete geometrical object.

So this is our proposal for the emergence of cosmic time. Constrained by the Einstein equation, cosmic time advances in discrete intervals, that might be multiple steps of microcosmic time, giant steps. With each giant step, yet another condensation occurs, as follows.

We consider a memory device, controlled by the cosmic-time function, T. Between cosmic times T_1 (corresponding to network time t_1) and T_2 (with its t_2) the memory device records all of the finite states of QX between network-time t_1 and network-time t_2, and condenses this finite set of QX states into a space-like pseudo-continuum corresponding to the discrete cosmic time T_2. One method for the condensation of a finite set of QX states is the sum algorithm. That is, we form a QX sum-state by adding the internal node states of all nodes, and all the bond states of all the bonds, of the set of QX states. In other words, fix a node of QX. Sum up the node-states of that one node for all the QX states with network time in the interval, (t_1, t_2), that is an integer. Do likewise for each bond of QX, but round down if this sum is greater than one, and round up if less than minus one.

Thus, spacetime is squeezed from the dynamical cellular network, QX, as toothpaste from a tube. As giant steps are still very small compared with the resolving power of macroscopic science, cosmic time appears to be continuous. The macroscopic system, QX, sparkles with activity on the scale of Planck space and time, while macroscopic spacetime unrolls essentially continuously. The past and present become known, while the future remains yet a mystery.

In summary, our scheme, QX → ST → 3ST is extended to the scheme QX → ST → 4ST, all in the context of the body, that is, the physical world. We now wish to apply this new scheme to the mind/body problem.

6. *The Mind/Body Problem Resolved*

We now consider two QX networks: QX1 (the body level), and QX2 (the mind level). Each of them might be the basis for an RRA process, one condensing to the body, or the physical world as we have considered up to this point, the other to a separate world of the mind.

However, we may prefer alternatively to join QX1 and QX2 into a single entwined network, QX*, on which two condensation processes operate. We might compare this approach to John Whitney's concept of digital harmony, in which a single mathematical algorithm is employed to compose a piece of music, and an abstract animated image, which then seem — when played together — to harmonize, due to deriving from a common archetypal process. But we will proceed now with QX1 and QX2.

After all this preparation, our approach to the perennial conundrum is now simple: we apply the idea of condensation from a QX network twice: once to the body level, as in the RRA model, and again by analogy to the mind level, as in Fredkin (2000). This results in the four-part scheme:

QX2 → Mind
QX1 → Body

The mystery connection between the disjoint mind and body systems now becomes an epiphenomenon of the connection between QX1 and QX2 which is not mysterious at all. For the nature of the QX model of RRA is that of a dynamical cellular network, and we may regard QX1 and QX2 as a single, entangled network, as directed links between the two systems will be allowed by our dynamical rules. In other words, we ask you to replace the mystery of the Mind/Body connection with the mystery of the QX1 Body connection. Mysterious as this may be, it is ubiquitous throughout the physical and biological sciences, as physical systems admit mathematical models.

7. Descartes Reconsidered

The traditional view of Descartes (1596-1650) as perpetrator of the mind/body problem deserves refinement. His main work on this subject is his book, *The Passions of the Soul*, written in 1646 at age 50, and published in 1649 just before his death. It is presented as a series of 212 articles collected in three parts. It is the 50 articles of the first part that most concern us here. Each article comprises a short caption with a paragraph of text. Here are the captions of the 16 most relevant articles of Part I of his text. Note: Soul in Descartes refers to what we have called Mind.

Part I. About the Passions in General, and Incidentally about the Entire Nature of man

> Article 17. What the functions of the soul are.
> Article 20. About imaginations and other thoughts that are formed by the soul.
> Article 25. About perceptions we refer to our soul.
> Article 27. The Definition of the Passions of the

soul.

Article 30. That the soul is jointly united to all the parts of the body.

Article 31. That there is a little gland in the brain in which the soul exercises its functions in a more particular way than in the other parts.

Article 32. How it is known that this gland is the principal seat of the soul.

Article 34. How the soul and the body act on one another.

Article 35. Example of the way impressions of objects unite in the gland in the middle of the brain.

Article 36. Example of the way the Passions are excited in the soul.

Article 37. How it becomes apparent that they are all caused by some movement of the spirits.

Article 43. How the soul can imagine, be attentive, and move the body.

Article 44. That each volition is naturally joined to some movement of the gland, but that by artifice or habituation one can join it to others.

Article 45. What the power of the soul is with respect to its passions.

Article 46. What the reason is on account of which the soul cannot completely control its passions.

Article 47. What the struggles consist in that people customarily imagine between the lower part of the soul and the higher.

Paraphasing the texts of these articles, we may say that the soul (mind) exists outside of space, while the body lives in spacetime. They are united whole to whole, but especially through the tip of the gland. The soul is characterized by volitions, thoughts, imaginations, and passions (emotions); and the body by movements. The soul has a structure, polarized between the sensitive (lower) and rational (upper) poles.

Altogether, we see that Descartes has not only posed the mind/body problem, but also proposed a solution which is surprisingly like our own.

8. Conclusion

In sum, then, the mind/body connections are completed in a circuit outside ordinary consensual reality in a submicroscopic atomic realm beyond our senses, but revealed by the progress of modern physics. This realm or matrix, an extension of the quantum vacuum into the realm of consciousness, is a finite, discrete, digital, cosmos, which condenses — in the human perceptual and cognitive process — into epiphenomena, the continuum illusion of mind/body, hypostases, koshas, cakras, tattvas, and so on, of the perennial traditions of consciousness studies.

Note that the QX level is a static point set with a dynamic network structure, changing in microscopic time, t. Meanwhile, the macroscopic body and mind have been constructed as complete spacetime worlds, with locally defined macroscopic times, T. This provides a background for psi phenomena such as telepathy and clairvoyance, but also leaves a window of opportunity for free will. Like a zipper closing, the past is zipped (or firmed) up, while the microscopic future is subject to interaction with the macroscopic body and mind, until the zipper closure arrives, and condensation (or collapse) occurs.

The end of our construction is an echo of the Two Ways of

A Digital Solution to the Mind/Body Problem

Parmenides, the atomic QX*, and the 4ST continua of body and mind, playing out in digital harmony.

Appendix. Summary of the RRA process

The RRA process, of Abraham and Roy (2007) is not a description of physical reality, but just a mathematical model that captures some aspects of our experience of physical reality. We will summarize this process in three stages. Full details, examples, and graphics, may be seen in Abraham and Roy (2010).

- A. We begin with microscopic system, QX.
- B. Then we extract from it our macroscopic system, ST.
- C. Finally, we describe the embedding of ST into Euclidean space.

A1. There is a finite, but huge, point set, which is static throughout the process. Let S denote this finite set. Enumerate this set by fixing a bijection from S to N, the cardinality of S. Thus, S is a set of points, $\{n_0, n_1, ..., n_{(N-1)}\}$. These points are called nodes.

A2. At each node and each moment of time there is an internal node-state, which is some integral number of quanta of information. Thus, we have a set of time-dependent node-states, $\{s_0, s_1, ..., s_{(N-1)}\}$.

A3. There are no bilateral connections. That is, for each pair of nodes, n_i and n_j, there may be a directed link from n_i to n_j, or none. We agree there cannot be a directed link from n_i to n_j if there is one from n_j to n_i.

A4. There is a global time clock for the system. The time variable, t, is a natural number, and increases by one at regular intervals, called clicks.

A5. The directed links may appear, disappear, or change direction, with each click. They change according to a fixed dynamical rule.

A6. With each click, each node n_i sends one quantum of information to the node n_j if there is a directed link from n_i to n_j.

A7. At each time there is a digraph, a directed graph on S, defined by the directed links. Let $D(t)$ denote the state of this digraph at clock time t, an integer. Associated with $D(t)$ is a graph $G(t)$, in which the directions of $D(t)$ are ignored.

This is our microscopic system, QX, exactly as described by Requardt and Roy (2001). Next we will describe the emergence of the macroscopic ST system from QX, or QX → ST, following Abraham and Roy (2007).

B1. For each node, n_i, of $D(t)$ let w_i denote its node-weight, that is, the number of directed links of $D(t)$ that either arrive at, or depart from, n_i. Thus, we have a finite sequence of node-weights, $\{w_0, w_1, ..., w_{(N-1)}\}$.

B2. Next, at each time, t, we may construct, from the digraph $D(t)$, a permutation of the set S of nodes, as follows. We reorder the nodes of S according to their nodeweights, in decreasing order. If several nodes have the same node-weight, we retain their original order. Let $P(t)$ denote the permutation of N obtained in this way.

B3. A *clique* of a permutation is a maximal inverse sequence. Compute the cliques of $P(t)$. This may be done by inspection if N is not too large. Let $K(t)$ denote the set of all cliques of $P(t)$. These cliques, which are simply subsets of $\{0, 1, ..., n-1\}$ in decreasing order, will be considered the supernodes of our macroscopic system, ST.

B4. If K is a finite set of natural numbers, let the *span* of K denote the filled-in interval, $span(K)=[min(K), max(K)]$. We define a superbond between two supernodes, or cliques, if and only if their spans are disjoint. Thus we have a graph $ST(t)$ defined by these supernodes and superbonds.

This is our macroscopic system, ST. Finally we will describe the pseudo-isometric embedding of ST into a Euclidean space, ST → EST, again following Abraham and Roy (2007).

C1. For every pair of disjoint cliques of $K(t)$, we define their *overlap*, a measure of the entanglement of the two cliques, by counting points in the intersection and union of the sets spanned by the two cliques. Details and examples may be found in Abraham and Roy (2007). These overlap measurements may be used to define distances, more entanglement corresponding to a smaller distance.

C2. Embed $K(t)$ in a Euclidean space, and relax the embedding to approximate as closely as possible an isometry. That is, the distance between the images of two cliques represents their entanglement.

The process QX → ST → EST may be called *condensation*.

Notes

1 Physics and Applied Mathematics Unit, Indian Statistical Institute, Calcutta.
2 (Hey, 1999)
3 (Popper, 1998)
4 (Hey, 1999)
5 The numbers in brackets are page numbers of the Stevens translation.
6 (Saraswati, 1998; p. 54)
7 (Probhananda, 2003, 2004; Dyczkowski, 1992; Singh, 1980.)
8 (Redondi, 1987)
9 (Shea, 1991; p. 181)
10 (Hey, 1999)
11 (2000 Draft Paper)
12 (Fredkin, 1992)
13 (Abraham and Roy, 2006)

Chapter 21
Consciousness and the New Math

Abstract

A brief report of some years of study of supramental activity using the metaphor of *vibration*, including recent joint work with Professor Sisir Roy of the Indian Statistical Institute, Kolkata.

Publication

Ms #128 written April 2, 2008. Presented at the Ramakrishna Mission Institute of Culture, the Mina Majumdar Lecture. Not previously published.

Contents

1. Introduction
2. Telepathy
3. Mind/Body Connection
4. Precognition
5. Conclusion
Acknowledgments
Notes

1. Introduction

Under the heading "consciousness" I mean to include the whole system: individual consciousness system, individual unconscious system, collective unconsciousness system, higher planes, and so on. We assume for the sake of discussion such a global supramental system, as proposed by Teilhard de Chardin for example, under the name *noosphere*, by Rupert Sheldrake as the *morphic field*, and in the Sanskrit literature as the *akasha* and by other names. Following Ervin Laszlo, who refers to this system as the *Akashic Field*, I will call this global system the *A-system*.

I became interested in this subject during my first visit to India, in 1972, when I stayed for seven months in the ambiance of Neem Karoli Baba, a local saint in the Himalayan foothills. During this time, and ever since, novel information seems to come to me in dreams and meditations. A key idea coming in this way is the metaphor of *vibration*. Well known in modern science in the context of physical systems — sound waves, radio waves, quantum waves, gravity waves, etc — the vibration metaphor is equally well known in Hindu philosophy in the literature on the akasha. On returning to my post as professor of mathematics in the University of California in 1974, I initiated a new line of research on vibrations and forms, which continues to this day.

Complex dynamical systems is a new branch of mathematics dealing with large networks of systems changing in time according to rules. And in this new subject a paradigm called *connectionism* has evolved, in which the intelligence of a system is thought to reside primarily in its network of connections, rather than within its collection of nodes. So as a mathematician interested in complex dynamical systems, my perspective on the A-system has been to focus on its linkages, rather than the nature of its subsystems or nodes. And it is in this perspective of the new math that I have studied the duality of vibrations and forms.

Thus a form in one level or subsystem of the global A-system emits a vibration in an interpolating medium, and this vibration crystalizes a form in another level of the A-system — that kind of link, from form to form. Under this paradigm I will now discuss three so-called paranormal phenomena. Here *paranormal* means along-side normal science, that is, challenging modern science, and therefore, denied by modern science. It is this habit of denial that we seek to change with our mathematical models.

2. *Telepathy*

Telepathy, like telegraphy and telephony, refers to the transmission from one individual consciousness to another through intervening space, over long distances, and with great speed. Unlike its electrical siblings, telepathy is thought to proceed without a material basis. Although not dependent on the electromagnetic field, it is nonetheless somewhat similar to radio transmission, and thus has been called *mental radio* by Upton Sinclair. Rupert Sheldrake, one of the great scientists working in this area, has proposed a new nonphysical field called the *morphic field* to account for telepathy and other like communication, functions of the natural world.

One of Sheldrake's many experiments aimed at breaking through the denial of the paranormal on the part of modern scientists concerns the ability of many pets to predict when their owners are coming home. As reported in his book,[1] videos of dogs in empty houses clearly show this predictive power, as their owners are told to start home at a computer-selected random time.

Consciousness and the New Math

In any case, considering the crucial role of mathematics in bringing understanding and thus acceptance to new scientific ideas in the past — like the electric and magnetic fields, universal gravitation, quantum probabilities and the like — I undertook a project with a colleague, Peter Broadwell, of mathematical modeling, computer simulation, and computer graphic animation of the setup of Sheldrake's experiment.

In this model the d'Alembertian wave equation of mathematical physics is repurposed as a model for the vibration of the A-system linking two individual conscious

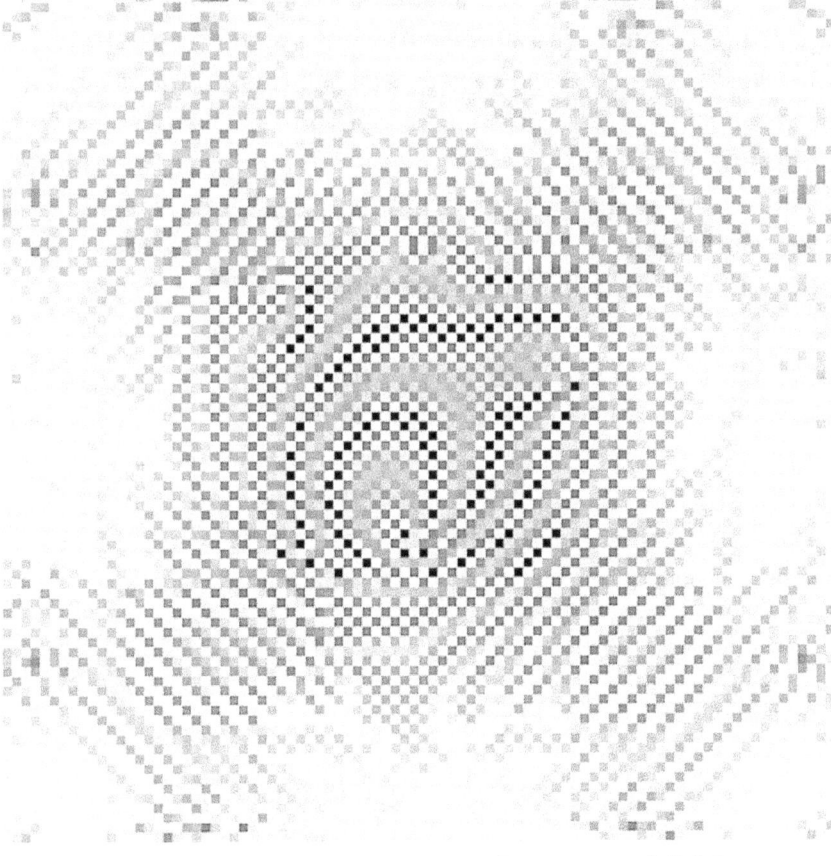

Figure 1. Vibration in a two-dimensional field.
A color image of this figure may be found on the front cover.

systems. Initially vibrating, as shown in Figure One, and on the front cover, the square may be regarded as an elastic membrane stretched over a horizontal frame, and struck with a stick. The ensuing vibration is indicated by blue if deflected down by a wave, red if deflected up, black if not deflected at all, and intermediate spectral hues for intermediate deflections. This image is a single frozen frame from a rapidly ongoing animation.

At a certain time in the simulation, a black square appears in the lower left of the image, as the dog's owner gets the call to start homeward, and the shape is considered to encode that thought. The entire vibratory pattern is greatly transformed by this event, as the black indicates that the membrane has been momentarily forced to its neutral position, in the plane of the bounding square frame. And then, soon after, a smaller black triangle appears in the upper right corner of the image. This is the dog's mental radio antenna coming up to test for good news. This perturbation also disturbs the vibratory pattern. Then the waves made by the owner's thought progresses through the A-field, changes patterns on a line segment called the *retina*, lies adjacent to the dog's antenna, and is registered by the dog as a *memory engram*, or space-time pattern in two dimensions — one spatial and one temporal. The engram pattern corresponding to the owners' homecoming signal is recognized by the dog, and she goes to the door in anticipation.[2]

3. Mind/Body Connection

It seems that modern science denies the existence of telepathy, possibly as it has no explanation or mechanism for it. However, the situation is rather opposite for the mind/body problem. How can the thought of a departed loved one beget tears? Even though modern science knows no mechanism at present, the phenomenon cannot be denied. For a certain sector of the scientific community, a thought is a physical state of the biological neural network including the brain and central nervous system — for them there is no mind/body problem, as the mind is assumed to be part of the body. For those of us unable to hold to this hypothesis, mind/body connection remains a conundrum.

In joint work with Sisir Roy, professor of quantum physics at the Indian Statistical Institute (Kolkata), we have proposed models for the mind and the body that admit a simple connection mechanism. While the connection we propose is simple, the models themselves require quite a stretch. Unless, of course, you are a quantum physicist! For our models are adaptions of a recent model for the quantum vacuum, due to Professor Roy and his German colleague, Manfred Requardt (2001). This whole line of thought partakes of the *digital philosophy* of Ed Fredkin, Steven Wolfram, and others, according to which ordinary reality is a fuzzy perception of quantum reality, which consists of an astronomically large yet finite set of points arranged in a gigantic cellular automaton! Thus, Roy and I have adapted and simplified the Requardt and Roy model for the quantum vacuum as a model for the body, taken a similar model for the mind, and connected up the two cellular automata-like objects by adding links between them. Computer graphic simulation of this model makes the complicated verbal/symbolic description easy to grasp, and the details are given in our joint papers,[3] Again, the new math is exploited to model an aspect of consciousness, and NetLogo, an agent-based modeling language, makes the computer simulation quite easy. These NetLogo models are posted on the website (see references below) along with the articles.

4. Precognition

We now take up our third and final application of the new math to aspects of consciousness, and its ambient A-system. But this one is conceptually more difficult: precognition. Even if the mind were a part of the body, modern science would still be challenged to accept telegrams from months in the future! One way many people have experienced such precognition is through their dreams. So let us assume this happens, for the sake of discussion.

The reason this is a challenge to our thinking, I conjecture, is that our entire planetary culture, for ages, contains an assumption so pervasive and taken for granted as to not even have a name! This assumption concerns the separation of the past from the future, which is universally considered to be done by a sharp knife, cutting very thin slices of the future, compressing an enormous living spectrum of possibility into a single dead fact of history. Slice by slice, eating away at the future, increasing the length of the past, each slice taking a turn at being the infinitesimal now. I call this view of time "step-time", after the Heavyside step function well-known to mathematicians.

Now that we have identified and named this hidden assumption of everyday life and thought, it is not so difficult to replace it with a variation, *slope-time*. In this view of time, the present moment, *now*, is expanded into a finite interval, its width measured in milliseconds, or perhaps months or years, as we wish. The infinite living possibilities of the future are still compressed into a single dead fact of history in the past. However, the flattening process now takes a finite interval of time.

During this interval, the spectrum of future possibilities is gradually reduced — perhaps nonlinearly in time — and during this compression process we may perceive some possibilities of relatively large probability.

Having made a new model of reality based on slope-time rather than step-time, we have to admit that, still, our perception is based on step-time, and that this is a sort of physiological or mental limitation, so it is convenient to maintain both models in side-by-side parallel universes, slope-time *and* step-time.[4] The flattening process has been modeled using the quantum vacuum, digital philosophy paradigm described above, in further joint work with Sisir Roy.[5]

5. Conclusion

Having seen three examples of the new math applied to aspects of consciousness, or the A-field, we may just end with the hope that more theoretical models of this sort might assist the scientific community to break through denial, and engage the subtle realms of Mind as an aspect of Nature to be explored with the usual, superb scientific apparatus. After all, mathematical physics did evolve in a giant step forward after the new math of Newton, and a new Enlightenment might serve us well at the present time.

Acknowledgments

I am enormously grateful to the Ramakrishna Mission Institute of Culture for extraordinary hospitality during my stays in 2006 and 2008, to the Fulbright Program, the Indian Statistical Institute (Kolkata), and the West Bengal University of Technology, for support, and Professors Sisir Roy (ISI) and Debabrata SenSharma (RMIC) for sharing ideas and friendship.

Notes

1 (Sheldrake, 1999)
2 More detailed descriptions of this work may be found in reference Ms #86.
3 Ms #119 and Ms #122.
4 This idea is explained in more detail in Ms #106.
5 See Ms #122.

Chapter 22
The Emergence of Spacetime from the Akasha

with Sisir Roy[1]

Abstract

In our recent book (Abraham and Roy, 2010) we have proposed a mathematical model for the quantum vacuum as a model of consciousness. We emphasized that the quantum vacuum is not identical to cosmic consciousness. The word *akasha* is translated in English as space, or ether. In the Eastern tradition, ether has two phases, subtle and gross. In our model, the nodes of the network correspond to subtle ether, while the physical space created in temporal slices by condensation corresponds to gross ether. In essence, the akasha is a subtle background against which everything in the material universe becomes perceptible. In this essay we expand on the self-organization of the gross ether from a subtle (submicroscopic) cellular network, with special emphasis on the illusion of time, and the apparent paradoxes such as precognition, retro-causation, and entanglement.

Publication

Ms #134, written September 20, 2011. Not previously published.

Contents

INTRODUCTION

PART ONE: PHILOSOPHY
1. Atomism before Bruno
    Eastern Atomism
    Western Atomism
2. Atomism of Bruno
    Life of Bruno
    Works of Bruno
    Atomism of the Triple Minimum
    Summary
3. Atomism after Bruno
    Galileo
    Descartes
    Cell Biology
    Yoga

PART TWO: MODELS
4. Cellular Dynamical Networks
5. Condensation
6. Time
    Precognition
    Retrocausation
    Entanglement

CONCLUSION

INTRODUCTION

Our proposed model for cosmic consciousness is made from a cellular dynamical network (CDN), a new category of discrete mathematical model.[2] From a master CDN in the abstract universe outside of space and time — called *QX*, corresponding to the subtle akasha, henceforth simply *akasha* — we construct another CDN — called *ST*, corresponding to the gross akasha, henceforth simply spacetime, the phenomenal world of space, time, matter, motion, and multi-leveled cosmic consciousness — in a process we have called *condensation*. In this work we extend our recent book with an explicit discussion of the construction of time as a sequential, discrete, or stepwise process, We begin with a review of the historical background of atomism and discrete time from the East (Buddhism and Vedanta) and the West (from Pythagoras to the Renaissance), with special attention to the 16th century philosopher Giordano Bruno, one of the last of the atomists to include spirit or soul in his cosmology.[3]

PART ONE: PHILOSOPHY

We begin with a review of atomism before, during, and after Bruno.

1. Atomism before Bruno

Atomism is a long and important thread in the history of science and philosophy,

> The conception of atomism has been the spearhead of the advance of science.[4]

Further, it is the backbone of our models for individual and cosmic consciousness. We now give a brief history of this thread in the East, then in the West.

Eastern Atomism

The concept of atomism had been widely discussed by various schools of Indian Philosophy several centuries before Bruno. We will focus our discussions mainly on Jaina, Buddhist, and Carvaka views on atomism, with special emphasis on the concept of discrete time by Jaina and Buddhist philosophers.

Indian philosophical systems can be broadly classified into two classes: *astika* and *nastika*. Astika establishes their authority by considering the Vedas as infallible, whereas nastika does not. Buddhist, Jain, and Carvaka belong to this nastika school, whereas Samkhya, Yoga, Nyaya, Vaisesika, Vedanta, and Mimamsa belong to the astika school.

Carvaka. The term Carvaka was first used in the 7th century. This word is perhaps a combination of *caru* (sweet) and *vak* (speech) and hence meaning sweet-tongued. It is claimed that pleasure is the ultimate aim of life for all human beings. They believe that the four elements or atoms — earth, water, air, and fire — exist, which make up the body and lead to consciousness. They did not consider the existence of akasha as a fifth element or atom.

Carvaka is considered to be a materialistic school. It has a significant objection to the necessity of introducing the idea of causality as the result of the relation between antecedent and consequent. That is, it opposes any ontological or logical connection between the antecedent and consequent as the basis of causality.

Jaina. The Jaina school is a distinct school of Indian philosophy as old as the Buddhist school. The metaphysical view of Jainism known as *anekantavada* is distinct from that of the Buddhist or Brahmanical schools. The atomic conception of time was elaborated in depth by the Jaina school.[5]

The characteristic of atomic time is different from that of atomic space or matter in the sense that time atoms cannot be combined or mixed, whereas those of space or matter can. In this framework atomic time, or *kalanu,* is different from the conventional time of minutes, day and night, months, years, etc. The former is considered as unconditioned or absolute time, whereas the later depends on outside factors like measurements. Conventional time has beginning and ending, whereas there is no beginning and ending for the instants comprising absolute time.

According to the Jaina view, instants or time atoms have no extension or volume and they are not simultaneous. Thus it agrees with the Yoga and Buddhist concepts of time atom. However, the instants or time atoms in the Jaina view are imperishable, in contrast to the Buddhist view. It is to be noted that whereas the atom of matter is said to have sense qualities like smell, color, etc, the time atom does not have any such sense qualities, but can be perceived through inference alone.

Discreteness vs Continuum. The concept of ksana or instant has been used and discussed by various schools of Indian Philosophy. According to Jaina or Yoga views, time as instant is real, whereas time as continuum is unreal. The Buddhists advocate that the discrete character of time and the sequence or *krama* of instants is a mental construction as in Yoga philosophy. In fact, the discrete nature of time made a profound impact on Buddhist understanding of metaphysics and perception. We shall discuss the discreteness of time and cognitive activities in the brain from a neurophysiological perspective next.

Timing in Cognition: Discreteness vs Continuity. The timing problem in cognitive neuroscience has drawn much attention from scientists in the last few decades.[6] The temporal structure of cognition and the activity of its neuronal network play a key role in understanding perception and information processing.

Magnetic and electric recordings from the human brain have revealed the existence of coherent oscillatory activity near 40 Hz. A magneto-encephalography (MEG) system was used by Joliot et al. to test whether the 40 Hz oscillatory activity relates to the temporal binding of sensory stimuli.[7] The results showed that the 40 Hz oscillations not only relate to primary sensory processing, but also reflect the temporal binding underlying cognition.

Experimental results have shown that there exists a time interval of 1014 ms (corresponding to the up trajectory of the 40 Hz oscillations) which is the minimum time required for the binding of sensory inputs to the cognition of any single event. This was proposed as the cognitive quantum of time. Again, the delay in conduction speeds along different axons and the integration time for individual neuronal elements in the circuit are both of the same order of magnitude as the temporal quanta. So, in spite of such delays, the concept of simultaneity of the external event will be considered valid for a functional space, that is, as an operational definition of simultaneity. In the present context, the operational definition has been used to study one event at a certain place and particular instant of time in the external world as cogitated by the brain. Here, the simultaneity is between the event in the external world and the event in the internal world. Broadly speaking, an operational definition specifies the type of observations that are relevant to making decisions about the applicability of the defined terms in a particular situation.

Western Atomism

We are now going to give a capsule history of atomism in the Western tradition, based on three important texts:

- *The Metaphysical and Geometrical Doctrine of Bruno*, by Serbian philosopher Ksenia Atanasijevic (1894-1981),
- *Essay on Atomism from Democritus to 1960*, by Scottish engineer Lancelot Law Whyte (1896-1972), and
- *A Short History of Atomism from Democritus to Bohr*, by historian Joshua Gregory (b. 1875).

Gregory begins his history of atomism with Mochus the Phoenician, of Sidon, 12th century BCE.[8] Atanasijevic begins her book on Giordano Bruno's Latin poem on atomism (discussed in our next section) with a brief historical chapter, *Forerunners of Bruno's Doctrine of the Minimum*. In her history, the earliest forerunners were the Pythagoreans of the 6th century BCE, noted for their ideas that number is the fundamental principle of all things, and the point (monad) is the principle of geometric bodies.

The second forerunners are the Greek atomists of Abdera, Leucippus and Democritus, 5th century BCE.[9]

According to these Greeks,

- movement is impossible without empty space,
- matter is composed of atoms, separated by empty space,

- atoms are full, that is, they do not contain empty space,
- atoms are impenetrable, continuous, and extended,
- atoms have parts, and yet are indivisible,
- atoms are so small that they cannot be perceived by the senses,
- changes in things are based on the union and separation of atoms,
- atoms are qualitatively equal, but differ in form, size, and position in space.[10]

Democritus appealed to interactions between atoms of things and atoms of souls for the qualitative richness of appearances.[11]

The views of the Greek atomists were popularized later by the Roman poet and philosopher, Lucretius, in *De Rerum Natura (On the Nature of Things)* of 54 BCE. According to Gregory,

> ... the *De Rerum Natura* presented the essential and uniform characteristics of the Greek atomistic tradition. We can know the Greek Atomism through Lucretius.[12]

Gregory includes an excellent paraphrase of Lucretius. For example,

> When the body walked the atoms of the soul had struck it within, and, helped by inrushing air, it was borne along like a ship by oars and wind.[13]

For Gregory, atomism was essentially dead (or in exile, as he says) from 200 CE until the 17th century.[14] Actually, Lucretius was rediscovered and translated in the Early Renaissance, in

1418.[15]

The third forerunner, according to Atanasijevic, comprised the medieval (late 9th century) Arab scholastics known as the *Mutakallimun* (Arabic for practitioners of *kalam*, or discourse; theologians). In this Islamic atomism, each body consists of atoms which are point-like monads. Bodies are formed by the association of atoms in empty space. According to this theory, time is also atomic, that is, is composed of discontinuous temporal instants.[16] Consequently, motion is discontinuous as well. This aspect of atomism, anticipated by Isadore of Seville (560 - 636),[17] is basic to our cellular dynamical network (CDN) model for consciousness.

Giordano Bruno, the 16th century Renaissance philosopher, represents the apex of the historical trajectory of spiritual and material atomism. According to Atanasijevic,

> Bruno, who was acquainted with all the doctrines of his predecessors, also knew, without a doubt, the doctrine of the Mutakallimun and was receptive to its influence.[18]

While Bruno is known for his support of the Copernican model, he is less known for his atomism, to which we now turn.

2. Atomism of Bruno

The Renaissance progressed from Italy to England by a slow process of cultural diffusion. The Early Renaissance in Italy was characterized by the philosophy of Marsilio Ficino, from 1470 or so. The Late Renaissance in Italy, shifting into the Baroque around 1500,[19] overlapped the Early Renaissance in the North, where John Dee was a central figure. One important vector in this diffusion was Bruno, our hero of atomism. We will begin here with his life and work, and then proceed to a detailed account of his atomism.

Life of Bruno

Bruno was born in Nola, near Naples, in 1548 [190].[20] At age 15 he entered a Dominican convent. After 13 years there, he was accused of heresy. He shed his robes and fled, becoming an itinerant philosopher and teacher of the memory arts. Thus began his professional career, in 1576, at age 28. He traveled during the next 16 years through Switzerland, to Toulouse, Paris [190], London [205], back to Paris [291], Wittenberg [306], Prague [313], Helmstedt [315], Frankfort [318, 325], Venice and Padua [346], ending in Venice in 1592, where he was jailed by the Inquisition [348]. After 8 years of interrogation, he was burned alive at the stake in Rome on February 17, 1600.[21] It is said that 100,000 thrill seekers flocked to the Campo de' Fiori to witness the event. The site, marked with an impressive statue of Bruno since 1887, is a venue for noisy parties even today. His itinerary is indicated in Figure 1.

Works of Bruno

Bruno's writings began in his first stay in Paris, in 1582, with two Latin works devoted to the memory arts [192]. After a number of other works in Latin, he arrived in London in 1582. Inspired by the emergence of vernacular literature there, he wrote six dialogues in Italian, published during 1583-1585:

1. The ash wednesday supper (*La cena de le ceneri*)

2. Cause, principle and unity (*De la causa, principio et uno*)
3. On the infinite universe and worlds (*De l'infinito universo et mondi*)
4. The expulsion of the triumphant beast (*Spaccio de la bestia trionfante*)
5. The kabbalah of the horse Pegasus (*Cabala del cavallo Pegaseo*)
6. The heroic frenzies (*De gl' heroici furori*)

all of which exist in English translations. He also wrote three poems in Latin:

1. On the triple minimum (*De triplici minimo et mensura ad trium speculativarum et multarum activarum*

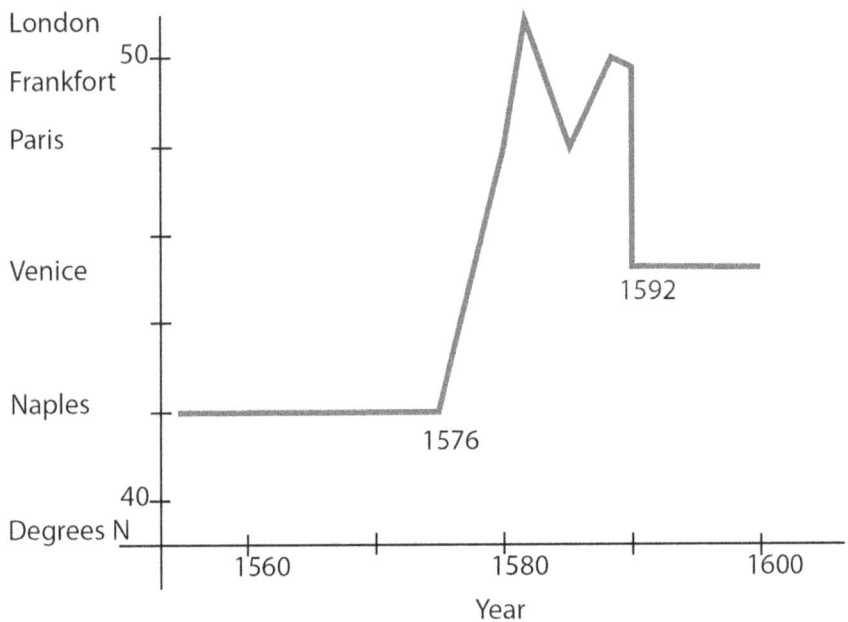

Figure 1. Travels of Bruno, 1576-1592.

principia libri V)
2. On the monad *(De monade, numero et figura liber consequens quinque de minimo magno et mensura)*
3. On the immense *(De innumerabilibus, immenso et infigurabili, seu de universo et mundis libri octo)*

which were published in Frankfort in 1591, and are as yet unavailable in English.[22] These appeared just as Bruno's philosophical career was coming to an end. It is the first of these which presents his atomistic ideas, and is of special interest to us here. Although there is no English translation, we have a detailed account in English by George Vid Tomashevich (1972) of the French paraphrase, and commentary of Ksenia Atanasijevic (1931), to which we now turn.

Atomism of the Triple Minimum

The Latin original of *De triplici minimo* has three sections, on atomism, angles, and triangles.[23]

The table of contents of the first section lists five books:

1. De minimi existentia. (On the existence of the minimum, 14 chs, 53 pp)
2. Contemplationes ex minimo. (Considerations starting from the minimum, 15 chs, 43 pp)
3. Inventio minimi. (Invention of the minimum, 13 chs, 34 pp)
4. De principiis mensurae ac figurae. (On the principles of measure and Figure, 10 chs, 40 pp)
5. De mensura. (On measure, 9 chs, 18 pp)

Of these 70 chapters we have explanations from Atanasijevic of 41 chapters: 8 of the 14 of Book 1, 7 of the

15 of Book 2, all 13 of Book 3, 9 of the 10 of Book 4, and 4 of the 9 of Book 5. We are indebted to her for the clarity of her exposition of Bruno's Latin, which, she generously states, *is surcharged with a complex and original, but sporadically very entangled, content.*[24] As Bruno is centuries ahead of his time, modern mathematics is really needed to clearly express his ideas, so the explanations of Atanasijevic are also rather demanding. From her text we now extract the few ideas of Bruno that we require.

Book 1, Ch. 2, p. 24.[25] The minimum is an indivisible unity, the element of everything composite, the principle and seed of everything existent. It is triple: (1) the general metaphysical minimum or monad, (2) the physical minimum or atom, and (3) the geometrical minimum or point.

Book 1, Ch. 7, p. 36. There are two smallest parts: the minima and the termini. The termini are the limits of the minima, and separate minima so that they cannot coincide.

Book 1, Ch. 9, p. 44. The minimum of nature is smaller than the minimum of sense perception. The minimum of nature cannot be perceived by the senses.

Book 1, Ch. 10, p. 46. Each category has its own minimum: the point for geometry, the letter for grammar, and so on.

Book 1, Ch. 11, p. 47. Each genus has its own minimum: force, order, faculty, affection, form, distance, time, moment, weight, and so on.

Book 1, Ch. 13, p. 50. The minimum is the first dimension of length and width; it is that of which dimension is composed.

The terminus has no dimension.

Book 1, Ch. 14, p. 51. The minimum cannot be perceived by the senses, and yet it can be observed as it becomes large through composition.

Book 2, Ch. 4, p. 63. The atom of the soul is the monad.

Book 2, Ch. 9, p. 68. An atom touches an atom through a terminus.

Book 2, Ch. 10, p. 69. Between atoms there must be empty space.

Book 3, Ch. 2, p. 75. Plurality increases through the minimum and can be decomposed into minima.

Summary

We may now synthesize Bruno's atomism. Every physical minimum (atom) has a corresponding soul minimum (monad). A body is an aggregation of atoms, and has a soul which is a corresponding aggregation of monads. A physical system is a network of interacting bodies, and has a soul which is a network of interacting souls. The motion of a physical system is comprised of a sequence of networks separated by discontinuous temporal instants.

All this suggests describing a system by a mathematical model which is a cellular dynamical network (CDN). The physical system and its soul may be modeled by isomorphic CDNs, and the body/mind connection modeled in turn by mathematical links between the two CDN models, as in fact we have proposed in our joint book of 2010. We have here a two-level tiered cosmology, body/soul or body/mind, which is common to the spiritual cosmologies of many different cultures.

3. Atomism after Bruno

The writings of Bruno, in his short career, had an enormous impact on philosophy and science right up to the present. In particular, his work on atomism, published in Frankfort in 1591, had an important impact on his immediate successors, Galileo, Kepler, Descartes, and Leibniz. Yet so suppressive was his public torture and execution of 1600 that he has never received the credit that he is due. Not only the spectacle made of Bruno, but a whole sequence of Inquisitional persecutions contributed to this suppression:[26]

- 1570, Cardano arrested and tried,
- 1592, Bruno arrested and tried,
- 1593, Telesio's works condemned,
- 1594, Patrizi's works condemned,
- 1594, Campanella arrested,
- 1615, Galileo's works banned.

Galileo

Galileo did not credit Bruno in his *Sidereal Messenger* of 1610, and Kepler remonstrated with Galileo for this omission in his *Conversation with Galileo's Sidereal Messenger* of the same year. Galileo's crime was repeated in 1623, with his publication of *The Assayer*, a text on atomism owing much to Bruno.[27]

Descartes

Another slight to Bruno may be detected in the works of Descartes (1596-1650). He is credited with the revival of atomism, in the form of his *corpuscular philosophy*.[28] In addition, Descartes is routinely blamed for creating the mind/brain problem.[29] Yet Descartes had a soul (mind) theory quite similar to that of Bruno. Descartes' final work, *The Passions of the Soul*, written in 1646 and published in 1649 just before his death in 1650, comprises 212 short propositions called *articles*. Part I, *About the Passions in General*, is devoted to the mind/body connection. Among its 50 articles we may select the titles of just a few to give an indication.

Article 20. About imaginations and other thoughts that are formed by the soul.

Article 30. That the soul is jointly united to all parts of the body.

Article 34. How the soul and the body act on one another.

Article 43. How the soul can imagine, be attentive, and move the body.

So Descartes was a close follower of Bruno.

Cell Biology

A realization of Bruno's atomistic scheme in the context of cell biology has been proposed by cell biologist Bruce Lipton in his book, *The Biology of Belief*. In an epilogue entitled *Spirit and Science*, Lipton identifies the individual soul of a living body with a complex of environmental signals that know the identity code of that body. This identity code is a unique set of identity receptors floating on the surface membranes of the cells of the body.[30] In terms of Bruno's atomism, this suggests that the identity receptor atoms are especially sensitive to communication from their monads.

Yoga

In our joint book, *Demystifying the Akasha*, we situated our CDN model for the mind/body system in the context of Kashmiri Shaivism. This philosophical system evolved from Advaita Vedanta in medieval Kashmir. The first distinction of Kashmiri Shaivism, according to Swami Lakshmanjoo, is in the practice of yoga. A second distinction concerns the relation between individual soul and the universal soul.[31] But the two systems agree in their multi-level cosmological models: the pancha-kosha, or five-sheaths model of the cosmos, and the simpler three-bodies model, of physical, astral, and causal body. Taking this simpler Vedantic approach, we may identify our mind/body problem with the question of connection between the physical and the astral bodies.

The Ramakrishna Mission Institute of Culture in Kolkata hosts a series of seminars on Science and Consciousness. The third of this series, in 2006, entitled *Consciousness: A Deeper Scientific Search*, was aimed at experiential reports. The first report in the published proceedings was from Swami Vidyadhishananda Giri, an experienced yogi from the Kriya-yoga (Vedanta) Giri tradition of Himalayan meditation with a Ph.D. in neurobiology. He wrote,

In the second part of this paper, I present to the

reader some very secret knowledge of the Himalayan yogis and mystics who are adept in advanced meditation or yogic methods.

Actually, in his presentation in 2006, he said that he had received permission from his order to present secrets never before made public. And his presentation was accompanied by highly sophisticated three-dimensional graphics showing the neurophysiology of all three bodies. Only three planar graphics were published in the proceedings. Based on these three graphics, his written report describes explicitly the information exchange among the three bodies. The personal ego plays the role of identity receptors in this exchange.

PART TWO: MODELS

Given this background on atomism, it is time to describe the category of mathematical models in which our work on consciousness and the mind/body problem resides.

4. Cellular Dynamical Networks

Rather than a full mathematical specification of our model, we wish simply to introduce, step-by-step, the cellular dynamical network, or CDN, category. We will proceed from graph, to network, to complex dynamical system, and at last to CDN.[32]

Graphs

This is math, but of the simplest sort: graph theory. We begin with a finite set of points. In the mathematical theory of point sets, unlike Euclidean geometry, a point is a totally abstract and basic thing, without an ambient geometric context. For example, a set of six points might be indicated symbolically as, $P_1, P_2, \ldots, P_6$. Here, P_1 is an abstract point, P_2 is another, and so on. While they may be totally abstract, it may still be helpful to visualize them in a geometric context. For example, let us think of them as geometric points around a circle in a plane. In the context of graph theory, the points are called *nodes*.

Having visualized our nodes in a circle, we may now visualize connections among them as line segments through the circle, as shown in Figure 2. These are called *links*. In this figure we have indicated three links. For example, the nodes P_5 and P_6 are connected by a link. A *graph* in graph theory is a finite set of *nodes*, some pairs of which are connected by *links*.

A directed graph, or *digraph*, is a graph in which each link has a direction. Thus P_1 may be linked to P_4 while P_4 is not linked to P_2, as shown in Figure 3.

CDNs

We begin with a positive number, N, possibly very large, and a digraph with N nodes, $P_1, P_2, \ldots, P_N$.

We assume that each node has an attribute, a natural number (zero or a positive integer), called its *charge*, or node-state.

Given any two nodes, P_i and P_j, if $i < j$, we then say P_i precedes P_j, or equivalently that P_j follows P_i.

We next assume that if P_i precedes P_j, then there is a directed link from P_i to P_j, called a *bond*.

Thus from any node, there are directed links (bonds) to all following nodes. For example, if $N=6$, there are 15 bonds:

- from P_5 to P_6,

- from P_4 to P_5 and to P_6,
- from P_3 to P_4, to P_5, and to P_6,
- from P_2 to P_3, to P_4, to P_5, and to P_6,
- from P_1 to P_2, to P_3, to P_4, to P_5, and to P_6,

Next, we assume that each bond has a state, its *bond-state*, which is *+1, 0,* or *-1*. If P_i and P_j are nodes with $i<j$, then the bond-state *+1* means charge may only flow along that bond in the positive direction, that is, from node P_i to its following node, P_j. If on the other hand the bond-state is *-1*, that means that charge may flow in the opposite direction only. And bond-state zero means that the bond is closed, that is, no flow may occur in either direction.

Finally, it is assumed that there is a master clock ticking off discrete instants of network time, and with each click, the charges flow according to some given rules, called the *dynamical rules*, thus the node-states change, and then the bond-states change.

Typical Rules

While we cannot know the dynamical rules for the entire akasha, we may give an example. These rules are from the CDN model of Requardt and Roy for the quantum vacuum.[33] Here, A_i denotes the node with index i, s_i its corresponding node-state (or charge), and $s_{ik} = s_k - s_i$ the difference in charge between two nodes.

- Each node-state is increased by the net amount of incoming information from all its bond neighbors
- Each bond-state, J_{ik},
  - is unchanged if the node-state at node A_i is equal to that at node A_k ($s_{ik} = 0$)

- becomes +1 if the difference is positive but not too much so ($0 < s_{ik} < \lambda_1$)
- becomes -1 if the difference is negative but not too much so ($-\lambda_1 < s_{ik} < 0$)
- becomes 0 if the difference of node state at A_i and that at A_k is too large ($s_{ik} > \lambda_2$ or $s_{ik} < -\lambda_2$)
- becomes +1 if J_{ik} is not 0 and the difference is medium positive ($\lambda_1 < s_{ik} < \lambda_2$)
- becomes -1 if J_{ik} is not 0 and the difference is medium negative ($-\lambda_2 < s_{ik} < -\lambda_1$)

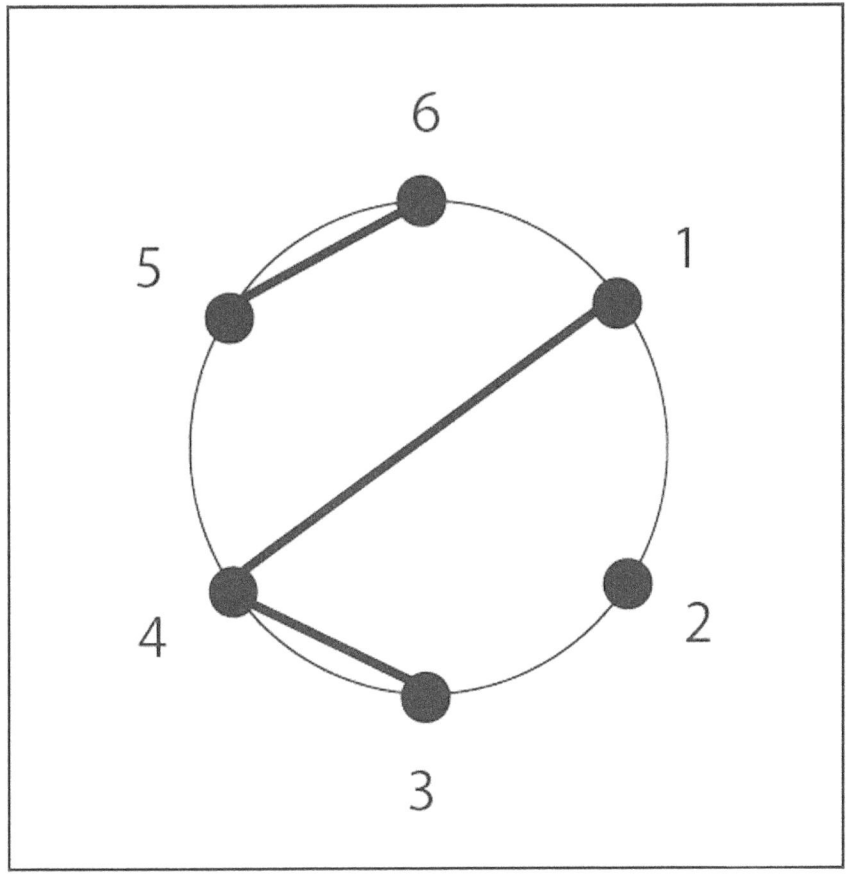

Figure 2. A simple graph.

- becomes 0 if $J_{ik} = 0$ and the difference is medium positive or negative

Of course, we must have some initial conditions, $s_i(0)$ and $J_{ik}(0)$ in order to begin a dynamical trajectory of the cellular network.

All this comprises the definition of a CDN. All CDNs are the same, except for the size, N, and the rules. **Note.** Digraphs are convenient, but not really needed, in the definition of a CDN.

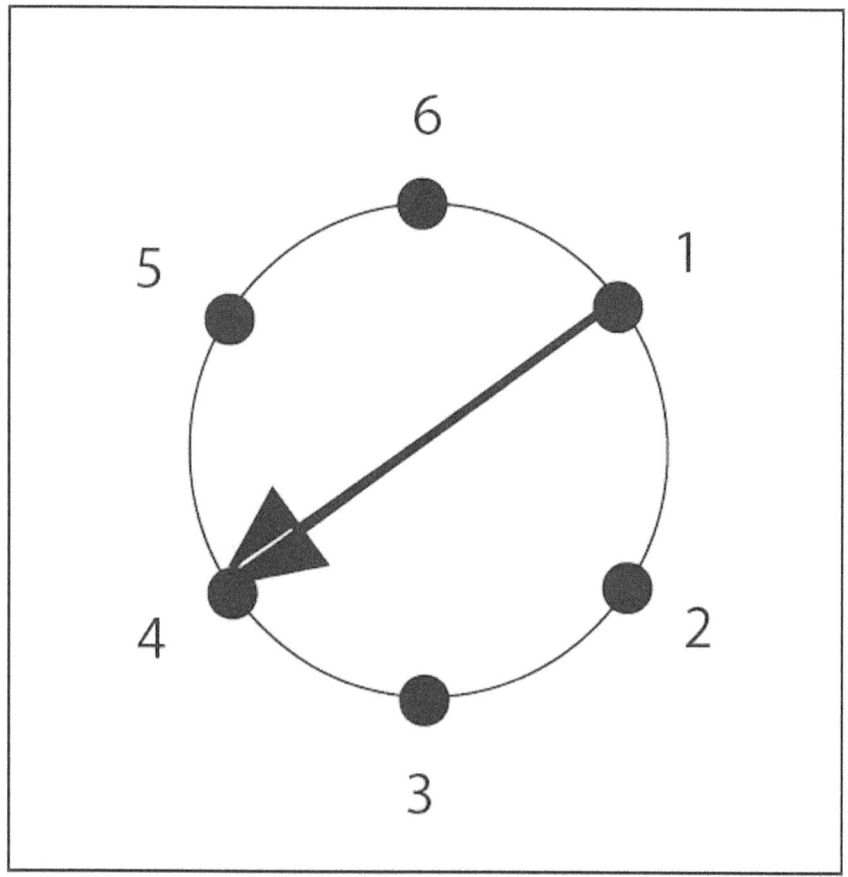

Figure 3. A simple digraph.

5. Condensation

We recall now the fundamentals of our mathematical model for cosmic consciousness.[34] There is a CDN, QX, which is similar to the model of Requardt and Roy (2001) for the quantum vacuum. It is outside of ordinary space and time, following the ideas of Vedanta (eg, Swami Vivekananda) and Kashmiri Shaivism. It has an enormous number of nodes, and its node-states and bond-states evolve with each tick of a very fast network clock, according to rules that we do not pretend to know.

Condensation is a multi-step process.

1. Firstly, given the state of the master CDN, QX, at network time, t, a second CDN, S_t, which has the characteristics of macroscopic three-dimensional space, is derived from QX by a graph-theoretic process.
2. Secondly, a continuous three-dimensional space, $3S_t$, is created by an isometric embedding of S_t into euclidean three-dimensional space, followed by a spatial smoothing process.[35]
3. After some large number of ticks, comprising an *occasion* or time-atom of macroscopic time, T, this two-step process is repeated, again and again.
4. The successive CDNs, S_t, combine to create a discrete CDN embedded in a four-dimensional spacetime, the gross akasha, ST,
5. The successive smoothed three-dimensional spaces, $3S_t$, combine to create four-dimensional continuous spacetime, $4ST$,

The illusion of continuous world-lines in space and time is a post-production special effect applied to a discrete or atomistic model.

Although the perspectives of quantum mechanics and general relativity might by accommodated by this modeling process, we have sought here the simple intuition of ordinary consciousness: the past is past, that is, condensed, the future is yet to condense, and the present moment is the last occasion to have condensed. Nevertheless, all times and events are known to QX, which exists outside (or above) space and time. We have described this situation previously as *two-dimensional time*.[36]

6. Time

Finally we have arrived at our main target in this essay, a model for time-anomalous phenomena. Throughout history there have been reports of mystics, yogis, and ordinary people as well, of time anomalies, for example: precognition, retrocausation, and entanglement. These are accommodated in our model as follows.

Firstly, recall that our models have evolved in the context of monistic philosophy: consciousness is primary, and consensual ordinary reality is secondary. The individual mind (conscious and unconsciousness) is a component of the individual soul (alternatively spirit, subtle body, and so on). Thus an individual consciousness is influenced by the states of the QX network, and vice versa.

Precognition

Precognition means an intuition of a future event before it happens, as in precognitive dreams and presentiment experiments. Such an intuition amounts to receiving a message from the future.

We are going to make an assumption here, that the individual may query the *QX* network for an advance or predictive condensation. Thus an approximation of a future occasion (time-atom snapshot of the whole spatial universe) may appear in the individual mind as a precognition. Of course, in the interval between the predicted occasion and the official present-moment condensation later on, the *QX* network, and its derivatives, will have greatly changed.

Retrocausation

Retrocausation refers to an event in the past which is caused by an action taken in the present. Or equivalently, an event in the present which is caused by an action taken in the future. In other words, the cause follows its effect, rather than the usual order, in which the cause precedes its effect. For example, a recorded computer tape containing a sequence of numbers in order is placed in a sealed vault, and later, a psychic changes some of the numbers out of order.

This may occur in our model because an actor in the present is part of the *QX* network, which is outside of space and time. The actor may influence the state of *QX*, which then is condensed into a past moment, overwriting all prior condensations.

Entanglement

Quantum entanglement is an aspect of subatomic particles, predicted by Schrödinger in 1935, in which two particles, having once interacted locally, are correlated forever, even nonlocally.[37] This prediction was verified experimentally by John Clauser in 1972, and subsequently by many others.[38] Ordinary (macroscopic) entanglement is sometimes called *synchronicity*, and appears as a startling coincidence.

Entanglement may occur in our model because of a strong network of bonds in QX created by local interaction, which then persist in QX, and manifest in correlation in all subsequent condensations.

CONCLUSION

And so, our CDN model provides for time-anomalous phenomena. Many other phenomena, also regarded as paranormal by conventional science, may also be accommodated in our model. But this is not the only justification for such a complex model. Our modeling strategy is consistent with the ancient atomistic traditions of both Eastern and Western philosophy, as well as with modern quantum theory and experiments. It fits closely with the connectionist paradigm of neural network theory. And finally, it provides for an evolutionary story of its own creation, as in the growing field of artificial life.

Notes

1 Physics and Applied Mathematics Unit, Indian Statistical Institute, Calcutta-700035, INDIA. *sisir@isical.ac.in*
2 Introduced in (Requardt and Roy, 2001).
3 (Michel, 1973; Ch. 4)
4 (Whyte, 1961; p. 3)
5 (Balslev, 2009)
6 (Fingelkurts, 2006; pp. 135-162)
7 (Joliot, 1994)
8 (1931; p. 1)
9 Whyte begins his chronology at this point, 450 BCE (1961; p. 31).
10 (Atanasijevic. 1972; pp. 13-15)
11 (Gregory, 1931; p; 18)
12 (Gregory, 1931; p. 5)
13 (Gregory, 1931; p. 8)
14 (Gregory, 1931; p. 20)
15 (Gregory, 1931; p. 23, and (Michel, 1973; p. 29)
16 Islamic atomism is thought to derive from Indian sources, rather than Greek. See (Sorabji, 1983; p. 399) and (Abraham and Roy, 2010; p. 44).
17 See (Whyte, 1961; p. 44), and also (Sorabji, 1983; chs. 5, 24, 25).
18 (Atanasijevic, 1972; p. 19)
19 (Abraham, 2011; p. 81)
20 Numbers in brackets indicate page numbers in (Yates, 1964), where full details may be found.
21 It was the custom in the Inquisition to behead victims in prison, and then to burn the dead bodies at the stake. Bruno was burned alive, exceptionally, as he refused to recant [349].
22 (Michel, 1973; p. 49)
23 Available online as *oplatI_III.pdf* from warburg.sas.ac.uk.

24 (1972; p. xvii)
25 These page numbers refer to (Atanasijevic, 1972)
26 (Schmidt, 1988; p. 253)
27 (Abraham and Roy, 2010; p. 47)
28 (Gregory, 1931; Ch. 4)
29 (Abraham and Roy, 2010; pp. 18, 111)
30 (Lipton, 2005; p. 189)
31 (Laksmanjoo, 2007; Ch. 15)
32 This is an expansion of (Abraham and Roy, 2010; Ch. 6).
33 (Abraham and Roy, 2010; p. 89)
34 This occupies about 40 pages, Chs. 6, 7, and 8, of our joint book of 2010.
35 (Abraham and Roy, 2010; pp. 83-87)
36 (Abraham and Roy, 2010; pp. 113-115)
37 (Kaiser, 2011; p. 33)
38 (Kaiser, 2011; p. 175)

PART 4
APPLICATIONS
2011-2018

Chapter 23
Shamanism and Noh

Abstract

In support of my theory on the evolution of mathematical ideas from paleolithic shamanism, we are interested in the survival of shamanic ritual elements in the classic theatre arts of Japan. In this short article we describe some of these elements in their historical contexts.

Publication

Ms #135, written 2012. Not previously published.

Contents

1. Introduction
    - My Noh Experiences
    - Background
    - Noh
2. From Shamanism to Noh
    - The Path of Shamanism
    - The Roots of Noh
3. The Music of Noh
    - The Roots of Music
    - The Instruments of Noh Music
    - The Characteristics of Noh Music
    - Shamanic Resurgence
4. Conclusion

Notes

1. Introduction

While researching the roots of chaos and fractals in our paleolithic past, I happened across book titles connecting shamanism with the classical theater arts of Japan. Among these arts, Gagaku and Noh seemed especially to preserve survivals of shamanism.[1]

To investigate this connection I made an exploratory one-week trip to Tokyo in November, 2010, with my assistant, Hiroko Tojo. Here is a brief report on that trip, and its sequel.

My short visit to Tokyo did not coincide with any Gagaku or Bunraku performances, but I was able to observe one Kabuki performance, and two Noh plays. Kabuki is of special interest as its birth is contemporaneous with the beginning of opera in the West. The example that I saw included the most incredible stagecraft I have ever seen.

Observing Noh theater was my first priority on this trip. I had never seen a performance, but had read several books (see the bibliography). My expectations were to see an early form of chaos art, perhaps the earliest: chaotic music and dance coordinated with poetic chant. This would be centuries earlier than the art of Kupka, which I have previously proposed as a prefiguration of the computer graphics of the chaos pioneer Yoshisuke Ueda, and the creator of fractal geometry, Benoit Mandelbrot.

There are several Noh theaters in Tokyo (also some in Osaka, Nara, and Kyoto).[2]

My Noh Experiences

With Hiroko Tojo, I went to the Kanze Noh (Shibuya area) on Sunday November 7th, and saw Kyogen *Shimai*, and Noh *Kanawa (Iron Trivet)*. Then we went to the National Theater (near Kokuritsu-Kyogijyo station) on Wednesday, November 10th, and saw Kyogen *Sakono Samuro*, and Noh *Aoi-no-ue (Lady Aoi)*. Lady Aoi exists in an excellent translation by Arthur Waley.[3]

As for the connection with shamanism, I was surprised by the difference between the two Noh performances. The first one (Iron Trivet) realized my expectations, while the second (Lady Aoi) was very tame in comparison. I will have to return to Tokyo (or perhaps Kyoto or Nara) to see Gagaku and Bunraku, in search of more such connections.

The production of Iron Trivet was splendid with masks, costumes, movements, and music. As for the story, it concerns people, demons, and a shaman. A woman visits a Shinto shrine every morning at two-o-clock to curse her ex-husband who has abandoned her. A priest receives a divine revelation in a dream that he should give her a message. When the woman appears he gives her the divine oracle, which says that if she puts on a red kimono, spreads red powder on her face, puts an iron trivet on her head which burns with three flames, and holds rage in her mind, she will be able to turn into a demon as she wishes.

Meanwhile the ex-husband has nightmares every night and visits a shaman, who predicts that he and his new wife will die from the curse of the ex-wife. The shaman transfers the curse to two dolls. The ex-wife appears with an iron trivet on her head, and transforms into a demon. She beats the two dolls, but the demon is exorcised by the shaman.[4]

The background in shamanism is evident in the cosmology, and the role of the shaman.

Background

I will make occasional references to the major eras of

Japanese history[5]
- Heian period (capital in Kyoto, 794-1191 CE)
- Kamakura period (capital in Kamakura, 1192-1333)
- Muramachi period (capital back in Kyoto, 1334-1573)
- Azuchi-Momoyama (1574-1600)
- Tokugawa (1600-1867)

The four traditional arts of Japan are, in chronological order:

- Gagaku, the court music (Kangen) and dance (Bugaku) of the Heian and Kamakura periods.
- Noh, the music and dance of the Muramachi period. Performances usually include short comedy (Kyogen) interludes.
- Bunraku, puppet theater, Muramachi period from 1500.
- Kabuki, song and dance from the Tokugawa period around 1600.[6]

Noh

Noh has several traditional troupes, from about 1400, the four best known being:

- Enamani-za, became Komparu,
- Sakado-za, became Kongo,
- Tobi-za, became Hosho, and
- Yuzaki-za, became Kanze.

Kan'ami, the first leader of the Yuzaki-za, moved to Kyoto and founded a new school, Kanze, which remains the most prestigious school today. Kan'ami's son Zeami, who succeeded him as head of Kanze, contributed greatly to the development of Noh as we see it today.[7]

In Noh we may recognize remnants of paleolithic shamanic rituals.[8] The shamanic cosmology of three levels of consciousness (subterranean, ordinary, and celestial) is especially relevant. This cosmology need not have been carried out of Africa by our earliest Homo sapiens ancestors, but could rather simply emanate from the same Ur source: altered states of consciousness. In addition, Noh has been related to the Enochian magic of the Elizabethan magus John Dee (1527-1608).[9]

2. From Shamanism to Noh

Shamanism is our oldest surviving religion, and has influenced all the later sacred movements. Mathematics, magic, ritual, medicine, the visual arts, and music — all may be traced from shamanism in the archeology of paleolithic times. While the shamanic tradition survives even today, in a continuous line of teacher and apprentice, many aspects are known only from cave paintings and other buried treasures. The decorated drums of Siberian shamans, seen *in situ* and in museums, inspired Kandinsky in his innovation of abstract painting around 1910.[10] It happens that, in terms of historical time, Japan is relatively close to its roots in shamanism as a living tradition. We will begin our investigation of shamanism with the evolution of the classical Noh theater of Japan.

The Path of Shamanism

The origin of shamanism is unknown, but the earliest surviving relics are found today in Western Europe. From which there may have been a cultural diffusion to Siberia (Northern Asia), or perhaps it went the other way. In any case, the connection between shamanism and psychedelics (entheogens) is sometimes credited to the Siberians, and otherwise to the Western Europeans. Characteristic of this thread in all times and places has been a cosmology of three tiers: the ordinary realm, the underworld, and the celestial sphere. Other characteristics include the ritual use of masks, drums, flutes, costumes, ecstatic dance, and abstract (symbolic) drawings. The trail from the frozen north to Japan, around 300 CE, is usually traced via China, and Korea.[11] Alternatively, Alaska, Siberia, and Japan are closely connected today by sea, and presumably in the Ice Ages, by land. To this northern source their may have been also an admixture of southern shamanism, from Polynesia.[12]

In any case, Japanese shamanism fused with Shinto and Buddhism in late prehistoric times, 5th or 6th centuries.[13]

The Roots of Noh

Turning now to the history of the classic theater and music of Japan, the oldest written source on the folk rituals seems to be around 300 CE.[14] Among these ancient records is found the myth of Ame-no Uzame-no-mikoto performing in front of a heavenly cave. This is associated with a shift in emphasis from shamanic ritual to artistic performance, and thus, the origin of the Japanese performing arts in a bifurcation from primitive shamanism. Myths, rituals, religions, the arts ... cultural history in general: all are characterized by the universal features of complex dynamical systems, such as bifurcations, or saltatory shifts from one plateau of evolution to another.

In the case of this shamanic bifurcation, the arts evolved from rituals to *kagura* — a dance performance involving *kami* (ghost, divine guest) — by the 8th century. In the same period *gigaku*, involving musical instruments, fanciful masks, and costumes which survive today — arrived from China. Next came *gagaku* (music from Korea) in the 5th century, and *bugaku* (dances from India, Tibet, and China) evolving in Japan continuously from the 8th century to the present.[15]

The further development of the Noh has been described in three stages:[16]

- Inception, from 11th century gagaku and bugaku.
- Earliest performances, from 15th century works of Kan'ami and Zeami.
- Preservation, from 17th century.

Again, these stages were punctuated by cultural bifurcations. The Noh theater came together from these roots (especially shamanic kagura) in the creative work of Kan'ami around 1400.[17] The history of Noh from that time consists of faithful adherence to tradition, and new works created within the traditional parameters. And thus, we may experience shamanic rituals in artistic recreation in the Noh theaters of Japan today. Besides the ritual dance, costumes, masks, and drama of the ancient tradition, the music integral to the performance stands out as preeminently shamanic.

3. *The Music of Noh*

As the music of Noh derives from that of the paleolithic shamanic traditions, we must be aware of these ancient roots.

The Roots of Music

From footprints found in paleolithic caves, it is plausible that chthonic rituals in the caves included ingestion of entheogens, improvisation on musical instruments, and ecstatic dancing. Shamans in historic times have very commonly been observed (and photographed) with frame drums, such as those that inspired Kandinsky for his abstract paintings. Stringed instruments are thought to have evolved from the hunting bow, attested in cave paintings throughout Western Europe. And the oldest musical instruments presently known are flutes made of bird bone and mammoth ivory, more than 40,000 years old. These were found in a cave in the Jura mountains, near the Danube in Germany.[18]

The Instruments of Noh Music

The music of Noh today is provided by the chorus and the orchestra. The chorus is seated on the right-hand side of the stage and sing in unison.[19] The orchestra, seated at the back of the stage, consists of four instrumentalists: a transverse flutist and three drummers.[20] The three drums are a shoulder drum and a side drum, both played with the hands, and a front drum, played with sticks.[21] The performance is punctuated by vocal cries by the drummers.[22]

The Characteristics of Noh Music

The music of gagaku comprises musical notes from the chromatic scale, harmonic intervals, and regular rhythms, much like the classical music of Europe.[23] As gagaku evolved into the music of Noh in the 15th century, these three principles were replaced by new principles of rhythm, tempo, and structure.[24] Note pitches were freed from the chromatic scale, intervals from Pythagorean harmonics, and rhythms from periodicity. In place of the traditional rules, a new structure of vocal and percussion cells emerged.

The vocal cells are short melodies, patterns of movement in

fluid, relative pitches.[25] The flutist also utilizes melody cells.[26] And each of the drummers plays from a set of rhythm cells, special to the type of drum.[27] A rhythm cell comprises drum beats and vocal cries.

Shamanic Resurgence

Here again, in the shift from gagaku to Noh, we have an example of cultural bifurcation. There is a special name for a bifurcation which repeatedly recovers an earlier state: *resurgence*. This term was introduced by cultural theorist Riane Eisler in the 1980s.[28] She studied *gylanic resurgence,* in which the prehistoric partnership form of social organization (equal partnership of the genders in human society) repeatedly breaks through the barriers of the dominator society. In our history of Noh, we have observed repeated incidents of *shamanic resurgence.*

4. Conclusion

While survivals of the shamanic practices of prehistoric times may be found in several cultures today, only the Noh theater of Japan recreates the full spectacle, including music, dance, drama, masks, costumes, integrated performance, and highly evolved stage art. The content — story, poetry, historic and mythical characters, ghosts, and elemental forces, relating to all three levels of the shamanic cosmos — is enhanced by chaotic music and surreal movements to invoke the ambiance of an authentic paleolithic cave spectacle.

Reading widely in world cultural history, informed by this exemplary case of shamanic resurgence, we may now recognize many other examples of this phenomenon. Particularly, in current events, we find ourselves amid a shamanic resurgence affecting mathematics, the sciences, the arts, politics, economics, the environment — everything — which is crucial to our choice of a future.

Notes

1. See (Blacker, 1975), (Ortolani, 1995), (LaFleur, 1983), and (Shigeo, 1984; Ch. 4).
2. (Kenny, 1974)
3. (Waley, 1921/1976; pp. 117-127)
4. This abstract is from http://www.the-noh.com/en/plays/data/program_026.html, which also has photos of a production very much like the one I saw.
5. See, for example, (LaFleur, 1983; p. xvi)
6. See (Kenny, 1974)
7. (Cavaye, 2004)
8. (Lewis-Williams, 2002; pp. 132-135)
9. (Lehrich, 2007; pp. 61-81)
10. (Abraham, Ms #131)
11. (Ortolani 1995; p. 2)
12. (Blacker, 1999; p. 27)
13. See (Blacker, 1999; p. 29), (LaFleur, 1983; p. 46), and (Ortolani, 1995; p. xii).
14. (Ortolani; 1995; p. 2)
15. (Ortolani, 1995; Ch. 4)
16. (Tamba, 1981; p. 16)
17. (Ortolani, 1995; p. 93)
18. Reported in the BBC News, 25 May 2012.
19. (Tamba, 1981; p. 29)
20. (Tamba, 1981; pp. 27, 141)
21. (Tamba, 1981; p. 159)
22. (Tamba, 1981; p. 165)
23. (Tamba, 1981; p. 5)
24. (Tamba, 1981; p. 6)
25. (Tamba, 1981; p. 63)
26. (Tamba, 1981; p. 171)
27. (Tamba, 1981; p. 172)

28 (Eisler, 1987)

Chapter 24
Mathematical Perception

Abstract

We extend the cognitive theories of Husserl and Poincaré up the cosmological chain to the Platonic world of ideas.

Publication

Ms #147, written 2015. Not previously published.

Contents

1. Introduction
2. Theories of Perception
    2.1. Phenomenology
    2.2. Hallucinations
        2.2.1. Common-kind theories
        2.2.2. Disjunctive theories
    2.3. Mathematics
3. Examplary Cases
    3.1. The genericity of transversal intersection
    3.2. The case of the homoclinic tangle
4. Conclusion
Notes

1. Introduction

Poincaré (1855-1912) was perhaps the most creative mathematician of all time. And he was among the first to write about his creative process. So naturally his article entitled *Mathematical Creativity* must be taken seriously. As the title indicates, he was a constructivist, believing that mathematics was a human creation. His article contains a theory of mathematical perception.

He was a contemporary of Husserl (1859-1938), who also wrote on perception. It is well-known that Husserl and Poincaré influenced each other on the philosophy of geometry, and here I contend that they also interacted on the theories of perception. Husserl's early ideas on perception appeared in his *Logical Investigations* of 1900 and 1902, while Poincaré's lecture on creativity in 1904 was the basis of his writing, published in 1908.

While Poincaré died prematurely at age 57, Husserl enjoyed a long and prolific life, developing his early ideas into phenomenology, his mature philosophy of perception.

Meanwhile, Poincaré's ideas were carried further by the mathematician Jacques Hadamard (1865-1963) in a book *The Psychology of Invention in the Mathematical Field*, of 1945. Briefly, the theory of Poincaré, reduced to an outline, amounts to these four stages.

1. Fully conscious work, without success.
2. Incubation, unconscious work by the *subliminal ego*.
3. Illumination, spontaneous emergence of an idea into consciousness.
4. Conscious verification and elaboration.[1]

During incubation, the subliminal ego performs

experimental combinations of ideas, filtering the outcomes by criteria of mathematical beauty.

This may be regarded as a specialization of phenomenology to the case of mathematical ideas, or objects. My project in this paper is to question this theory from a Platonic perspective. The problem, as I see it, is posed by the universality of mathematical ideas, as supported by the many cases of independent discovery. I say discovery, rather than creation or invention, due to my personal preference for Platonism. The problem may be resolved by the cosmological concept of the *great chain of being*, common to both Eastern and Western philosophies.

The crux of the problem lies in the nature of the perception of objects in the mathematical world.

2. Theories of Perception

We may begin with the ideas of Poincaré and Husserl, and attempt to update them, following developments in the philosophy and psychology of perception since their time a century or so ago.[2]

2.1. Phenomenology

The trajectory of phenomenology has advanced from Husserl through the work of Merleau-Ponty, Francisco Varela, and their followers.[3] But the problem remains: How are mathematical objects perceived?

Recall Poincaré and Husserl. In Step 1, we have the manipulation of mathematical objects by the conscious mind. These presumably have been learned through reading the literature of the subject, and talking with colleagues. They are established as mental objects, and have no counterparts in the real world, no sense-data, no conventional perceptions. Thus, they skirt the central ideas of phenomenology completely.

To apply these central ideas, we must suppose the mathematical object received is a presentation of an existing external prototype object, but this is not in the physical world of matter and energy that may be sensed by the usual senses. Instead we must posit a Platonic world of ideas. And then the semiotic triangle may be applied to the perceptual process. This process of transcendental perception may be regarded as a kind of resonance process, as in the *morphic resonance* of Rupert Sheldrake,[4] or the *spanda* of Kashmiri Shaivism.[5]

In Step 1 of Poincaré we have a sort of concentration exercise, or meditation, on mathematical objects selected from the collective storehouse of mathematical ideas. They are manipulated, or combined, according to established rules. Then Step 2 becomes a shadow of the conscious process of Step 1 in the unconscious system of the mathematician's mind. The process of trial combination of ideas and aesthetic evaluation proceeds in the background, and perhaps a discovery is made by the subliminal ego. Finally, in Step 3, a rent in the curtain between the conscious and unconscious systems allows the new object to be perceived in consciousness. This is similar to the recovery of a dream upon waking from sleep.

Mathematical perception more resembles a dream or an hallucination than a sense-perception. We may summarize the fundamental setup with the semiotic triangle shown in Figure 1. Here we have shown the semiotic connection as a bidirectional channel, in consideration of the enactive approach of Varela, Thompson, and Rosch. Hence, math objects may be immortal as in Plato, or human creations as in Poincaré, or a combination of these.

2.2. Hallucinations

Psychedelics used to be called hallucinogens, but fans objected. It was thought that psychedelic visions are more real than hallucinations. In earlier writings, I compared mathematical perceptions and psychedelic visions. Here I am relating them to hallucinations.[6] Although hallucinations have been with us forever, they comprise a branch of the philosophy of perception only since Descartes. And this recent explosion of articulate works on non-veridical (un-real) perception provides us a wealth of concepts that we may adapt to the problem of mathematical perception. Here I will briefly summarize some of these ideas, following Fiona Macpherson (2013).[7] There are many schools of thought, here are a few of them.

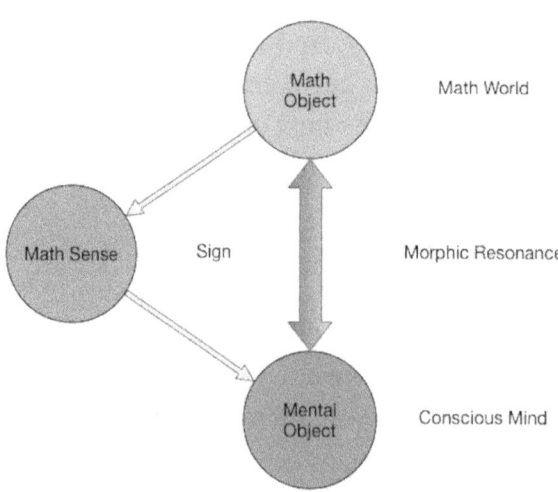

Figure 1. Mathematical perception, semiotic view.

2.2.1. Common-kind theories

This category comprises most of the traditional writings on hallucinations before the advent of the divergent views called disjunctivism. A visual perception of a physical object, for example, is regarded as a causal chain of reactions:

- light from the object, passing through the eye, impinges the retina,
- retinal cells fire through the optic nerve to the primary visual cortex,
- a complex of brain states is instantiated,
- a visual experience occurs via an unknown brain/mind process.

According to common-kind theories, if an intermediate step in the chain is caused somehow, the same visual experience will result as if it had resulted from the entire chain being involved. Thus, an observation of a red teacup will be indistinguishable from an hallucination of a red teacup. This is the common-kind view of hallucinations and dream experiences.[8] The sameness of the kind of the mental states in the two cases is the source of the name, common-kind.

According to this way of thinking, a mathematical visualization might be regarded as a sort of hallucination, in which the math object, a mental object, must impinge on the causal chain via a mind/brain process, proceed down the chain like a veridical perception, and then be returned to the mental world by an inverse brain/mind process. Such a morphic resonance chain seems possible, but perhaps unnecessarily complicated.

2.2.2. Disjunctive theories

The disjunctivists, on the other hand, view the two cases of perception (veridical and hallucinatory) as mental states of different kinds, even though the perceiver may not be able to distinguish them. The common causal chain of the common-kind theories is dropped. One may imagine instead that there are two disjunct causal chains, one starting from the physical world, another that is entirely within the mind.[9]

This conception is better suited to an understanding of mathematical perception. A special chain may have its source in the world of mathematical objects, belonging to the collective consciousness perhaps, and its target in a mental zone that has evolved in the individual mind (conscious or unconscious) through the history and prehistory of mathematical thinking.

2.3. Mathematics

So here is a theory of mathematical perception. This is a theory, not a theorem, that is, there can be no proof, it is just an opinion, a cognitive strategy. We may use it to understand mathematical creativity in a way that is compatible with Poincaré's theory.

We begin by enlarging the world so as to include several levels, like Plato's cosmology, or the five kosas, or 36 tattvas, of the Sanskrit philosophers. Among them are the physical world of traditional theories of sense perception, and Plato's world of ideas, including mathematical ideas.

Then, as in the disjunctive theory of hallucination, we propose two chains of communication, or morphic resonance. Each begins in a level of the enlarged world, and terminates in the individual mind of the mathematician. As in the enactive theory of phenomenal perception, these channels may be bidirectional. Further, they may have cross connections, empowering synesthesias such as mathematical visualization.

Some support for this model is provided by the work of the mathematical biologists Bard Ermantrout and Jack Cowan. They showed in 1979 that a mathematical model for the reaction and diffusion of morphogens over the visual cortex may produce morphodynamic patterns of chemotaxis mimicking the visions seen during a migraine attack. This suggests a chain from an idea or mental state to a physicochemical brain state and thence to a visual perception. This also indicates cross-links among the levels of the cosmological model.

The five kosas of classical Vedanta philosophy possibly preceded and inspired Plato and the Neoplatonic traditions. These are:

- Annamaya Kosa (Physical Body)
- Pranamaya Kosa (Energy Body)
- Manomaya Kosa (Mind)
- Vijnanamaya Kosa (Intellect), and
- Anandamaya Kosa (Bliss)

These five evolved — in the two hundred years from Shankar to Abhinavagupta — into the 36 tattvas of Kashmiri Shaivism, about 1000 years go.

It seems likely that the five kosas evolved from the three bodies — causal, subtle, and gross — that may in turn derive from the Shamanic traditions of the Epipaleolithic caves. The three bodies and the five kosas are usually correlated thus:

- Gross body = Annamaya Kosa (Physical)
- Subtle body = (Pranamaya, Manomaya, and

Vijnanamaya) Kosas (Energy, Mind, Intellect)
- Causal body = Anandamaya Kosa (Bliss)

In any case, we may use the three bodies as the basis for an analysis of the work of Ermantrout and Cowan. The mathematical model and the computer model may be assigned the subtle body, the neurochemical morphogens to the gross body, and the hallucinatory visual perception back again in the subtle.

It will be helpful to use the five kosas as a framework for the disjunctive view of mathematical perception, as shown in Figure 2.

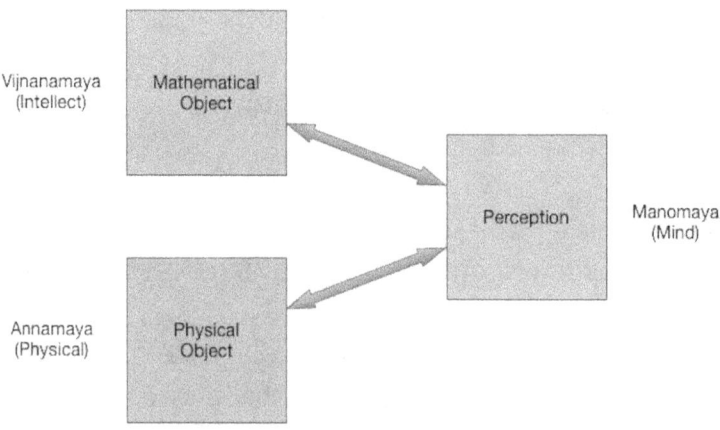

Figure 2. Mathematical perception, disjunctive view.

3. Exemplary Cases

We have considered the theories of perception as a foundation for the analysis of mathematical creation (from the human-centered point of view), or equivalently, discovery (from the Platonic view). We now consider two exemplary cases.

3.1. The case of the homoclinic tangle

This mathematical object came into consciousness along with Poincaré's founding of chaos theory in 1890. A rough sketch of a tangle is shown in Figure 3. Poincaré intuited a fuzzier image in the context of his famous work on the stability of the solar system.[10]

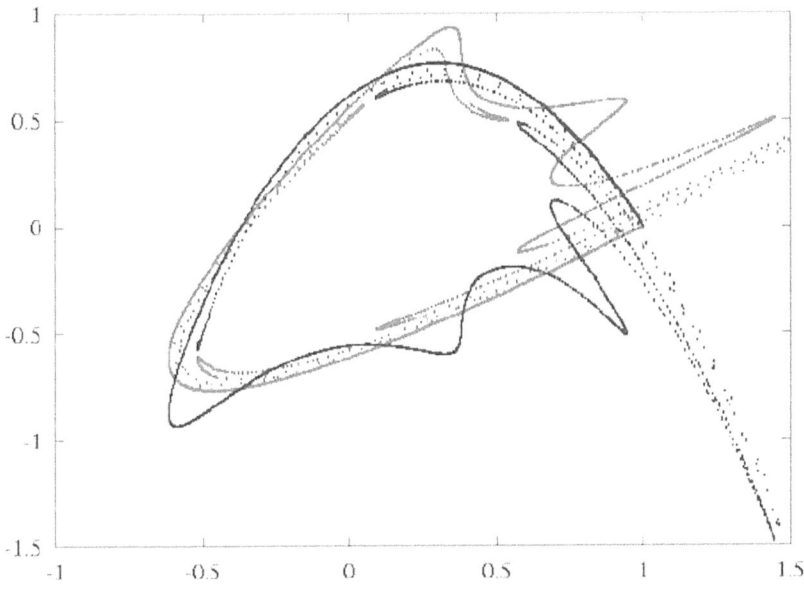

Figure 3: A typical homoclinic tangle in two dimensions.

The first drawings came a generation later, in a publication of the American mathematicians George D. Birkhoff and Paul Smith in 1928.[11] The firm connection with chaos theory came only after another generation, in the original discovery of chaotic behavior by Yoshisuke Ueda in 1961.[12]

In both cases, Poincaré in 1890 and Birkhoff and Smith in 1928, the image must have popped into consciousness after hard work by the subliminal ego. No such image had previously been known to mathematics, nor seen in Nature.

3.2. Genericity of transversal intersection

Transversal intersection is a property of geometric objects seen only in the imagination of mathematicians specializing in differential topology, a branch of mathematics created by Poincaré. This particular property, first studied by the American mathematician Hassler Whitney around 1940, may be exhibited by subspaces in Cartesian three-dimensional space. For example two planes, when their intersection is as simple as possible, such as crossing each other in a common line.[13]

In 1960, the Fields Medalist Stephen Smale proved that dynamical systems were characterized by curved surfaces called stable manifolds, which might have multiple intersections. He conjectured that these intersections, in general, were transversal. He presented this work at a conference in Urbino, Italy, in 1961, where I was in the audience. Shortly after, I was scheduled to present my own proof of this generic property of transversal intersection at another international conference in Bonn, Germany. The day before my scheduled talk, as I was reviewing my rather complicated proof, I realized there was a gap. I was petrified, because if I had to cancel my talk my reputation would be ruined.

I went into the library of the Institute where the conference was gathered to have some private time to collect my thoughts. I felt dizzy, and grasped the library shelves on both sides of the aisle, and there was a flash like a thunderbolt. Instantly there popped into my mind a totally new and very simple proof, complete with details of the presentation such as drawings for the blackboard and hand gestures to indicate the movements of the surfaces. Like Poincaré, I was so certain of the argument that I completely relaxed, and went out to dinner and dancing with some of the other participants. The next morning I gave the talk from memory with great success. The printed version of the proof filled an entire book that was published in 1967.

4. Conclusion

Attempts to model mathematical perception following in the footsteps of Poincaré and Hadamard after 1945 in the tradition of common-kind theories were foiled by the fact that most of the writings of this tradition seemed to identify a mental state with a brain state, whereas a mathematical object and its presentation in the mind (conscious or unconscious) are equally mental. This obstacle disappeared with the advent of the disjunctive theories in the 1960s. Now it is possible to speculate on mathematical perception using the tools of the disjunctive theories of hallucination, as we have done here.

However, a problem remains: what is the nature of the link between a mathematical object in the Intellect (Vijnanamaya Kosa, or Plato's World of Ideas). and its mental representation in the Mind (Manomaya Kosa)? This is the upper link in Figure 2. It is a subtle version of the mind/body problem, the lower link in Figure 2, and we have glossed over it with the mysterious metaphor of morphic resonance. In Kashmiri Shaivism this problem is addressed explicitly with the notion of *spanda*, or vibration in the *akasha*, an immaterial field that connects all 36 tattvas. We have attempted an atomic model for this vibratory field elsewhere,[14] but the problem remains.

Notes

1 (Hadamard, 1954; pp. 31, 56)
2 (Abraham, 2015)
3 See (Varela, 1991), (Thompson, 2007), and (Thompson, 2015).
4 (Sheldrake, 2009)
5 (Abraham and Roy, 2010)
6 I am grateful to my friend Dr. Paul A. Lee for suggesting this line of approach.
7 See her 36-page introduction in (Macherson and Platchias, 2013).
8 (Macpherson, 2013; pp. 8-18)
9 (Macpherson, 2013; pp. 18-25)
10 For better drawings with interpretations see (Abraham and Shaw, 2005), and for more of the surrounding history, see (Abraham, 2013).
11 Smith was my department chair when I was an assistant professor at Columbia University, 1962-64.
12 (Abraham, and Sisir Roy, 2007).
13 I am sorry that this example contains technical jargon, which may be ignored.
14 (Abraham and Roy, 2010)

Chapter 25
Hip Santa Cruz and the Chaos Revolution

Abstract

The genesis of Hip Culture in the 1960s is described as a bifurcation of a complex dynamical system, triggered by psychedelics.

Publication

Ms #150, written 2016. Based on a talk at the Logos bookstore in Santa Cruz, October 6, 2016, introducing my new book, *Hip Santa Cruz*. Not previously published.

Contents

Introduction
1. The Chaos Revolution
    Chaos, Gaia, Eros (1994)
    Complex Dynamical Systems
    The Santa Cruz Hip History Project (2002)
2. Hip Santa Cruz
    The Beats
    From Beat to Hip
    Ken Kesey
    The Seeds of Santa Cruz Hip
Conclusion
Notes

Introduction

I have to wonder what it is about this book about Santa Cruz in the 1960s — *Hip Santa Cruz* — that could actually bring us all together. I think it is something about this 50-year interval. It's not only the passage of a certain amount of time that demands remembering, but also the themes of the 1960s seem to be coming up again, coming up again as they came up then, for more or less unknown reasons. And its those unknown reasons that I have been pursuing, especially during these past two months. There is a book by Mark Kurlansky (2004), entitled *1968: The Year That Rocked The World*. Its a rather thick book entirely devoted to this one year. In the introduction it says:

> There has never been a year like 1968, and it is unlikely that there will ever be one again.

And from the back cover,

> To some, 1968 was the year of sex, drugs, and rock and roll. Yet it was also the year of the Martin Luther King, Jr., and Bobby Kennedy assassinations; the riots at the Democratic National Convention in Chicago; Prague Spring; the antiwar movement and the Tet Offensive; Black Power; the generation gap; avant-garde theater; the upsurge of the women's movement; and the beginning of the end for the Soviet Union.

For me, personally, it was also an important year, because that is the year I moved from the East Coast to the West Coast, from Princeton, New Jersey to Santa Cruz, California, and from Princeton University to UC Santa Cruz. In all my days and many transformations, this has been my largest dislocation. Astrologically, it somehow coincided with all these other big things that happened in 1968.

My official title here is *Hip Santa Cruz and the Chaos Revolution*, so I want to start with these two questions: Why should we be interested in Hip Santa Cruz? And: What is the Chaos Revolution? I'll start with the Chaos Revolution.

1. The Chaos Revolution

At Princeton University, before I moved, I was studying chaos theory. I gave a graduate course on it in 1966. The lecture notes became a book, my first book,[1] and in that course I encountered for the first time the idea of a revolution or paradigm shift, such as a revolution in the sciences, or in mathematics. For example, I came to understand the origin of chaos theory as a major revolution in the history of mathematics.

Chaos, Gaia, Eros (1994)

After coming to Santa Cruz, chaos theory had a brief moment of fame. For a year or two from 1987 it was all in the news, and then of course forgotten. But while the subject was hot I was besieged by journalists asking me: What is chaos theory and why should we care? How did it happen? Is it really revolutionary? They naturally wondered: Is it news or not? In trying to answer these questions, I had to dig into the history of the chaos concept over the ages. This resulted in my first historical book, *Chaos, Gaia, Eros*.[2]

In looking at this history, I had to look at the data and consider it from my own point of view, which was the point of view of chaos theory, that is, history as a series of paradigm shifts. In other words, chaos theory, looking at itself.

Complex Dynamical Systems

Chaos theory is not well named, as it is not about chaos. It is about complex dynamical systems. These comprise a class of mathematical models which are similar somehow in their structure to the systems within which we live, also called complex dynamical systems. In the mathematical systems, virtual experience may be obtained through computer simulation, in which the chief characteristic feature is discontinuity, or major transformation, which mathematicians call *bifurcation*.

So I saw the beginnings of chaos theory as a bifurcation in the history of mathematics, radiating outward into the sciences, the arts, and popular culture, and coinciding with the major cultural transformations that took place in the 1960s.

The Chaos Avant-garde (2000)

After the wave of chaos curiosity passed, I wanted to record the origins of chaos theory before the principals passed away. Jointly with the first chaos pioneer, Yoshisuke Ueda of Kyoto University, most of the pioneers were asked for a memoir. And these became a book, *The Chaos Avant-garde*.[3] This is a collection of first-person accounts by the mathematicians who actually initiated and carried through the Chaos Revolution, which happened to coincide with the 1960s.

This became a prototype for my current book, *Hip Santa Cruz*, which comprises first-person accounts of the pioneers of Hip Culture in Santa Cruz in the same time frame, the 1960s.

Chaos theory is about the specific mechanics of bifurcation, that is, the major transformations of history, machines, chemistry, or whatever. And my idea now, on the history of Santa Cruz in the 1960s, is to apply the mathematical ideas of bifurcation theory to this data.

The Santa Cruz Hip History Project (2002)

Within a year or two of *The Chaos Avant-garde*, it occurred to me to apply this same idea to the Hip Culture of Santa Cruz. So I began the Santa Cruz Hip History Project. This is about a group of people who experienced Santa Cruz in the 1960s. These people participated in an oral history project in which people took turns, sitting in a circle of 15, 20 or more people, telling their story into a recording device. Then the stories were transcribed and posted to a website, which is the virtual home of the project. And recently, I decided to bring some of the collected material together as a book.

2. Hip Santa Cruz

The period of Hip Culture in Santa Cruz spanned from about 1964 to 1970. It was a relatively short period, with a definite beginning and ending. When I arrived in Santa Cruz in 1968 it was almost over. So considering my mathematical question — How did it start? — I had to rely on the observations of other people. This was the motivation of my Hip History Project: I wanted to find out from the 1960s pioneers how it all began in Santa Cruz.

From the thirteen chapters of the book, written from different perspectives and times and places, you may piece together the anecdotes to get a picture of what was going on, including the beginning of Santa Cruz Hip History.

From the testimonies of the pioneers whom I had known, I came up with my theory that Hip Culture derived from the Beat Generation by a major social transformation.

The Beats

When you read about the Beat Generation and Hip Culture, its amazing how similar their ideas were. It is clear that Hip evolved from Beat. In their outré ideas and behavior, the Beats were even more extreme than Hippies. The Beat movement began with the meeting of three people at Columbia University in 1944, the Beat KGB: Jack Kerouac, Allen Ginsberg, and William Burroughs. These three people were the skeleton of the group that came to be called the Beat Generation.

Two years after they met, a fourth important actor joined them in New York City, Neal Cassady. He wrote little but talked a lot, and he had a great influence on other people. He had a very close relationship with Kerouac, and they traveled together. That is the story of Kerouac's *On the Road*, and subsequent books. Kerouac wrote twenty-one books in eighteen years, all autobiographical. His role carried a different name in each book.

He had a great knack for telling true stories. Each of his novels is written in a different style. One of them, *The Subterraneans*, was written as a stream of consciousness with little punctuation, the style in which Cassady was famous for speaking. A little over 100 pages, it was written in three days. Well, the principal drugs of the Beat Generation were alcohol and Benzedrine,

The Beat Generation emerged into the limelight in 1955, when the three principals (and two others) gave a poetry reading at the Six Gallery in San Francisco. One of the works was a poem by Allen Ginsberg, read by himself, called *Howl*. This poem, like most of his work, was obscene to a degree, so of course it was attacked for obscenity by the law-and-order people. Thus it became famous thanks to the obscenity laws, and the Beats emerged into the media.

Later they hung out at the newly (1953) formed City Lights Bookstore co-founded by Lawrence Ferlinghetti, a French-speaking intellectual from Morocco. It was the first bookstore in the United States that carried paperback books exclusively. The Hip Pocket Bookstore in Santa Cruz was modeled on it. The Beat Generation came to an end around 1970, when some of the principals died.

From Beat to Hip

Now let's consider the question: What is the transmission from the Beat Generation to the Hip History of Santa Cruz? So now I have to tell you my main idea here: In the chemical reaction that turned Beat into Hip, there was a special catalyst called LSD.

Other psychedelics were involved in the cultural history of twentieth century North America: mushrooms and psilocybin, peyote and mescaline, yage and DMT. But LSD specifically called forth the Hippie cultural features from the confusion of the Beat psyche. And two vectors carried it: Allen Ginsberg and Ken Kesey, of Merry Prankster fame. Ken Kesey himself said,

> I'm too young to be a Beat.
> I'm too old to be a Hippie.

That suggests that he is, in fact, a vector from the Beats to the Hippies.

The LSD story is particularly interesting because of the role played by the CIA. Our heroes — Ken Kesey and Allen Ginsberg — were given LSD through the CIA in 1959, two years before Timothy Leary turned on with LSD. Allen Ginsberg had gone to Boston to read *Howl*, and told Leary, who had already established a research project on psilocybin, about LSD.

Ken Kesey

Kesey's story is particularly amazing. From the unique charisma and power of this one personality grew up a whole phenomenon, the so-called Acid Test, which was a prototype for the emerging Hip Culture.

First he was given LSD in the Palo Alto Veterans Hospital. Then he was living on Perry Lane, where a group of friends were already morphing into the Merry Pranksters. When Perry Lane was sold to a developer who bulldozed all the houses, Kesey and company moved to La Honda, a hamlet between Palo Alto and Santa Cruz, and the idea evolved for a bus trip to New York and back. The idea was to spread the news about LSD to everyone, to leapfrog cultural diffusion through the media.

Back in those days, people read magazines. You know, the Gordon Wassons' story about the psilocybin mushrooms in Oaxaca was published as a 17-page spread in LIFE magazine in 1957, and because of that a lot of people turned on. But Ken Kesey and his Merry Pranksters wanted to turn on the whole of North America without delay.

What had been happening in their La Honda living room evolved into a public ritual, the Acid Test. There was a series of Acid Tests in California. By making a spectacle of themselves, performing Acid Tests all across the country and all the way back, they would turn on a nation.

The first Acid Test was here in Santa Cruz. There were about forty or fifty Pranksters, including those on the bus and others off the bus. Of those forty or fifty people, there were seven that were, for awhile, residing in Santa Cruz. One of them, Ken Babbs, number two in the Prankster hierarchy, took over when Ken Kesey was put in jail. Babbs lived in Soquel, a suburb of Santa Cruz. So the first Acid Test was held here, almost exactly 51 years ago.

The Seeds of Santa Cruz Hip

The germinal event in Santa Cruz was the opening of the Hip Pocket Bookstore in 1964 by Pranksters Peter Demma and Ron Bevirt. And Neal Cassady, who (like Allen Ginsberg) had moved from Beat to Prankster, helped out in the store. The bookstore served as a staging ground for the first Acid Test, giving people directions to the event.

Then Cassady brought in his friend and housemate, Leon Tabory, who started The Barn. The bookstore opened in 1964, the first Acid Test was in 1965, and the Barn opened in 1966, when the bookstore closed. The Barn became a stationary Acid Test. It was there every day, every night, with 300 people stoned on LSD, weird music, psychedelic art, and light shows by Dr. Richard Smith, a dentist in Scotts Valley. The Barn became the nucleus of Hip Culture in Santa Cruz.

Conclusion

So from Beat to Hip: a bifurcation in which Santa Cruz played a crucial role. From the Acid Tests outward, LSD catalyzed a spreading wave of major cultural transformation.

Notes

1. (Abraham, 1967)
2. (Abraham, 2011)
3. (Abraham and Ueda, 2000)

Chapter 26
Theosophy and the Arts

Abstract

The cosmology of Ancient India, as transcribed by the Theosophists, contains innovations that greatly influenced modern Western culture. Here we bring these novel embellishments to the foreground, and explain their influence on the arts.

Publication

Ms #151 written January 17, 2017. Not previously published.

Contents

1. Introduction
2. The Esoteric Planes and Bodies
    2.1. Sinnett
    2.2. Blavatsky
    2.3. Besant
    2.4. Leadbeater
    2.5. Thought-forms and the arts
3. The Akasha
    3.1. The ancient Akasha
    3.2. The Akasha in Theosophy
    3.3. The Akasha in Science
4. Conclusion
Notes

1. Introduction

Following the death of Madame Blavatsky in 1891, Annie Besant ascended to the leadership of the Theosophical Society. The literature of the post-Blavatsky period began with the very influential *Thought-Forms* by Besant and C. W. Leadbeater, of 1901.

The cosmological model of Theosophy is similar to the classical Sanskrit of 6th century BCE. The *pancha kosa*, in particular, is the model for these authors. The classical pancha kosa (five sheaths or levels) are, from bottom up: physical, vital, mental, intellectual, and bliss.

The related idea of the *akashic record* was promoted by Alfred Sinnett in his book *Esoteric Buddhism* of 1884.

2. The Esoteric Planes and Bodies

The Sanskrit model was adapted and embellished by these early Theosophists.

2.1. Sinnett

Alfred Percy Sinnett (1840-1921) moved to India in 1879, where he was the editor of an English daily. Sinnett returned to England in 1884, where his book, *Esoteric Buddhism*, was published that year. This was based on his correspondence with masters in India.

2.2. Blavatsky

Helena Petrovna Blavatsky (1831-1891) — also known as HPB — was a Russian occultist and world traveler. While reputedly in India in the 1850s, she came under the influence of the ancient teachings of Hindu and Buddhist masters. She co-founded the Theosophical Society in New York City in 1875. In 1877 she published her first book, *Isis Unveiled*, which is basic to Theosophy. The following year, Blavatsky (traveling with Henry Steel Olcott, journalist and co-founder of the Theosophical Society) arrived in India and stayed for some time with the Sinnetts in Simla. She then returned to Europe, where her second book, *The Secret Doctrine*, was written and self-published in 1888, in two volumes.

2.3. Besant

Annie Besant (1847-1933), leader of the Theosophical Society after the death of HPB, wrote many books and pamphlets on Theosophy and related matters. One of the basic themes regards the cosmological model of several planes or bodies.

From the point of view of the individual seer, the elements are experienced as ascending levels of consciousness. These are the planes of consciousness.

But to a clairvoyant, they appear as three-dimensional sheaths, which surround a physical body with successively larger and interpenetrating sheaths. These are the esoteric bodies of existence.

The planes according to Theosophy

The Theosophical scheme is clearly laid out in *The Ancient Wisdom* of Annie Besant (1897). There are seven planes, of which the first five (counting from the lowest or most dense) are the Physical, Astral, Mental, Buddhist. and Nirvanic. These are worlds which emanate from a manifested Divine Being, the Logos. Their attributes are these, in brief:

1. The Physical Plane consists of spirit and matter: solid, liquid, gas, and ether. There are seven grades of physical spirit-matter.
2. The Astral Plane is the region next to the Physical. Its spirit-matter is more highly vitalized and finer than that of the Physical Plane. Astral matter permeates the Physical Plane. Feelings appear as shapes in the Astral, and propagate as vibrations from mind to mind. The personal aspect of the Astral is a body that surrounds a living being, its Astral Body. The Astral Body serves as a bridge between the individual consciousness and the physical brain.[1]
3. The Mental Plane is the region next above the Astral. It is the world of thoughts, intelligence, intellect, the mind. Mental spirit-matter permeates the Astral, but is more vital, more fine. It has seven subdivisions. Thoughts manifest as vibrations of forms, thought-forms. Spirits, elementals, and helpers also inhabit this plane. Vibrations create thought-forms which interact via resonance.
4. The Buddhist Plane is the stage for the interaction of the individual mind, or Mental Body, with the universal mind. There are individuals, but without separation. This Mental Body is the same as the anandamayakosa of the pancha kosa of the Taittiriya Upanashad.
5. The Nirvanic Plane is the locus of the highest aspect of the god within.
6. and 7. The final two levels are hidden from our view.

Of all these, the Astral and Mental receive the most attention in the Theosophical literature.

The Bodies

Clairvoyance was an important ability for these writers, and it was believed that it could be developed by training, which they offered. As seen by the clairvoyant, a Physical Body was surrounded by its Astral Body, and that in turn by its Mental Body. And more, there were Astral Bodies without Physical Bodies, and Mental Bodies with or without Astral Bodies.

The innovations of the Theosophists

Thus the clairvoyant, with all faculties activated, might gaze about and observe all kinds of lively activities in the astral and mental fields. This view extended the classical literature somewhat.

2.4. Leadbeater

Charles Webster Leadbeater (1854-1934), in his book, *The Astral Plane: It's Scenery, Inhabitants, and Phenomena* (1896), went into great detail in his clairvoyant observations. And in his later book, *Clairvoyance* (1889), following Sinnett, he identified the Akashic Records as something a clairvoyant could read.

2.5. Thought-forms and the arts

In their book *Thought-Forms* (1901), Besant and Leadbeater present 49 paintings in full color plates. These are indicated not as abstract expressions, but rather as realistic images of alternate realities. This radical idea of thoughts and feelings as real things animating the Astral and Mental Planes inspired a whole generation of modern painters, most notably Mondrian (after 1908) and Kandinsky (after 1910). In fact, several of Kandinsky's works incorporate images from this book. An exemplary case appears on the cover of the 1999 edition of *Thought-Forms*.

In addition to modern painting, other arts were influenced: sculpture, music, architecture, and so on. Conferences on these influences were held in Amsterdam in 2013 and at Columbia University in 2015. Early pioneers of visual music, such as Thomas Wilfred, explicitly tried to reproduce the clairvoyance of Astral light.

3. The Akasha

In Kolkata on a short visit in 2005, I was invited to speak at the Indian Statistical Institute. There I met Professor Sisir Roy, who showed me his recent paper on the quantum vacuum. It occurred to us that the atomistic model of the quantum vacuum of that article might be applied to cosmic consciousness. Our subsequent work on this idea led to a joint book, *Demystifying the Akasha*, in 2010. As I was studying Sanskrit philosophy while in India, the Akasha in this title was intended as a reference to the ancient cosmology of India. But it also appears in the Western Esoteric Tradition, specifically in the idea of the Akashic Record in Theosophy.

3.1. The ancient Akasha

In *Demystifying the Akasha*, we described in some detail the cosmology of Kashmiri Shaivism. This highly evolved system, dating from around the year 1000 CE, has 36 planes of existence. For comparison with the planes of Theosophy it will be convenient to refer to the earlier Sanskrit system of the five koshas, and that of Neoplatonism.

3.2. The Akasha in Theosophy

The idea of the akashic record appears in HPB's first book, but without the name. Such planes have figured in the occult cosmologies of the West since Plato.

Sinnett, 1883

In his *Esoteric Buddhism*, he wrote,[2]
> Early Buddhism, then, clearly held to a permanency of records in the Akasha, and the potential capacity of man to read the same when he has evoluted to the stage of true individual enlightenment.

Bailey, 1887

Alice Ann Bailey (1880-1949) wrote, in her book *The Light of the Soul*, inspired by the Sanskrit of Patanjali,
> The akashic record is like an immense photographic film, registering all the desires and earth experiences of our planet.

Blavatsky, 1888

It is in the first volume of *The Secret Doctrine*, entitled *Cosmogenesis*, that HPB's concept of the akashic record first appears, but without the name already applied by Sinnett. In the *Cosmogenesis*, HPB summarizes the central points in six "items of cosmogony." The first two items concern the "first fundamental proposition" —
> "the One homogeneous divine SUBSTANCE-PRINCIPLE, the one radical cause. It is called "Substance-Principle." ... a "principle" in the

> beginningless and endless... SPACE.³ That is, the
> divine radical cause is essentially the Akasha.

She characterized it as a sort of life force; she also referred to "indestructible tablets of the astral light" recording both the past and future of human thought and action.

She further described it as a part of an element:

> Next we see Cosmic matter scattering and forming itself into elements; grouped into the mystic four within the fifth element — Ether, the lining of *Akasa*, the *Anima Mundi* or Mother of Kosmos.⁴

and also:

> It will only be in the next, or fifth, Round that the fifth Element, *Ether* — the gross body of *Akasa*, if it can be called even that — will, by becoming a familiar fact of Nature to all men, as air is familiar to us now ...⁵

Finally, she wrote that the *Aether* of the ancient Greeks was the *Akasa* of the Hindus.⁶

Besant, 1897

In the *Ancient Wisdom*, Annie Besant indicated that the Akasha was a plane of existence between the Etheric Plane (above) and the Mental Plane (below). This is similar to the cosmology of Marsilio Ficino, the Renaissance Neoplatonist. For the earlier Theosophists, the Akasha was located in the Astral Plane. We are left with this important ambiguity.

3.3. The Akasha in Science

The origin of the field concept in the sciences is shrouded in antiquity, but it came to the foreground with the gravitational field of Kepler (1600) and Newton (1660), and again with the magnetic field of Gilbert (1800) and Faraday (1812). But after the publication of *Isis Unveiled* in 1877, the applications of the field concept multiplied rapidly.

From the records of the Nobel Prize from 1901 to 1935, we see the field concept leading the advances of physics in these developments:

- 1890, Thompson, radiation experiments (prize of 1906)
- 1895, Roentgen, x-rays (1901)
- 1896, Curie, radioactivity (1903)
- 1905, Einstein, photoelectric effect (1922)
- 1915, Einstein, general relativity (no prize)
- 1910, Millikan, electron charge (1923)
- 1913, Bohr, hydrogen atom (1922)
- 1917, Einstein, cosmology (no prize)
- 1925, Heisenberg, matrix mechanics (1932)
- 1926, Schroedinger, wave equation (1933)
- 1931, Dirac, positron (1933), also quantum vacuum
- 1932, Chadwick, neutron (1935)

Concurrently, the evolution of field concepts in biology began with the *elan vital* of Henri Bergson (1907), and continues today in the work of Rupert Sheldrake on *morphogenetic fields*.

4. Conclusion

The occult investigations of the early Theosophists advanced the received wisdom of the ancients with novel insights, including visual representations of higher consciousness. Advances in color printing around 1900 enabled the widespread distribution of these visual images of thought-forms, catalyzing the new styles in the visual arts now regarded as abstract expressions. Painting, visual music, and lightshows were particularly transformed by the Akasha of the ancient philosophers, augmented and popularized by the Theosophists.

Whether located in the Astral Plane, between the Mental and the Etheric, or surrounding them all, the atomic model of the Akasha developed in our book, *Demystifying the Akasha*, supports the idea of the Akashic record, including the future as well as the past in a mammoth mathematical system.

Notes

1. (Besant, 1887; p. 79)
2. (Sinnett, 1885; p. 44)
3. (Blavatsky and Gomes, 2009; p. 233)
4. (Blavatsky and Gomes, 2009; p. 31)
5. (ibid; p. 57)
6. (ibid; p. 139)

Chapter 27
Vibrations and Spiritual Communication

Abstract

A host of phenomena, usually labeled paranormal — including many spiritual practices — may be regarded as forms of communication with a higher intelligence, by means of *vibrations* of a *mental field*, in the ambiance of mystical cosmologies, or models of consciousness: *spiritual communication*. In this note we focus on some of these phenomena, and propose mechanisms based on the cymatic concept: vibrations create forms. In the present application, vibrations in a mental field are imagined to create mental forms, or ideas.

Finally, a mathematical model for a vibrating mental field is proposed, based on my book, joint with Sisir Roy, *Demystifying the Akasha*. This model is an atomistic, rather than continuum-based, model, and belongs to the emerging field of mathematical cosmology. A mathematic ladder is constructed, ascending and descending the levels of consciousness, much like a transatlantic telegraph cable. Mathematical theories of information transmission may be applied to this channel.

Publication

Written July 30, 2018. Not previously published.

Contents

1. Introduction
2. The Evolution of Aristotelian Cosmology
3. Prophecy
4. The Placebo Phenomenon
5. Meditation, Prayer, Dreams, and Psychedelics
6. Conversing with Angels
7. Physical Models
8. Math Models
9. Conclusion
Notes

1. Introduction

The phenomena to be considered here are from alternative medicine (the placebo effect, homeopathy, acupuncture) and from spiritual practices (prophesy, meditation, prayer, psychedelics, and conversing with angels). Several conversations with friends contributed to the ideas presented here. I am especially indebted to Raymond Trevor Bradley, Scott Clements, Frank Galuszka, Kelley Landaker, Jason Louv, Rupert Sheldrake, and Rick Strassman. A talk with Rick Strassman gave the initial impetus for this article.

Rick Strassman and super-placebos

During November, 2017, I visited Santa Fe, New Mexico, on holiday with my family. At this time there was great interest in new research on psychedelics as medicines. It was in the air. Here I met with psychotherapist Rick Strassman. Rick is the author of two recent books on DMT which are relevant to this new wave of research.[1]

Rick had noticed that the converging results of new medical research with psychedelics — MDMA, LSD, DMT, psilocybin, ayahuasca, ibogaine, and mescaline — reveal that several of these were effective with several of the afflictions studied — PTSD, addiction, depression, anxiety, etc. For this reason he had begun calling the substances *super-placebos*. As Rick explained his idea to me, a possible mechanism for it and related phenomena occurred to me, which I will now describe.

Philosophies of mind

Neuroscience and most cognitive studies are fundamentally *materialist*. That is, perceptions, sensory representations, memories, and thoughts, are all regarded as physical states of the biological brain.

Idealism is an opposing view, in which states of the individual intelligence are regarded as the basis of reality. Here we have a broader view, in which states of the active intelligence are the basis of reality. We might call this *cosmic idealism*.

Nondualism emphasizes the connection, or unity, of the individual and the cosmic. In these systems of thought, cosmic consciousness is primary.[2] This perspective is the basis of the current work.

This viewpoint is regarded as *paranormal* by materialists, especially traditional scientists. After all, the scientific method is based upon repeatable observations, and therefore must focus mainly on the material aspects of nature. Meanwhile, our concerns are fundamentally inscrutable. Some circumstantial evidence for the mental field concept comes from phenomena such as telepathy, precognition, and so on, which are our primary concern in this article.

The mental field concept

Transcendental philosophies of mind have an individual soul or mind closely connected to the biological brain, and usually a cosmic soul or mind as well. The nature of the mind, and its connection to the brain, is conceived in terms of fields. The fields of physics (gravitational, electromagnetic, nuclear) may be inadequate, in which case, additional fields may be hypothesized — mental fields.

The cymatic concept

The evolution of cymatics, beginning from the Renaissance,

is described in a later section. The current form, which is the basis of the vibrating mental field concept developed here, is due to Hans Jenny in the 1960s. He studied the forms realized in liquids under the influence of a physical vibration. The translation of this idea to vibrations and forms in a mental field occurred to me during my stay in India in 1972.[3]

Models of consciousness

In prior writings I have based my models along the classical Sanskrit line: planes and vibrations of consciousness and the like. With up to 36 planes, the details tended to obscure my ideas. Here, I will resort to the simplest model, which has evolved from Plato and Aristotle through ancient, medieval, and Renaissance philosophers — Greek, Islamic, Jewish, and Italian.[4] I will begin with a cosmological model due to Aristotle, and then apply the model to prophesy and the other paranormal phenomena mentioned above.

Disclaimer

Regarding the philosophies of mind and all the theories put forward here, I am agnostic. Everything is pure speculation.

2. The Evolution of Aristotelian Cosmology

The philosophy of Plato was elaborated in the Neoplatonic line — Ammonius Saccas, Plotinus, Porphyry, and Proclus — which reached us, after a lapse, in the Greek/Arabic translations of Baghdad around 800 CE. The Platonic Corpus itself reached the West only later, in the Latin translations of Ficino around 1400. Meanwhile the philosophical writings of Aristotle were read and translated continuously from the time of Christ. It fell to the Medieval Islamic philosophers to harmonize Plato and Aristotle.

Here I will be interested especially in the two intellects — active and passive — introduced by Aristotle, the idea of emanation introduced by Plotinus, and on their combination by Alfarabi into a basic model of consciousness. It is this basic model that I will elaborate into a mathematical model for prophesy, the placebo effect, spiritual practices (meditation, prayer, and psychedelics), and conversing with angels.

Aristotle

In *Alfarabi, Avicenna, and Averroes on Intellect*, Herbert A. Davidson wrote,

> The most intensely studied sentences in the history of philosophy are probably those in Aristotle's *De anima* that undertake to explain how the human intellect passes from its original state, in which it does not think, to a subsequent state, in which it does. ... he found the intellect to be a "part of the soul" ... Aristotle brought to bear a dichotomy pervading his entire philosophy, positing that the various domains of the physical universe disclose both a "matter" and a "cause" or "agent", which leads the matter from potentiality to actuality; and he inferred that the same distinction must also be "present in the soul." ... The intellect that is what it is "by virtue of becoming all things" came to be known as the *potential* or *material intellect*, and the intellect that is what it is "by virtue of making all things," as the *active intellect (nous, active mind, active intelligence, active reason, agent intellect, productive*

intellect).[5]

While Aristotle's meaning of the potential and active intellects remains obscure, the concepts have evolved over the centuries in the treatments of many philosophers who followed in the Aristotelian tradition.

Plotinus — whose cosmology comprised four hypostases: the One, from which emanated the Intellect, and from that the Soul, and from that the Body — identified his Intellect with the active intellect of Aristotle.[6] Into this sequence, Ficino interpolated the Spirit between the Soul and the Body.

Alfarabi

Alfarabi (872-951) was a Persian or Turkic philosopher, scientist, cosmologist, and music scholar. In his philosophy he harmonized Plato and Aristotle. To each of Aristotle's nine nested celestial spheres he added causal connections in the form of Neoplatonic emanations. Each sphere has an intelligence which emanates the intelligence of the next sphere nested within. The ninth intelligence, belonging to the lunar sphere, emanates a tenth intelligence which rules the sublunar realm, which contains the stationary Earth, at the center of the whole scheme. It is this tenth intelligence which is identified, by Alfarabi as the active intelligence of Aristotle, in his *Al-Marina al-Fadila*, finished shortly before his death in Damascus.[7]

Thus with Alfarabi we have arrived at a fusion of the emanation idea of Plotinus with Aristotle's idea of the active intelligence as the agent behind the arising of thoughts in an individual human soul or mind. It was the Medieval Jewish philosophers who took the next step: the application of this model to prophesy.

3. Prophecy

The connection between higher mind, (the active intelligence, intellect, or cosmic soul), and the lower mind (the individual human mind or soul) is manifest in all so-called paranormal phenomena, including prophesy. In the Renaissance Neoplatonism of Ficino, this connection between the cosmic soul and the human intellect is made through the mental field he called spirit. We now consider prophesy within this context. Prophesy is the epitome of this spiritual connection, in which divine information is downloaded through the field into the receptive mind of an adept, the prophet. This phenomenon was a special concern of medieval Jewish philosophers, including: Saadiah Gaon (933), Judah Halevi (1140), Ibn Daud (1160), Maimonides (1190), Gersonides (1329), Hasdai Crescas (1410), Joseph Albo (1425), and Baruch Spinoza (1670). Their contributions are studied in depth in the work, *Prophecy: The History of an Idea in Medieval Jewish Philosophy*, by Howard Kreisel (2001).[8] Here I shall select a few details from Kreisel's chapter on Maimonides.

> It was Ibn Daud's misfortune that shortly after the appearance of his work [*Exalted Faith*] a different work was to push it aside almost completely — Maimonides' *Guide of the Perplexed*. Ibn Daud in many ways should be considered the pioneer in the introduction of Aristotelian thought into Judaism, particularly along the lines laid down by the great Islamic philosophers, Alfarabi and Avicenna. It was Maimonides' more widespread efforts in this area, however, which carried the day. The *Guide* became the focus for all subsequent Jewish philosophical

approaches.⁹

Kreisel omitted Ibn Daud from his book because he was eclipsed by Maimonides, thus he had limited influence on later philosophy. Thanks to Wikipedia, we may easily find Ibn Daud's theory of prophecy.

> The connection between the mind of the prophet and the higher intellects, principally with the Active Intelligence, furnishes a sufficient explanation of the higher cognitive faculty of the prophet, as well as his power of transcending natural law. Appointed to become an intermediary between God and man, the prophet is elevated almost to the plane of the separated intelligences, or angels.
> (*Emunah Ramah*, Solomon Ben Labi, Hebrew transl. p. 73; S. Weil, German transl. p. 91)

In his *Commentary on the Mishnah* (1145-1169) Maimonides gives this definition of prophecy.

> The sixth principle — prophecy. That is, one should know that there are human beings possessing a superior nature and great perfection. They prepare their souls till they receive the "form of the intellect." The human intellect then conjoins with the Active Intellect. From it, a noble emanation emanates upon them. These are the prophets; this is prophesy and this is its essence.[10]

For a more complete description of the mechanisms of prophesy in Medieval Jewish Philosophy, including the role of the Active Intellect, see Strassman, *DMT and the Soul of*

Prophesy.[11]

4. The Placebo Phenomenon

Observed commonly in medical research and practice — in drug trials with pills and injections, recovery from surgery, and so on — this phenomenon is usually considered normal, rather than paranormal.

Placebos

The word placebo is from *placere*, Latin, to please. Traditionally, the placebo, a fake medicine, was given to spoof a patient into an improvement. Nocebo, from *nocere*, Latin, to harm, is used for the analog with a negative effect, as in a magical or voodoo curse.

Placebos are used as controls in clinical trials on the effectiveness of medical procedures. For example, two groups of subjects are given pills, with one group taking the drug being tested, and the other group taking sugar pills that seem identical. This pattern may be followed also to test injections, or surgical procedures. The placebo effect has been offered as an explanation for alternative medical procedures, such as acupuncture and homeopathy.

The placebo effect

In experiments, placebos are supposed to produce no outcome. However, the experimental findings frequently show a mysterious result: The placebo acts to some degree like the agent it is supposed to mimic. This is the placebo effect. The mystery is: How does it work? The usual explanation is suggestion. But then, how does suggestion work? Remote prayers have been shown to improve recovery from surgery. Not even suggestion is able to explain this.

Placebo studies is an academic field, begun at Harvard Medical School in 1954, to study the placebo effect.[12] Studies have shown that placebos, even simple suggestions, affect neurotransmitters, and these in turn affect the patients health, pain, anxiety, etc. Thus, the placebo effect might be subsumed under the larger category of *suggestibility*. The mystery remains: How does a thought affect the brain? This mystery, action from mind to body, is the inverse of the mystery of the psychedelic effect, in which an ingested chemical, interacting with neurotransmitters, changes the state of the mind. What is lacking is a model of the mind/body system in which these effects are understandable. One such model is the complex dynamical system described in *Demystifying the Akasha*.[13]

Super-placebos

The super-placebo idea of Strassman goes beyond the theory of suggestibility, as one psychedelic may be found effective for certain health problems but not others. This is the seed for the idea presented here, of a medical college in the sky. According to this idea, the Active Intelligence (or higher realms) knows of cures for diseases before earthly medical science discovers them, and communicates the needed information to the human intelligence of the patient via prophesy.

5. *Meditation, Prayer, Dreams, and Psychedelics*

While these practices may have medical applications, we are usually more interested in them for their spiritual applications. That is, we regard them, like prophesy, as spiritual practices.

Meditation

In the first chapter of his recent book, *Spiritual Practices*, Rupert Sheldake explains, in his typically clear style,[14]

> Of all the spiritual practices discussed in this book, meditation is the most inward. When meditating, people withdraw from normal activities. and usually sit still with their eyes closed. ... Meditation is not about intentions or requests: it is to do with letting go of thoughts.

Nevertheless, letting go of thoughts is not easy, and from time to time, thoughts may arise. In the 1980s, several Buddhist monks from Burma visited Santa Cruz, and involved me in studies of the *Abhidamma*, from the Pali Canon.

I came to understand that dhamma theory was discovered through insight meditation, by watching carefully the arousal of an idea into the quiet mind through a dynamical process.

Thus, the apprehension of the chain of being, that is, the connection of the individual mind to the active intelligence and higher realms, occurred in the spiritual practice of meditation, perhaps over 600,000 years, of adepts and shamans among the Neanderthals and early homo sapiens.

Prayer

In *Spiritual Practices*., Sheldrake continues,

> I both meditate and pray, and I think of the difference between them as being like breathing in and breathing out. Meditation is like breathing in, directing the mind inwards; and prayer like breath-

ing out, directing the mind outwards.

Prayers function as a dialogue with a higher mind, asking for an intercession or reply. A line of communication up the chain of being is tacitly assumed. Some sort of vibratory or digital transmission up the chain is requested, and to the degree the prayer succeeds, the transmission is validated.

But not all prayers initiate a dialogue,

> ... obviously many prayers don't; so much depends on state of consciousness and intentionality to produce creative vibrations.[15]

Dreams

The dream state has many functions, some discovered recently through dream research and imaging technology such as the MRI.[16] Two of these functions are of special interest here: creative dreams and precognitive dreams. Many creative dreams have been recorded. Those of Dmitri Mendeleev (the periodic table), Otto Loewi (Nobel prize for synaptic communication), Paul McCartney (the song Yesterday), Keith Richards (Satisfaction), and Mary Shelley (Frankenstein) are detailed in Walker (2017).

Precognitive dreams have been experienced by many people, including myself. A spectacular case is described in detail in J. W. Donne's *An Experiment with Time*, of 1927. These dream functions are closely related to prophesy.

Psychedelics

The experience of a psychedelic trip is like meditation on steroids. At least in my experience of multiple explorations with LSD and DMT during the 1960s and 70s, the connection from my mind upwards one or more levels of the cosmic mind structure were manifest as direct perceptions, with visual, aural, and emotive aspects, in an apparent download of information with a heightened sense of reality. To some extent, questions could be posed and answered. The visual phenomena in particular suggested the vibration metaphor of the Vedic literature and Yogic tradition of India.[17]

The psychedelic experience, an opening of the spiritual channel, was my original motivation for my writings on this subject, which began in 1973 after my return from seven months in India.

6. *Conversing with Angels*

A *grimoire* is a textbook of magic. The magic tradition has ancient roots, and the Alexandrian library from the time of Aristotle likely contained such textbooks. An early and extant exemplar is the *Hermetic Corpus*. Several Medieval grimoires were influential, such as the 13th century *Picatrix*. The lore of angels, devils, demons and so on, based on the Bible, is fundamental to the practice of magic, in which angels are called, spells cast, and so on.

John Dee

John Dee (1527-1608), mathematician, alchemist, and astrologer to Queen Elizabeth I, was important to the history of mathematics as the sponsor of the first translation of the *Elements* of Euclid into English. This book, among the best editions of Euclid ever to appear in print, begins with a Preface by Dee, in which the future of applied mathematics was forecast with amazing clairvoyance.

In the second half of his life, Dee turned to magic in search of the secrets of nature, and the hidden future of science. His practice, now called angelic magic, or sometimes Enochian magick, involved calling angels, and then conversing with them. Dee, working with various scryers, would call angels, pose questions to them, and apparently receive answers. Many of these conversations were recorded in diaries and published in Latin as *The Five books of Mystery*.[18]

While the language and nomenclature of these conversations are very strange, it does seem that valid information was encoded within them. Thus, we have here a novel paranormal phenomena in which the contact between the active intelligence or cosmic mind and the individual human mind is a bidirectional link, like an undersea telegraph cable.

Here is an example, from the spirit diaries of John Dee, in Prague, 1584.[19]

> By October 1, Jane Dee was grievously ill; Dee and Kelly consulted the angels to ask why, and how to cure her. Gabriel asked them who they were to dare seek after science, and reminded them to grovel and to turn away from the sin of the world. After this chastening, Dee and Kelly were given a magical theory of disease; if sickness came from sin, Gabriel explained, it could be cured by prayer, or by the angels, as ministers of God's justice. He offered to spend forty days teaching them medicine, and offered a diagnosis of Dee's pregnant wife. The next day, they were given a recipe for a folk remedy by the angels, but told that they would have no more until they were repentant, and made apt again for the angels' school.

We now turn to physical and mathematical models of this connection by emanation.

7. Physical Models

Several physical models share a common feature: the creation of forms by vibrations in a field. Some physical systems are highly suggestive of the informatics link between the active intelligence and the individual mind. Here are some of them.

Cymatics

Early in 1972, I discovered the book, *Kymatik, Band 1*, published 1967 in German (also in English as *Cymatics*) by Dr. Hans Jenny (1904-1972). I was inspired to go to see him as soon as possible. We met at his home in Dornach (near Basel) shortly before his death, where he showed me his laboratory, and some films of his research results similar to the photographs in his book. See Figure 1.[20]

On returning to Santa Cruz in 1974, I reproduced his laboratory with modifications. The main instrument, dubbed the *Jenny Macroscope*, was a device to study the evolution of form from vibrations in the context of catastrophe theory.[21]

The history of cymatics includes the following milestones.

- 1490, Leonardo da Vinci observed patterns formed in the dust on a tabletop on which he drummed with his hands.[22]

- 1787, Ernst Chladni, the founder of acoustics, used patterns of sand (*Chladni patterns*) on vibrating glass plates to design better sounding glass harmonia.

- 1831, Michael Faraday observed standing wave patterns on the surface of beer on the tops of barrels being transported by a horse-drawn wagon.

- 1967, Hans Jenny, a medical doctor in the anthroposophic movement, studied Chaldni patterns in sand, lycopodium powder, and liquids on an acoustically vibrated plate.

- 1974, the Santa Cruz macroscope extended the work of Jenny to study the bifurcations of Chladni patterns in the chaotic regime of the control parameters (acoustic frequency and amplitude).

- 2017, Merlin and Rupert Sheldrake extended the work of Jenny with extraordinary precision.[23]

The macroscope may serve us now as a physical metaphor for the link between a human mind and the active intelligence.[24]

The macroscope

This is a simple device built for cymatics research. It manifests the emergence of form under the influence of a vibrating field.

In Figure 2, a schematic view of the first Santa Cruz macroscope, the upper two elements (xenon arc light and condenser lens) and the lower three elements (objective lens, color filter, and projection screen) comprise the optical system. This makes deformation waves on the surface of the object (a thin layer of transparent liquid) visible as a colored animation on the screen.

Removing these five elements from the schematic, the physical heart of the system remains: a heavy brass plumbing tee for four-inch pipe connecting four elements,

- top: the transparent liquid in a dish with a flexible and transparent bottom,
- side: a vibrating loud speaker driven by an electrical oscillator,
- bottom: a rigid plate closing the interior of the plumbing tee, and
- within: air at ambient pressure.

This subsystem of the macroscope is a physical model for the link from the active intelligence to the individual human mind/brain, as:

- loud speaker ←→ active intelligence
- enclosed air ←→ spirit or mental field
- layer of liquid ←→ mind/brain system

Organs of perception

A sound wave in the atmosphere is perceived by the mammalian cochlea in a cymatic process. The basilar membrane is deformed by the sonic vibration, and its deformation measured by the hair cells of the organ of Corti, as discovered by Georg von Bekesy, 1926.

Similarly, smells are identified by the mammalian nose by pattern recognition of a transitory wave of electrical activity on the olfactory bulb, as discovered by Walter Freeman, 1960s.

Taste and the tactile sense may be similar, but vision is more complicated. In any case, the human mental sensitivity to waves emanating from the active intelligence may be regarded as a sixth sense, analogous to the five material senses.

Electric field waves

Imagine an electric field freely vibrating in a two-dimensional plane. Now suppose the field is clamped by two grounded conductors, one a square, the other a triangle. The field continues to vibrate between and around the clamps.

Alternatively, imagine a bed sheet stretched horizontally by springs. Two small clamps near the center prevent the sheet from moving. Figure 3, taken from a computer simulation of a waving sheet or field, shows a birds-eye view of this configuration.

Consider the square the sender, and the triangle the receiver. Imagine that the receiver has a recording device along a boundary line segment, recording the signal strength as a function of time. The recording is the signal received from the sender, and contains a signature of the shape of the sender.

If the sender suddenly changes shape, for example from square to circular, then the receiver can detect the change in the signal. This idea has been proposed as a model for telepathy from a human to a dog.[25] It may similarly be a model of the link from the active intelligence to human intelligence, in all the phenomena considered here.

Mental field waves

Combining ideas here, we may begin with the cosmology of Aristotle: the active intelligence or cosmic consciousness (A) is coupled to an individual human consciousness or mind (M) by an intervening mental field such as the spirit of Ficino (F). An idea or new pattern in A propagates through F and is recorded by M as a space-time pattern. Or vice versa, an idea in M propagates through F and is recorded by A.

Such a conversation might be the basis of phenomena such as prophesy, the placebo effect, communications with angels, and so forth.

8. Math Models

Two exemplary models will suffice to demonstrate the power of computational mathematics in the study of consciousness. These models extend far beyond the usual static models, such as parallel planes or concentric spheres: they are dynamical systems. The computational versions of these models provide for computer graphic simulation of the vibratory process.

Discrete Poisson equation

The first example begins with the final physical model of the preceding section, the vibrating electric field in the plane. The standard model from mathematical physics is a two-dimensional partial differential equation (PDE) called the Poisson equation. For computational purposes the three dimensions of time and space are discretized. That is, each continuous variable is replaced by a discrete approximation, a finite set of points equally spaced in the line segment chosen for that coordinate variable for the simulation.[26]

The computer graphic video generated by this model illustrates how the change in shape of the sender is recorded as a space-time pattern in the optical memory of the receiver. One frame from the video made for this is shown in Figure 3.[27]

The digital Akasha

The second example is also from mathematical physics. The computational version of a PDE, as above, belongs to the mathematical category of cellular dynamical systems. But this category is much larger than the subcategory of discrete PDEs. This example is based on a cellular system that has been proposed as a model for the quantum vacuum (QV).

The QV may be regarded as a physical field filling the universe, like the electromagnetic (EM) field of the preceding model. The QV has been proposed as a model for cosmic consciousness by some authors, most notably, by Ervin Laszlo.[28]

The adaption of an historical QV model to the cosmology of Kashmiri Shaivism is the subject of the 2010 book, *Demystifying the Akasha*.[29]

Akashic information theory

Telegraphy was born in 1839, and the first transatlantic telegram was successfully transmitted from Ireland to Newfoundland in 1858. Alexander Graham Bell was awarded the first patent for the invention of the telephone in 1878. These technologies, the digital and the analog, are basic to our conceptions of spiritual communication.

Dennis Gabor, born in Budapest in 1918, studied engineering in Berlin and fled the Nazis to Britain in 1933. There he invented holography in 1947, for which he was awarded a Nobel Prize in 1971. His paper *Theory of Communication* appeared in 1946 in three parts. The first part applies a modified Fourier analysis to information conveyed through channels of communication. Time and frequency have symmetrical roles, and quanta of information called *logons* are introduced. In the second part, the theory is applied to hearing. The third part applies to the compression of speech and music.

Karl Pribram was born in Vienna in 1919, and moved to the USA in the 1930s. Known for many fundamental contributions to neuroscience with more than 700 papers and 25 books from the 1940s until his death in 2015, he may be best remembered for his application of holography theory to the neurophysiology of perception and memory, beginning in 1966. He adapted ideas of Gabor from optical holography (as in MRI technology) to the biological neural network in a theory he eventually called *holonomic brain theory*. Due to the special role of quanta of information, Gabor's logons, this theory is also known as *quantum holography* or *QH*. A careful history is given in Pribram's Lecture 2 of his *Brain and Perception* of 1991.

From Raymond Trevor Bradley's manuscript, *The Lens of Love*:

Quantum Holography — A Recap

Before proceeding, it is necessary to reiterate Gabor's concept of a quantum of information — the fundamental informational unit in quantum holography. As previously noted, Gabor's concept is radically different from, though related to, the more commonly used measure of information, the BIT — the Binary digit — developed by Claude Shannon (1949). While Shannon dealt with a *reduction in uncertainty*, Gabor designates the *minimum uncertainty* — a limit beyond which a message cannot be compressed. Drawing on the mathematics of Heisenberg's concept of uncertainty in quantum physics, Gabor determined that there exists a restriction to communication of a "message" encoded in a signal due to the limit of precision in concurrent measurements of the signal's energy spectral components (frequency, amplitude, and phase) and its (space) time epoch. Treating energy — frequency and (space) time — as orthogonal coordinates, Gabor was able to show mathematically that, at the *limit*, accurate measurement of the signal can be obtained only by minimizing uncertainty on both ordinates ... This limit of precision defined *the minimum uncertainty with which a signal can be encoded as a pattern of energy oscillations across a waveband at any frequency*, as in the encoding and transmission of vocal conversation for telephonic communication.

As previously noted, Gabor called this minimum area of measurement a *logon*, or a *quantum* of information — hence the term *"quantum holography"* ...[30]

In Pribram's collaboration with Raymond Trevor Bradley since 1997, QH is extended from an internal neural network to external behavior of a social group. QH has been further extended to nonlocal communication by Bradley.[31]

All of this information theory is obviously relevant to the math models described above, as they may be interpreted as a sort of transatlantic telegraph cable connecting an animal intelligence or soul and the active intelligence or oversoul. The discrete akashic model described above may be interpreted as the digitization of a generalized cable equation from mathematical physics. And the existence of this model outside of conventional space and time suggests a Gabor holographic transformation from the space-time representation of ordinary reality.

9. Conclusion

So we now have on the one hand this host of paranormal phenomena, and on the other hand, a cognitive strategy, a simple vibrational cosmology, which may unite them. This cosmology comprises the active intelligence or oversoul and billions of individual intelligences or souls, all having bidirectional links to the oversoul that are cymatic in nature: vibrations create forms. For example, a vibration emanating from the active intelligence or cosmic mind realizes a form, an idea, in an individual mind.

We have proposed spiritual communication as a way of understanding several phenomena: prophesy, placebos including homeopathy and acupuncture, meditation, prayer, psychedelic exploration, and angelic conversation. Similarly, telepathy might be accommodated by spiritual communication in either of two ways: a direct transmission through the mental field from one individual mind to another (M1 to M2), or, from one individual up through the field to the active intelligence and down through the field to another individual (M1 to AI to M2).

In either case, the population of interlinked minds (some incarnate, others perhaps not — angels, entities, gurus, demons, or whatnot) may be regarded as a giant neural network, the active intelligence network, or AIN. The collective intelligence of the AIN depends upon the strength or bandwidth of its links. In this model, the action of an idea, a placebo, a psychedelic, or a suggestion may be to adjust the strength of an individual's link in the AIN so as to tune in certain vibrations. The active intelligence is a master hub within the AIN, and may be the repository of all knowledge, as for example, the cure of diseases. The AI or master hub might hold a quantum holographic memory of the universe, as in David Bohm's *implicate order*.

Recall Jacob's ladder, from *Genesis*:

> And Jacob went out from Beersheba, and went toward Haran. And he lighted upon the place, and tarried there all night, because the sun was set; and he took one of the stones of the place, and put it under his head, and lay down in that place to sleep. And he dreamed, and beheld a ladder set up on the earth, and the top of it reached to heaven; and beheld the angels of God ascending and descending on it.

436   Vibrations and Forms

Figure 1. Dr. Hans Jenny in his lab in Dornach. (Jenny, 1972; frontis).

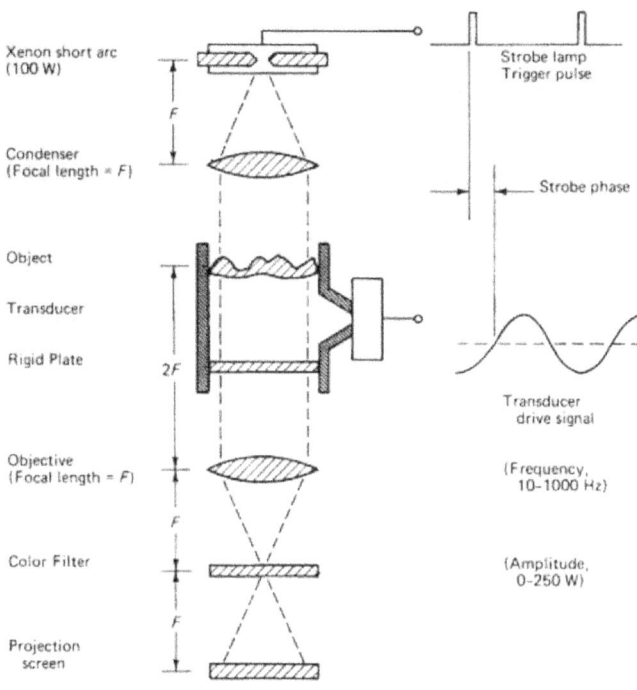

Figure 2. Schematic view of the four-inch Jenny macroscope of the University of California, Santa Cruz (Abraham, 1974). The darker bold lines comprise a cross-section of the brass plumbing tee.

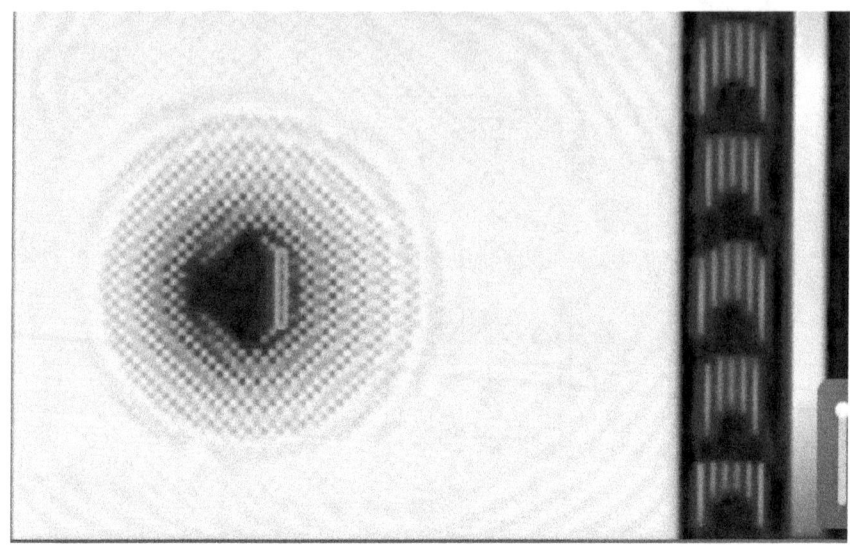

Figure 3. One frame from a computer simulation video of the morphic field linking a dog and its owner. See (Sheldrake, 1999), Chapter 17 (Abraham and Broadwell, 1997).

This is a monochrome version of a frame from a full-color video. See the website (Abraham, Broadwell, and Radunskaya, 1997). In the original, the colored vertical band at the right shows the color code for deformations of the field. The green area shows the outer portion of the fluid object, only slightly deformed. The black area contains the triangular receiver, including the violet recording retina.

Notes

1   *DMT, the Spirit Molecule* (2001), and *DMT and the Soul of Prophesy* (2014)
2   See for example, (Sheldrake, 1981), (Goswami, 1993), (McTaggert, 2001), and (Laszlo, 2009).
3   See (Abraham, 1973) and sequels.
4   The roots of these ideas in ancient India, from the Vedic literature (1500 BCE) have had an independent evolution in the Sanskrit tradition, and also in Western Esoteric tradition, such as Theosophy.
5   Davidson, 1992; p. 3
6   Davidson, 1992; p. 14
7   Davidson, 1992; pp. 45-46
8   For thumbnails of some of these, see (Strassman, 2014; pp. 302-304).
9   (Kreisel, 2001; p. 22, fn 10).
10   This is Kreisel's translation from the Arabic original, p. 169
11   (Strassman, 2014; pp. 243-247).
12   For a detailed history of the placebo effect, see (Dispenza, 2014; Ch. 2).
13   (Abraham and Roy, 2010)
14   (Sheldrake, 2017; p. 23)
15   John Allen, author of *Me and the Biospheres*, personal communication.
16   A wonderful account is given in (Walker, 2017).
17   The ancient vibration metaphor was revived in the late 18th century in the Theosophic tradition of Madame Blavatsky and Annie Besant. See (Besant, 1900; p. 31).
18   An excellent summary of Dee's angelic diaries may be found in (Louv, 2018).

19   Quoted from (Louv, 2018; p. 273).
20   (Jenny, 1772; frontis.)
21   (Abraham, 1974)
22   See (Capra, 2007; pp. 231–235).
23   (Sheldrake and Sheldrake, 2017)
24   From (Abraham, 1975; p. 143).
25   (Abraham and Broadwell, 1997)
26   See the Wikipedia page for "Discrete Poisson equation."
27   (Abraham, Broadwell, and Radunskaya, 1996)
28   For an excellent review, see (Laszlo, 2004; Ch. 4).
29   The akashic field has been proposed as a mechanism for the cosmic mind in a series of books by Ervin Laszlo; eg: 2003, 2009.
30   (Bradley, 2018; Ch. 5)
31   (Bradley, 2007)

Epilogue

These chapters have been written quite independently over a period of almost 50 years. Only now, having collected and reread them all at once, can I grok the emerging ideas. Looking at them in order, a metapattern emerges.

Part 0: Background, 1967-1971

These three chapters, from 2008, 2015, and 2017, are the only chapters that are out of chronological order. I selected them to come first to provide a chronicle of the origin of my fascination with psychedelics, vibrations, and cosmic consciousness, which fill the rest of this book.

Part 1: Physical Models, 1972-1982

My psychedelic period culminated in 1972 with my meetings with Hans Jenny and his *Cymatics* in Switzerland, with Neem Karoli and the *Vedas* in India, and with Terence McKenna and his mushrooms in California, as described in Part 0. The four chapters in this Part are my earliest writings on vibrations and consciousness after these meetings in 1972. Although I did not believe that the individual mind was inside the biological brain, the models I described in these ten years were neurological. I imagined that the larger world above the physical, spirit and soul and all, had a mysterious connection with the brain.

Part 2: Spiritual Models, 1982-2005

This epoch was initiated by my meeting with Rupert Sheldrake and his book, *A New Science of Life*. The gap between soul and brain was filled in by his proposed morphic field and morphic resonance.

The thirteen chapters in this Part fill in details of my vibratory model of cosmic consciousness, all in the metaphors of continuum mechanics. Successive layers of higher conciousness, individual consciousness, and the biological brain were connected by vibrations in a field transmitting forms from one layer to another.

Part 3: Atomic Models, 2005-2011

Following my meeting with Sisir Roy and his model for the quantum vacuum in Kolkata in 2005, and in connection with my mathematical works on cellular dynamical systems, my thinking shifted into the discrete atomistic thought-style of quantum mechanics. An atomic model evolved in our joint work, as described in the three chapters of this part.

In this final model, the continuum layers were replaced by atomic layers — cellular dynamical systems, that is, networks of mathematical models evolving in discrete time — connected by network links between nodes of adjacent layers.

Part 4: Applications, 2011-2018

In this final part, five applications of the layered models to various metaphysical domains are presented.

The Psychedelic Hypothesis

I have presented a number of examples of schismogenesis, that is, bifurcations along a time-line of human cultural history. In each case, I have been curious as to possible triggers of these events. According to the psychedelic hypothesis, or stoned ape theory, psychedelics have figured as significant triggers of some of these events.

One such event is of crucial importance in my journey chronicled in this book: the 1972 beginning of my writings on mathematical modeling of cosmic consciousness. And the triggers in this case are three: LSD/DMT, Neem Karoli Baba, and Terence McKenna. In addition to my personal bifurcation, there were concomitant transformations in cultural history, also triggered in part by psychedelics: Hip culture, civil rights, feminism, chaos theory, and of course, the psychedelic revolution itself.

Conclusion

I now think that this 50 year journey was all about bringing the atomic model into being. Since 2007 and my first presentation of the atomic model, and my 2010 book with Sisir Roy entirely devoted to this model and its relations with Sanskrit literature, there has been no similar sequel in the literature until Andrew Gallimore's book *Alien Intelligence* of this year.

I hope this literature will evolve further in the coming years.

Books by R. Abraham and coauthors

Abraham, Ralph, and Jerrold E. Marsden (1967/1978). *Foundations of Mechanics*, Second Edition. Reading, MA: Benjamin/Cummings.

Sheldrake, Rupert, McKenna, Terence, and Abraham, Ralph (2001). *Chaos, Creativity, and Cosmic Consciousness*. Rochester, VT: Inner Traditions.

Sheldrake, Rupert, McKenna, Terence, and Abraham, Ralph (2005). *The Evolutionary Mind: Conversations on Science, Imagination, and Spirit*. Rhinebeck, NY: Monkfish Books.

Abraham, Ralph, and Sisir Roy (2010). *Demystifying the Akasha: Consciousness and the Quantum Vacuum*. Rhinebeck, NY: Epigraph.

Abraham, Ralph (1994/2011). *Chaos, Gaia, Eros: A Chaos Pioneer Uncovers the Three Great Streams of History*. Rhinebeck, NY: Epigraph.

Abraham, Ralph and Christopher Shaw (1981/2016). *Dynamics the Geometry of Behavior, Part 1, Periodic Behavior*. Santa Cruz, CA: Aerial Press.

Abraham, Ralph, ed. (2016). *Hip Santa Cruz: First-person accounts of the Hip Culture movement in Santa Cruz, California in the 1960s*. Rhinebeck, NY: Epigraph.

Articles by Ralph Abraham

Abraham, Ralph (1972). Introduction to Morphology. *Publ. du Dept. de Mathématique*, 9, pp. 38-174. Lyon: Université de Lyon. (Ms #12.)

Abraham, Ralph (1973). Psychotronic Vibrations. In: *Proc. First Intl. Cong. Psychotronics*. Prague. (Ms #14, Ch. 4 in this book.)

Abraham, Ralph (1976). Vibrations and the Realization of Form. In: Erich Jantsch and Conrad H. Waddington (eds), *Evolution and Consciousness: Human Systems in Transition.* Reading, Mass.: Addison Wesley. (Ms #15, Ch. 5.)

Abraham, Ralph (1976). Macrodynamics and Morphogenesis. In: Erich Jantsch, Conrad H. Waddington (eds), *Evolution in The Human World.* (Ms #15A, Ch. 6)

Abraham, Ralph (1976). Macroscopy of Resonance. In Peter Hilton (ed), *Structural Stability, the Theory Catastrophes, and Applications in the Sciences.* New York: Springer. Reprinted in: Themistocles M. Rassias and George M. Rassias. *Selected Studies: Physics-Astrophysics, Mathematics, History of Science.* Amsterdam: North-Holland, 1982. (Ms #16)

Abraham, Ralph (1976). Simulation of cascades by videofeedback. In: Structural Stability, *The Theory of Catastrophes, and Applications*, Springer, New York (Lecture Notes in Mathematics, Vol. 525, pp. 10-14. (Ms #17)

Abraham, Ralph (1976). Dynasim: exploratory research in bifurcations using interactive computer graphics. *Ann. N.Y. Acad. Sciences* 316, 673-684. (Ms #18)

Abraham, Ralph (1981). The function of mathematics in the evolution of the noosphere. In Erich Jantsch, (ed) *The Evolutionary Vision: Toward a Unifying Paradigm of Physical, Biological, and Sociocultural Evolution.* AAAS Selected Symposium, 61. Boulder, CO: Westview Press; pp. 153-168. (Ms #20, Ch. 7)

Abraham, R. H. (1984). Complex dynamical systems. In X. J. R. Avula, R. E. Kalman, A. I. Leapis, & E. Y. Rodin (Eds.), *Mathematical Modeling in Science and Technology.* Elmsford, NY: Pergamon Press; pp. 82-86. (Ms #29)

Abraham, Ralph (1985). Dynamical models for thought, *J. Social Biol. Structures*, pp. 13-26. (Ms #25, Ch. 8)

Abraham, Ralph (1986). Vibrations in math, music and

mysticism. *Intern. Synergy Journal* 1, 1(0): pp. 7-8. (Ms #42, Ch. 9)

Abraham, Ralph (1987). Mechanics of resonance. *Revision*, 10(2): 13-19 (1987). (Ms #44, Ch. 10)

Abraham, Ralph. (1987). Dynamics and Self-organization. In: F. Eugene Yates (ed.). *Self-organizing Systems: The Emergence of Order.* New York: Plenum; pp. 599-613. (Ms #22)

Abraham, Ralph (1988). Visual musical instruments, *High Frontiers*, Fall, 1988. (Ms #47, Ch. 11)

Abraham, Ralph (1990). Visualization techniques for cellular dynamata. In: *Introduction to Nonlinear Physics*, Lui Lam, ed., Springer-Verlag, 1990. (Ms #58)

Abraham, Ralph (1991). Erodynamics and cognitive maps. In: *New Paradigms for the 21st Century: The Evolution of Contemporary Cognitive Maps*. Ervin Laszlo and Ignazio Masulli, eds., Gordon and Breach, 1991. (Ms #60)

Abraham, Ralph (1993). Cellular dynamata. In: *From Topology to Computation: Proceedings of the Smalefest*. M.W. Hirsch, J.E. Marsden, M. Shub, eds. New York: Springer-Verlag, 1993. (Ms #64)

Abraham, Ralph (1993). Human fractals, the arabesque in our mind. *Visual Anthropology Review*, 9, 1993, pp. 52-55. Reprinted in *IS Journal* #15/16, Summer 1995, pp. 75-79. (Ms #73)

Abraham, Ralph (1995). Erodynamics and the dischaotic personality. In: *Chaos Theory in Psychology*. F. D. Abraham, and A. R. Gilgen, eds. Westport, CN: Greenwood ; pp. 157-167. Reprinted in *IS Journal* #15/16, Summer 1995, pp. 80-85. (Ms #76)

Abraham, Ralph (1996). Vibrations: communication through a morphic field. *Proc. Intl. Conf. Synthesis of Science and Religion*, Calcutta. (Ms #86, Ch. 13)

Abraham, Ralph (2000). Vibrational resonance and

cognitive internalization. In: *Proceedings of Einstein Days in Visva Bharati University, Santiniketan, West Bengal, India, March 15-18, 2000: International Seminar on Cognitive Processes of Internalization in Humanities and Sciences.* (Ms #105, Ch. 14)

Abraham, Ralph (2000). A two worlds model for consciousness. Unpublished. (Ms #106, Ch. 15)

Abraham, Ralph (2005). The death and rebirth of the world soul, 2500 BCE-2005 CE, a concise overview. In: Ervin Laszlo. *Science and the Reenchantment of the Cosmos: The Rise of the Integral Vision of Reality*. Rochester, VT: Inner Traditions. (Ms #116)

Abraham, Ralph (2006). Vibrations and Forms. In: *Consciousness: A Deeper Scientific Search*. Proceedings of the 3rd Int'l. Conf. on Science and Consciousness. Kolkata: Ramakrishna Mission Institute of Culture, 2006. (Ms #118, Ch. 16)

Abraham, Ralph (2008). Mathematics and the Psychedelic Revolution. *MAPS Bulletin*, 18:1, Spring 2008: Special Edition: Technology and Psychedelics; pp. 8-10. (Ms #124, Ch. 1)

Abraham, Ralph (2009). Recent Progress in Dynamical Systems Theory. In: *Journal of the Calcutta Mathematical Society*, 5:1; 63-73. (Ms #129)

Abraham, Ralph (2011). The Paleolithic Birth of Geometric Thinking, preprint. Ms #131)

Abraham, Ralph (2011). Geometry of the Early Neolithic. (Ms #132.)

Abraham, Ralph (2013). The Peregrinations of Poincare. In: Christophe Letellier and Robert Gilmore, eds., *Topology and Dynamics of Chaos: In Celebration of Robert Gilmore's 70th Birthday*. Singapore, World Scientific; pp. 23-38. (Ms #136)

Abraham, Ralph (2015). Mysticism in the History of Mathematics. *Progress in Biophysics and Molecular Biology*.

(Ms #146)

Abraham, Ralph (2017). Entheogens in the Himalayan Foothills. In: *One Toke to God*, 2017; pp. 127-133. (Ms #148, Ch. 2)

Abraham, Ralph (2017). Chaos Math, Brain Science, and Mind Philosophy. *Chaos and Complexity Letters*, vol. 11, no. 1, September; pp. 179-182. (Ms #152, Ch. 3)

Articles by R. Abraham and coauthors

Abraham, Ralph, and Peter Broadwell. Vibrations: communication through a morphic field, Pt 2. (with Peter Broadwell). Preprint. (Ms #86B)

Abraham, Ralph, Corliss, John B., and Dorband, John E. (1991). Order and Chaos in the Toral Logistic Lattice. *Int. J. Bifurcation and Chaos*, 1(1): pp. 227-234. (Ms #52)

Abraham, Ralph H., and Sisir Roy, 2010. *Demystifying the Akasha: Consciousness and the Quantum Vacuum*. Rhinebeck, NY: Epigraph Books.

References, Others

Abraham, Fred and others (1973). Spectrum and discriminant analyses reveal remote rather than local sources for hypothalamic EEG: could waves affect unit activity?, *Brain Research*, 49 (1973) 349-266.

Adey, W. (1974). The Influence of Impressed Electrical Fields at EEG Frequencies on Brain and Behavior. Math. Inst. Univ. of Warwick, preprint.

Anthony, P. (1969). *Macroscope*. New York: Avon.

Arbib, M. (1972). *The Metaphorical Brain*. New York: Interscience.

Atanasijevic, Ksenia (1923/1972). *The Metaphysical and Geometrical Doctrine of Bruno: As given in his work De Triplici Minimo*. St. Louis, MO: Warren H. Green.

Bailey, Alice Ann (1887/1927). *The Light of the Soul: Its Science and Effect: A Paraphrase of the Yoga Sutras of Patanjali*. New York: Lucis Publishing Company.

Balslev, Anindita Niyogi (2009). *A Study of Time in Indian Philosophy, Third Edition*. Delhi: Motilal Banarsidass.

Bateson, Gregory (1936/1958). *Naven*. Stanford, CA: Stanford University Press.

Bateson, Gregory (1972). *Steps to an Ecology of Mind: A Revolutionary Approach to Man's Understanding of Himself*. New York, NY: Ballantine.

Bateson, Gregory (1979/1980). *Mind and Nature: A Necessary Unity*. New York, NY: Bantam.

Bateson, Gregory (1991). *A Sacred Unity: Further Steps to an Ecology of Mind*. New York, NY: HarperCollins.

Békésy, G. von (1960). *Experiments in Hearing*. New York: McGraw-Hill.

Bennett, Chris (2010). *Cannabis and the Soma Solution*. Walterville, OR: TrineDay.

Berman, M. (1981). *The Reenchantment of the World.* Ithaca, NY: Cornell University Press.

Besant, Annie (1897). *The Ancient Wisdom: An Outline of Theosophical Teachings.* London: Theosophical Publishing Society.

Besant, Annie (1900). *The Evolution of Life and Form: Four Lectures Delivered at the Twenty-third Anniversary Meeting of the Theosophical Society at Adyar, Madras, 1989.* London: Theosophical Publishing Society.

Besant, Annie, and C. W. Leadbeater (1901). *Thought-Forms.* London: Theosophical Publishing Society.

Black, Stephen (1969). *Mind and Body,* Wm. Kimber, London.

Blacker, Carmen (1975/1999). *The Catalpa Bow: A Study of Shamanistic Practices in Japan.* London: Routledge Curzon.

Blumenthal, David R (1978). *Understanding Jewish Mysticism: A Source Reader. The Merkabah Tradition and the Zoharic Tradition.* New York: Ktav.

Blavatsky, Helena Petrovna (1877). *Isis Unveiled: Secrets of the Ancient Wisdom Tradition.* London: Theosophical Publishing Society.

Blavatsky, Helena Petrovna (1888). *The Secret Doctrine.* London: Theosophical Publishing Society.

Blavatsky, Helena Petrovna, and Michael Gomes (1997). *Isis Unveiled: Secrets of the Ancient Wisdom Tradition, abridged.* Wheaton, IL: Theosophical Publishing House.

Blavatsky, Helena Petrovna, and Michael Gomes (2009). *The Secret Doctrine, abridged.* New York: Jeremy Tarcher.

Blumenthal, David R. (1978). *Understanding Jewish Mysticism: A Source Reader. The Merkabah Tradition and the Zoharic Tradition.* New York: Ktav.

Bradley, Raymond Trevor (2007). Psychophysiology of intuition: A quantum-holographic theory of nonlocal commmunication. *World Futures, The Journal of General Evolution*, 63(2); pp. 61-69.

Bradley, Raymond Trevor (2018). *The Lens of Love: Holographic Eye of Universal Consciousness*. Preprint.

Mary A.B. Brazier, Ed., (1963). *Brain Function: Cortical Excitability and Steady Potentials; Relations of Basic Research to Space Biology*. Berkeley, CA: UCPress.

Brazier, M. and D. Walter, ed. (1969). *Advances in EEG Analysis*, New York, Elsevier.

Brisac, Catherine (1986). *A Thousand Years of Stained Glass*. London: Macdonald.

Brown, Sarah, and David O'Conner (1991). *Glass-Painters (Medieval Craftsmen)*. London: British MuseumPress.

Buckley, R. (1985). *Oscillations and Waves*. Bristol, England: Adam Hilger.

Cannon, J. T., & Dostrovsky, S. (1981). *The Evolution of Dynamics: Vibration Theory from 1687 to 1742* (p. 26). Berlin, W. Germany: Springer-Verlag.

Capra, Fritjof (2007). *The Science of Leonardo: Inside the Mind of the Great Genius of the Renaissance*. New York: Doubleday.

Cavaye, Ronald, Paul Griffith, and Akihiko Senda (2004). *A Guide to the Japanese Stage: From Traditional to Cutting Edge*. Tokyo: Kodansha.

Chakrabarti, Arindam (2004). Matter, memory, and unity of the self. In: Prabhananda, p. 67.

Chakravarty, Amiya, ed. (1961). *A Tagore Reader*. New York: Macmillan.

Corbett, Jim (1944). *Man-Eaters of Kumaon*. Oxford: Oxford University Press.

Cowan, Painton (1990). *Rose Windows (Art and imagination)*. London: Thames & Hudson.

Crutchfield, James (1987). *Video Feedback*, video cassette,

Aerial Press, Santa Cruz. CA.

Davidson, Herbert A. (1992). *Alfarabi, Avicenna, and Averroes on Intellect: Their cosmologies, theories of the active intellect, and theories of human intellect*. Oxford: Oxford University Press.

Davis, Erik (2019). *High Wiredness: Drugs, Esoterica, and Visionary Experience in the Seventies*. Cambridge, MA: MIT Press.

Davis, P. J., & Hersh, R. (1986). *Descartes' Dream: The World According to Mathematics*. New York: Harcourt Brace Jovanovich.

Descartes, René (1649/1989). *The Passions of the Soul*. Stephen H. Voss, transl. Indianapolis, IN: Hackett.

Dispenza, Dr. Joe, (2014). *You Are the Placebo: Making Your Mind Matter*. Carlsbad, CA: Hay House.

Dostrovsky, Sigalia C., Ernst Florens Friedrich Chladni. In: Charles Coulton Gillispie, ed., *Dictionary of Scientific Biography*, Scribner. New York, 1970, pp. 258-259.

Duffing, G. (1918). *Erzwungene Schwingungen bei veränderlicher Eigenfrequenz und ihre technische Bedeuling*. Berlin, W. Germany: Braunscheig Vieweg Verlag.

Dunne, John William, (1939/1958). *An Experiment with Time*. London: A. & C. Black, 1927. London: Faber and Faber.

Dyczkowski, Mark S. G., tr. (1992). *The Stanzas on Vibration: The Spandakarika with Four Commentaries*. Albany, NY: State University of New York Press.

Dyczkowski, Mark S. G. (1992). *The Stanzas on Vibration*. Albany, NY: SUNY Press.

Eden, Frederick Sydney (1913). *Ancient Stained and Painted Glass*. Cambridge, UK: Cambridge University Press.

Einstein, Albert (1921). Geometry and Experience. *Idea and Opinions*. Dell Publishing Co., 1954. Note: Lecture before the Prussian Academy of Sciences, Jan. 27, 1921.

Eisler, Riane (1987). *The Chalice and the Blade: Our History, Our Future.* San Francisco: Harper.

Finamore, John F. (1985). *Iamblichus and the Theory of the Vehicle of the Soul.* Chico, CA: Scholars Press.

Fingelkurts, Andrew A., and Alexander A. Fingelkurts (2006). Timing in Cognition and EEG Brain Dynamics: Discreteness versus Continuity, *Cognitive Processing*, Vol. 7, no. 3; pp. 135-162. Berlin: Springer.

Finkenbeiner, Gerhard with Vera Meyer, The Glass Harmonica: A Return from Obscurity. *Leonardo*, 20(1087). 139-142.

Fleck, Ludwik (1935/1979). *Genesis and Development of a Scientific Fact.* Chicago, IL: Univ. Chicago Press.

Freeman, W. (1975). *Mass Action in the Nervous System.* New York: Academic Press.

Freeman, W. (1972). Waves, pulses, and the theory of neural masses, *Progr. Theor. Biol. 2*, 87-165.

Freeman, W. I. (1981) *Perspect Biol. Med.* (summer).

Fussbudget, Hectoring and Rueful Znarler (1979). Sagacity theory, a critique. *The Mathematical Intelligencer, 2,* 56-59.

Gallimore, Andrew R. (2019). *Alien Information Theory: Psychedelic Drug Technologies and the Cosmic Game.* Strange Worlds Press.

Gaukroger, Stephen (1995). *Descartes: An Intellectual Biography.* Oxford: Clarendon Press.

Gatti, Hilary (1999). *Giordano Bruno and Renaissance Science.* Ithaca, NY: Cornell University Press.

Gatti, Hilary (2011). *Essays on Giordano Bruno.* Princeton, NJ: Princeton University Press.

Giri, Swami Vidyadhishananda (2006). The internal instruments of the witness-consciousness. In: (Shear, 2006), pp. 47-69.

Goswami, Amit (1993). *The Self-Aware Universe: How*

Consciousness Creates the Material World. New York: J. P. Tarcher.

Gregory, Joshua C. (1931). *A Short History of Atomism from Democritus to Bohr.* London: A. & C. Black.

Hadamard, Jacques (1945/1954). *An Essay on the Psychology of Invention in the Mathematical Field.* New York: Dover. Reprint of 1st edition, Princeton University Press.

Haeckel, E. (1974). *Art Forms in Nature.* New York: Dover.

Halberstam, David (1993). *The Fifties.* New York: Random House.

Hesse, Mary B. (1961). *Force and Fields: The Concept of Action at a Distance in the History of Physics.* London: Nelson.

Herbert, Nick. *Quantum Reality: Beyond the New Physics.* Garden City, N.Y.: Anchor Press/Doubleday, 1987, 1985.

Hey, Anthony J. G. ed. (1999). *Feynman and Computation: Exploring the Limits of Computers.* Reading, MA: Perseus Books.

Hirsch, M., and Smale, S. (1974). *Differential Equations, Dynamical Systems, and Linear Algebra.* New York: Academic Press.

Hoffman, William C. (1989). The visual cortex is a contact bundle, *J. Appl. Math. Computation,* 32:137-167.

Hoffman, W. C. (1977). *Cahiers de Psychologie* 29, 135-174.

Howard, L. and Kopell, N. Pattern formation in the Belousov reaction. *Proc. AMS - SIAM symp.* (to appear)

Howard, L., and Kopell, N. (1976). Pattern formation in the Belousov Reaction," Proc. *AMS-SIAM Symp.*

Isnard, C. A., and Zeeman, E. C. (1975). Some models from catastrophe theory in the social sciences. In: *The Use of Models In the Social Sciences.* Lyndhurst, Collins, ed. Boulder, CO: Westview Press.

Inselberg, A., R. Chadwick, and K. Johnson (1975). Mathematical model of the cochlea, *SIAM J. Appl.* Math.

Jantzen, Hans (1984). *High Gothic: Classic Cathedrals of Chartres, Reims and Amiens*. London: Constable.

Jaspers, Karl (1964). *Three Essays: Leonardo, Descartes, Max Weber*. New York: Harcourt, Brace and World.

Jenny, Hans. *Kymatik, Band 1* (1967) and *Band 2* (1972). Basilius: Basel.

Joliot, M., U. Ribary, and R. Llinás (1994). Human oscillatory brain activity near 40 Hz coexists with cognitive temporal binding. *Proc. Natl. Acad. Sci. U.S.A.*, Vol. 91, pp. 11748-11751.

Julianus. (1989). *The Chaldean Oracles*, transl. T. Stanley. Berkeley Heights, NJ: Heptangle Books.

Kaiser, David (2011). *How the Hippies Saved Physics: Science, Counterculture, and the Quantum Revival*. New York: Norton.

Kargon, Robert Hugh (1966). *Atomism in England from Hariot to Newton*. Oxford: Clarendon Press.

Katchalsky, A. & Neumann E. (1972). *Int.J. Neurosci.* 3, 175-182.

Kennedy, J. (1959). A possible artifact in the EEG. *Psych. Rev.* 66, 347-353. See also Oswald, I., On the origin of the alpha rythym, *Psych. Rev.* 68 (1961) 360-362.

Kent, James L. (2010). *Psychedelic Information Theory: Shamanism in the Age of Reason*. Seattle, WA: PIT Press.

Kepler, Johannes (1997). *The Harmony of the World*. Transl. A. J. Aiton, A. M. Duncan, and J. V. Field. New York: American Philosophical Society.

Kenny, Don (1974). *On Stage in Japan: Kabuki, Bunraku, Noh, Gagaku*. Tokyo: Shufunotomo.

Kline, Morris (1985). *Mathematics and the Search for Knowledge*. New York, NY: Oxford University Press.

Kolmogorov, A., Petrovski I. & Pikunov, N. (1937), Etude de l'equation de la diffusion avec croissance de la quantite de matiere et son application a une probleme biologique, *Bull Univ. d'Etat Moscou, Ser. Intern.*, I(A), 1-25.

Komparu, Kunio (1983). *The Noh Theater: Principles and Perspectives.* New York: Weatherill.

Kreisel, Howard (2001) *Prophecy: The History of an Idea in Medieval Jewish Philosophy.* Dordrecht: Kluwer Academic.

Kuhn, Thomas (1962/1970/1996/2012). *The Structure of Scientific Revolutions.* Chicago, IL: Univ. Chicago Press.

Kurlansky, Mark (2004). *1968: The Year that Rocked the World.* New York: Random House.

LaFleur, William R. (1983).*The Karma of Words: Buddhism and the Literary Arts in Medieval Japan.* Berkeley, CA: University of California Press.

Lakatos, Imre (1976). *Proof and Refutations.* Cambridge University Press. Note: First published in 4 parts in *The British Journal for the Philosophy of Science, 14* (1963-64.)

Lakshmanjoo, Swami (1985/2007). *Kashmir Shaivism: The Secret Supreme.* Universal Shaiva Fellowship.

Laszlo, Ervin (2003). *The Connectivity Hypothesis: Foundations of an Integral Science of Quantum, Cosmos, Life, and Consciousness.* Albany, NY: State University of New York Press.

Laszlo, Ervin (2004). *Science and the Akashic Field: An Integral Theory of Everything.* Rochester, VT: Inner Traditions.

Laszlo, Ervin (2009). *The Akashic Experience: Science and the Cosmic Memory Field.* Rochester, VT: Inner Traditions.

Lattin, Don (2017). *Changing Our Minds: Psychedelic Sacraments and the New Psychotherapy.* Santa Fe, NM: Synergetic Press.

Leadbeater, C. W. (1896). *The Astral Plane: It's Scenery, Inhabitants, and Phenomena.* London: Theosophical Publishing Society.

Leadbeater, C. W. (1899). *Clairvoyance.* London:

Theosophical Publishing Society.

Leadbeater, C. W. (1902). *Man Visible and Invisible.* London: Theosophical Publishing Society.

Lehrich, Christopher I. (2007). *The Occult Mind: Magic in Theory and Practice.* Ithaca, NY: Cornell University Press.

Lewis-Williams, David (2002). *The Mind in the Cave.* London: Thames and Hudson.

Lewy, Hans (1956). *Chaldean Oracles and Theurgy: Mysticism, Magic, and Platonism in the Later Roman Empire.* Cairo: l'Institute Francais d'Archeologie Orientale.

Lipton, Bruce (2005). *The Biology of Belief: Unleashing the Power of Consciousness, Matter, and Miracles.* Santa Rosa, CA: Mountain of Love/Elite Books.

Lorenz, E. (1962). The statistical prediction of solutions of dynamic equations. *Proc. Internat. Symp. Numerical Weather Prediction*, Tokyo, 629-635.

Louv, Jason (2018). *John Dee and the Empire of Angels: Enochian Magick and the Occult Roots of the Modern World.* Rochester, VT: Inner Traditions.

Lovelock, James (1991). *Healing Gaia: Practical Medicine for the Planet.* New York, NY: Harmony Books.

Lucretius (54 BCE/2010). *On the Nature of Things*, tr. William Emery Leonard. New York, NY: Greenbook Publications.

Male, Emile (1913/1972). *The Gothic Image: Religious Art in France of the Thirteenth Century.* London: Taylor & Francis.

Manin, Yu. I. (1979). A Digression on Proof. *A Course on Mathematical Logic.* New York: Springer. Also printed as: How Convincing is a Proof? *The Mathematical Intelligencer, 2,* 17-18.

Markus, Parvti (2015). *Love Everyone: The Transcendent Wisdom of Neem Karoli Baba, Told Through the Stories of the Westerners Whose Lives He Transformed.* New York: Harper

Collins.

Marsden, J., and McCracken, M. (1976). *The Hopf Bifurcation and its Applications*. New York and Berlin: Springer.

McKenna, Dennis (2012). *The Brotherhood of the Screaming Abyss*. St. Cloud, MN: North Star Press.

McKenna, Dennis J. and Terence K. McKenna (1975). *The Invisible Landscape: Mind, Hallucinogens, and the I Ching*. Ndw York: Seabury.

McKenna, Terence (1993). *True Hallucinations: Being an Account of the Author's Extraordinary Adventures in the Devil's Paradise*. New York, NY: Harper.

McTaggert, Lynne (2001). *The Field: The Quest for the Secret Force of the Universe*. New York: Harper.

Meinhardt, Hans (1982). *Models of Biological Pattern Formation*. London, New York: Academic Press.

Michel, Paul-Henri (1962/1973). *The Cosmology of Giordano Bruno*. Ithaca, NY: Cornell University Press.

Moore, Thomas (1982). *The Planets Within: Marsilio Ficino's Astrological Psychology*. Lewisburg: Bucknell Univ. Press.

Moritz, William (1986). Abstract film and color music. In: Maurice Tuchman, ed., *The Spiritual In Art: Abstract Painting 1980-1985*. Abbeville, New York, NY, 1986; pp. 297-311.

Murray, J. D. (1989). *Mathematical Biology*. Berlin; New York: Springer-Verlag.

Ortolani, Benito (1990/1995). *The Japanese Theater: From Shamanistic Ritual to Contemporary Pluralism*. Princeton, NJ: Princeton University Press.

Oswald, I. (1961). On the origin of the EEG alpha rhythm, *Psychol. Rev.*, 68, 360-362.

Penrose, Roger (1989). *The Emperor's New Mind: Concerning Computers, Minds, and the Laws of Physics*. Oxford; New York: Oxford University Press.

Peterson, Erik L. (2016). *The Life Organic: The Theoretical Biology Club and the Roots of Epigenesis*. Pittsburgh, PA: University of Pittsburgh.

Pollan, Michael (2018). *How to Change Your Mind: What the New Science of Psychedelics Teaches Us About Consciousness, Dying, Addiction, Depression, and Transcendence*. New York: Penguin.

Popper, Karl R. (1998). *The World of Parmenides: Essays on the Presocratic Enlightenment*. London: Routledge.

Poston, Tim and Renfrew, Colin (1979). Discontinuities in the endogenous change of settlement pattern. In: Kenneth L. Cooke and Colin Renfrew (eds.), *Transformations: Mathematical Approaches to Culture Change*. New York: Academic Press.

Poston, Tim and Stewart, Ian (1978). *Catastrophe Theory and its Applications*. London: Pitman.

Pound, Ezra, and Ernest Fenollosa (1959). *The Classic Noh Theater of Japan*. New York: New Directions.

Prabhananda, Swami (2003). *Philosophy and Science: An Exploratory Approach to Consciousness*. Kolkata, India: Ramakrishna Mission Institute of Culture.

Prabhananda, Swami (2004). *Life, Mind, and Consciousness*. Kolkata, India: Ramakrishna Mission Institute of Culture.

Pribram, Karl H. (1991). *Brain and Perception: Holonomy and Structure in Figural Processing*. Hillsdale, NJ: Lawrence Erlbaum.

Rabin, Sheila J. (1987). *Two Renaissance Views of Astrology: Pico and Kepler*. Ph.D. thesis, City University of New York.

Radin, Dean I. (1997). *The Conscious Universe: the Scientific Truth of Psychic Phenomena*. New York, N.Y.: HarperEdge.

Rashevsky (1940). *Advances and Applications of Mathematical Biology*. Chicago, IL: The University of Chicago press.

Rayleigh, W. S. (1882/1960). *Theory of Sound*. New York: Dover.

Redondi, Pietro (1987). *Galileo Heretic*. Princeton, NJ: Princeton University Press.

Reizer, Oliver (1966). *Cosmic Humanism*, Cambridge, Mass.

Requardt, Manfred, and Sisir Roy (2001). (Quantum) space-time as a statistical geometry of fuzzy lumps and the connection with random metric spaces. *Classical and Quantum.Grav.*, vol. 18; p. 3039.

Richards, William A. (2015). *Sacred Knowledge: Psychedelics and Religious Experiences*. New York: Columbia University Press.

Rosen, R. (1970). *Dynamical System Theory in Biology*, Vol. 1. New York: John Wiley.

Rowland, Ingrid D. (2008). *Giordano Bruno: Philosopher / Heretic*. Chicago, IL: University of Chicago Press.

Roy, Prasun, Dutta Majumder, and Sisir Roy (1996). Man's internal world or psychocosm as a fractile, non-euclidean, multi-dimensional space, *J. Consciousness Studies*.

Roy, Sisir (1998). *Statistical Geometry and Applications to Microphysics and Cosmology*. Boston, MA: Kluwer Academic.

Roy, Sisir (2003). Quantum information and levels of consciousness. In: Prabhananda, pp. 223-241.

Ruelle, D., and Floris Takens (1971). On the nature or turbulence, *Communs. Math. Phys.*, 20, 167-192; 23, 343-344.

Sadler, A. L. (2010). *Japanese Plays: Classic Noh, Kyogen and Kabuki Works*. Rutland, VT: Tuttle.

Sansom, G. B. (1931/1973/1997). *Japan, A Short Cultural History*. Tokyo: Tuttle. No plays, pp. 236, 387, 479, 508.

Saraswati, Swami Satyananda (1998). *Yoga Nidra*. Munger, Bihar, India: Yoga Publications, Bihar School of Yoga.

Saraswati, Swami Satyananda (2002). *Four Chapters on Freedom*. Munger, Bihar, India: Yoga Publications, Bihar

School of Yoga.

Schmidt, Charles B., ed. (1988). *The Cambridge History of Renaissance Philosophy*. Cambridge: Cambridge University Press.

Scholem, Gershom (1974/1978). *Kabbalah*. New York: New American Library.

Schwenk, Theodor (1968). *Bewegungsformen des Wassers*, Triades, Paris.

SenSharma, D. (2003). Consciousness in Indian philosophical thought with special reference to the Advaita Saiva School of Kashmir. In: Prabhananda, 2003; pp. 207-222.

SenSharma, D. (2004). Concept of prana in Kashmir Saivism. In: Prabhananda, 2004; pp. 515-517.

Settles, G., The amateur scientist, *Sci. Amer.* (May, 1971). See also Strong, C., The amateur scientist, *Sci. Amer.* (Aug., 1974).

Shea, William R. (1991). *The Magic of Numbers and Motion: The Scientific Career of Rene Descartes*. Canton, MA: Science History Publications.

Shear, Jonathan (1990). *The Inner Dimension: Philosophy and the Experience of Consciousness*. New York: Peter Lang.

Shear, Jonathan and S. P. Mukherjee, eds. (2006). *Consciousness: A Deeper Scientific Search*. Kolkata, India: The Ramakrishna Mission Institute of Culture.

Shear, J. (1978), Plato, Piaget, and Maharishi on cognitive development (preprint).

Sheldrake, Rupert (1981/1985/1995). *A New Science of Life: The Hypothesis of Formative Causation*. London : Blond & Briggs, 1981; Los Angeles: J.P. Tarcher, 1981; New edition. London: A. Blond, 1985; Rochester, Vt. : Park Street Press, 1995.

Sheldrake, Rupert (1981/1995/2009). *Morphic Resonance: The Nature of Formative Causation*. 4th Edition, Revised and

Expanded Edition of A New Science of Life. Rochester, VT: Park Street Press.

Sheldrake, Rupert (1988). *The Presence of the Past, morphic resonance and the habits of nature*. New York: Times Books, 1988; London: Collins.

Sheldrake, Rupert (1990/1991/1992). *The Rebirth of Nature: the greening of science and God*. London : Century, 1990; New York: Bantam Books, 1991; New York: Bantam Books, 1992.

Sheldrake, Rupert (1994/1995). *Seven Experiments That Could Change the World: a do-it-yourself guide to revolutionary science*. London : Fourth Estate, 1994; New York : Riverhead Books, 1995.

Sheldrake, Rupert (1999/2011). *Dogs That Know When Their Owners Are Coming Home: and other Unexplained Powers of Animals*. London: Hutchinson. New York: Three Rivers Press.

Sheldrake, Rupert (2017). *Science and Spiritual Practices*. London: Coronet.

Sheldrake, Merlin, and Rupert Sheldrake (2017). Determinants of Faraday wave-patterns in water samples oscillated vertically at a range of frequencies from 50-200 Hz. *Water*, Vol 9.

Sheldrake, Rupert (1981). *A New Science of Life: the Hypothesis of Formative Causation*. London: Blond & Briggs.

Sen Sharma, D. (2003). Consciousness in Indian philosophical thought with special reference to the Advaita Saiva School of Kashmir. In: Prabhananda, pp. 207-222.

Sen Sharma, D. (2004). Concept of prana in Kashmir Saivism. In: Prabhananda, pp. 515-517.

Shigeo, Kishibe (1984). *The Traditional Music of Japan*. Tokyo: Ongaku No Tomo Sha.

Singh, Jaideva (1980). *Spanda-karikas: The Divine Creative Pulsation*. Delhi: Motilal Benarsidass.

Sinnett, Alfred Percy (1885). *Esoteric Buddhism*. London: Chapman and Hall. Fifth edition of the 1883 original.

Smale, Stephen (1967). Differentiable dynamical systems, *Bull. Amer. Math. Soc.*, 73. 747-817.

Smith, W. R. (1980). *Bull. Math. Biol*, 42, 57-78.

Spruit, Leen (1994). *Species Intelligibilis: From Perception to Knowledge*. Leiden: Brill.

Sorabji, Richard (1983). *Time, Creation and the Continuum: Theories in Antiquity and the Early Middle Ages*. Chicago, IL: University of Chicago Press.

Sorabji, Richard (1988). *Matter, Space, and Motion: Theories in Antiquity and their Sequel*. London: Duckworth.

Stein, P. and Stanislaw Ulam (1964). Nonlinear transformation studies on electronic computers, *Rosprawy Mat.*, 39, 66.

Strogatz, Stephen H. (1994). *Nonlinear Dynamics and Chaos: With Applications to Physics, Biology, Chemistry, and Engineering*. Reading, MA: Addison-Wesley.

Strong, C. (1974). The amateur scientist," *Scientific Amer*.

Strassman, Rick (2001). *DMT the Spirit Molecule: A Doctor's Revolutionary Research into the Biology of Near-Death and Mystical Experiences*. Rochester, VT: Park Street Press.

Strassman, Rick (2014). *DMT and the Soul of Prophesy: A New Science of Spiritual Revelation in the Hebrew Bible*. Rochester, VT: Park Street Press.

Swaraswati, Swami Satysangananda (2003). *Sri Vijnana Bhairava Tantra, The Ascent*. Munger, Bihar, India: Yoga Publications, Bihar School of Yoga.

Tagore, Rabindranath (1931). *The Religion of Man: Being the Hibbert Lectures for 1930*. London: George Allen and Unwin.

Tamba, Akira (1974/1981). *The Musical Structure of Noh*. Tokyo: Tokai University Press.

Thom, René (1972). Stabilité structurelle et morphogénèse;

Essai d'une théorie générale des models. New York: Benjamin.

Thom, R. (1973). *Stabilité structurelle et morphogenése* (3rd printing, with corrections). New York: Benjamin.

Thom, René (1975). *Structural Stability and Morphogenesis: An Outline of a General Theory of Models*. David Fowler, trans. Rev. and updated by the author. New York: W. A. Benjamin.

Turing, (1952). *The Chemical Basis of Morphogenesis*, Philosophical Transactions of the Royal Society of London. Series B, Biological Sciences, Vol. 237, No. 641. (Aug. 14, 1952), pp. 37-72.

Thompson, D'Arcy (1969). *On Growth and Form*, Cambridge: Cambridge Univesity Press.

Thompson, D'Arcy (1945). *On Growth and Form*, 2 vols. Oxford: Cambridge Univ. Press. Second ed, 1963; abridged ed., 1961.

Thompson, Evan (2007). *Mind in Life: Biology, Phenomenology, and the Sciences of Mind*. Cambridge, MA: Harvard University Press.

Thompson, Evan (2015). *Waking, Dreaming, Being: Self and Consciousness in Neuroscience, Meditation, and Philosophy*. New York, NY: Columbia University Press.

Thompson, Michael (1979), *Rubbish Theory*. Oxford: Oxford University Press.

Truesdell, C. (1960). *The Rational Mechanics of Flexible or Elastic Bodies: 1638-1788, Introduction to Leonhardi Euleri Opera Omnia, Vol. X et Xi seriei secundae*. Turici, Italy: Orell Fuessli.

Turing, A. (1952). A chemical basis for biological morphogenesis, *Phil. Trans. Roy. Soc.* (London), Ser. B., 237 (1952) 37.

Varela, Francisco J., Evan Thompson, and Eleanor Rosch (1991/1993). *The Embodied Mind: Cognitive Science and Human Experience*. Cambridge, MA: MIT Press.

Venkatesananda, Swami (1989). *Vasishta's Yoga*. Albany, NY: SUNY Press.

Volkers, V. and Candib, W. (1960). Detection and analysis of high-frequency signals from muscular tissues with ultra-low-noise amplifiers, *Intern. Conv. Radio Eng.*

von Békésy, G., *Experiments in Hearing*, McGraw-Hill, New York (1960).

Waddington, C. H., ed., (1968). Towards a Theoretical Biology. In: *Nature*, v. 218, May 11, 1968; p. 526.

Waddington, C. H. (ed.). (1968–1972). *Towards a Theoretical Biology*. 4 vols. Edinburgh: Edinburgh Univ. Press; Chicago: Aldine (Vols. 1, 2); New York: Halsted Press (Vol. 3).

Walker, D. P. (1958/2000). *Spiritual and Demonic Magic from Ficino to Campanella*. University Park, PA: Pennsylvania Univ. Press.

Walker, E. H. (1970). The nature of consciousness,' *Math. Biosci.*, 7, 131-178.

Walker, E. H. (2000). *The Physics of Consciousness: Quantum Minds and the Meaning of Life*. Cambridge, Mass.: Perseus Books.

Walker, Mary D. (1961). *Chladni Figures: A Study In Symmetry*, Bell, London.

Walker, Matthew (2017). *Why We Sleep: Unlocking the Power of Sleep and Dreams*. New York: Scribner.

Waley, Arthur (1998). *The Noh Plays of Japan*. Rutland, VT: Tuttle,.

Webber, Renee, ed. (1986/1999). *Dialogues with Scientists and Sages*. London: Routledge, 1986; New York: Viking Penguin; Arkana.

Whitehead, Alfred North (1929). *The Function of Reason*. Princeton: Princeton University Press.

White, Lynn Jr. (1979). The Ecology of our Science, *Science 80*, 1, 72-76

Whitney, John H. (1980), *Digital Harmony: On the Complementarity of Music and Visual Art*. Peterborough, NH: Byte Books.

Whyte, Lancelot Law (1961). *Essay on Atomism: From Democritus to 1960*. Middletown, CN: Wesleyan University Press.

Wigner, Eugene (1960). The unreasonable effectiveness of mathematics in the natural sciences. Richard Courant lecture in mathematical sciences delivered at New York University, May 11, 1959. *Comm. Pure and Appl. Math*, 13:1-14.

Winfree, Arthur (1972).Spiral waves of chemical activity, *Science*, 175 (1972) 634-636.

Wolfram, Stephen (2002), *A New Kind of Science*. Champaign, IL: Wolfram Media.

Yates, Frances A. (1964). *Giordano Bruno and the Hermetic Tradition*. Chicago, IL: University of Chicago Press.

Yukawa, H. (1966), Atomistic and the divisibility of space and time. *Supplements of the Progress of Theoretical Physics*, Nos. 37 & 38; p. 512.

Zeeman, E. C. (1971). The geometry of catastrophe, *Times Lit. Suppl.*, 1556, London (Dec. 10).

Zeeman, E. C. (1972). Differential equations for the heartbeat and nerve impulse. In: Waddington, 1972; pp. 8-67.

Zeeman, E. C. (1976). Catastrophe theory. *Scientific American*, 234(4), April 1976, pp. 65-83.

Zeeman, E. C. (1977). *Catastrophe Theory: Selected Papers, 1972-1977*. Reading, MA: Addison-Wesley.

Zeeman, E. C. and C. A. Isnard (1976). Some models from catastrophe theory in the social sciences. In: E. C. Zeeman (1977), Ch. 10.

Index

A

Abraham, F. 13, 53, 55, 56, 57, 58, 63, 90, 143
Abraham, R. 91, 107, 108, 144, 164, 169, 171, 175, 198, 199, 200, 204, 255, 292, 297, 306, 313, 314, 315, 327, 438
Adey 90
Albert 13
Albo 418
Alfarabi 416, 417, 418
Alpert 27, 272, 276
Anthony 71, 86
Arbib 123, 142
Arguelles 13, 150
Aristotle 415, 416, 417
Atanasijevic 333, 335, 338
Auribindo 35, 280
Avicenna 418

B

Babbs 396
Bailey 406
Banchoff 180
Bateson, G. 10
Bateson, M.C. 199
Batish 178, 184
Beethoven 185
Bekesy 428
Bell 431
Benjamin, B. 29, 274
Bergson 290, 408
Berman 155
Bernoulli 238
Berry 199
Besant 401, 402, 404, 407
Bevirt 396
Bierman 63
Birkhoff 382
Blavatsky 30, 275, 401, 402, 406

Blumenthal 292
Bohm 435
Bohr 408
Bradley 413, 432, 433
Bragdon 185, 203
Brennen 14
Broadwell 184, 198, 201, 205, 232, 233, 235, 289, 291, 321, 438
Bruno 155, 329, 333, 335, 336, 338, 339, 340, 341, 342, 343
Buckley 165
Burnham 13
Burroughs 393

C

Calatrava 190
Campanella 341
Candib 67
Cannon 167
Cardano 341
Cartan 110
Cassady 393, 396
Castel 184, 203, 204, 217
Catastrophe 456
Chadwick 408
Chaitanya 46
Chakrabarti 292
Chladni 168, 178, 185, 186, 228, 247, 251, 255, 285, 286, 426
Clark 184
Clarke 13
Clauser 351
Clements 413
Conways 305
Cooper 13
Copernicus 303
Corbett 33, 44, 278
Corliss 215
Corra 185, 203
Cousteau 88
Cowan 379, 380
Crescas 418
Crutchfield 181

Curie 408

D

d'Alembert 165, 171, 229, 238, 251
Dalton 304
Daud 418, 419
Davidson 416
da Vinci 155, 159, 165, 169, 171, 426
Davis 155
de Chardin 319
Dee 336, 362, 424, 425
Demma 396
Democritus 297, 302, 303
Descartes 297, 301, 304, 310, 312, 341, 342
de Silvestris 222
Devi 27, 272
Dharmakirti 302, 303
Dignaga 303
Dirac 304, 408
Dockum 185, 203
Donne 423
Dorband 215
Dostrovsky 167
Draves 30, 275
Duffing 156, 162, 164, 166, 167
Dunne 189, 259, 261
Dyczkowski 292
Dynamical System 456

E

Einstein 243, 245, 254, 304, 307, 308, 408
Eisler 366
Ermantrout 379, 380
Euclid 255
Euler 171, 251

F

Faraday 229, 247, 251, 255, 408, 427
Ferlinghetti 394
Feynman 304, 305

Ficino 285, 300, 335, 407, 417, 418
Fickas 13
Finamore 292
Fischer 228
Fischinger 185, 203, 204
Fourier 251
Fracastoro 155
Franklin 178, 185, 247
Fredkin 297, 305, 323
Freeman 53, 57, 58, 90, 123, 142, 428
Furnald 14, 92

G

Gabor 431, 432, 433
Gabriel 425
Galileo 155, 156, 157, 158, 171, 303, 341
Gallimore 443
Galloway 13
Galuszka 413
Ganesh 280
Gaon 418
Garfinkel 113, 143
Germain 186
Gersonides 418
Gilbert 408
Ginna 185, 203
Ginsberg 393, 394, 395, 396
Gleick 175
Gödel 109
Govinda 33, 278
Graboi 14
Greenewalt 185, 203, 204
Gregory, J. 333, 334
Griffiths 150, 228
Gupta 287

H

Hadamard 109, 373
Halevi 418
Hansen 14
Hazelip 13, 63
Heisenberg 408, 432

Index 471

Hersh 155
Hertz 229
Hesse 292
Hirsch 79
Hirsh 55
Hoffman 123, 136, 138, 142
Homer 298
Hoyle 253
Husserl 371, 373, 374
Huyghens 155, 157, 158, 159, 160, 171

I

Isnard 86

J

Jacob 435
Jantsch 14, 233, 243
Jaspers 298, 301
Jenny 8, 13, 24, 29, 36, 63, 71, 74, 77, 79, 84, 87, 88, 92, 177, 186, 187, 194, 228, 233, 248, 249, 255, 274, 282, 285, 286, 287, 289, 415, 426, 427, 436, 437, 441
Jordan 304
Julianus 292

K

Kanad 303
Kan'ami 361, 364
Kandinsky 365
Katchalsky 117, 123, 142
Kedarnath 280
Kelly 425
Kennedy 90
Kepler 285, 341, 408
Kerouac 393
Kesey 394, 395
Knecht 175
Koa 193
Kolmogorov 123, 128, 142

Kramerson 13, 14, 92, 184
Kreisel 418, 419
Kuiper 143, 184
Kupka 359

L

Labi 419
Lagrange 155
Lakatos 104
Lakshmanjoo 343
Landaker 413
Laszlo 15, 319, 431
Leadbeater 401, 404
Leary 13, 22, 27, 272, 395
Leblanc 186
Lee 13, 26, 271, 297
Leibniz 341
Levi 184
Levy 13
Lewin 29, 274
Lewy 292
Li 56
Lipton 342
Loewi 423
Lorenz 56, 111
Louise 14
Louv 413
Lovelock 192, 194, 199
Lucretius 334
Lunney 14

M

Machado 149
Macpherson 376
Macroscope 451
Maimonides 418, 419
Majumdar 317
Malcolm X 55
Mandelbrot 359
Margulis 190, 191, 199
Marsden 83, 107, 108
Max 180
Maxwell 230, 246

May 56
Mayer-Kress 13
McCartney 423
McCracken 83
McKenna, T. 9, 14, 21, 24, 113, 184, 233, 243, 441, 443
Meinhardt 229
Mendeleev 423
Merleau-Ponty 374
Metzner 13, 27, 272
Millikan 408
Moore 13, 184, 292
Morgenstern 13
Moritz 184
Morton 189, 190, 215
Mozart 185, 209, 210
Mu 175
Murray 229

N

Napoleon 186
Neem Karoli 8, 14, 31, 32, 35, 36, 42, 43, 44, 47, 50, 57, 63, 71, 177, 184, 228, 233, 276, 277, 280, 281, 282, 288, 319, 441, 443
Neumann 123
Newton 165, 229, 246, 325, 408
Noller 13

O

O'Connell 43
Olcott 402

P

Parmenides 301, 302, 306
Patrizi 341
Pauli 304
Peixoto 55
Planck 304
Plato 97, 109, 119, 120, 142, 284, 285, 290, 297, 298, 299, 300, 375, 379, 415, 417

Plotinus 415, 417
Poincaré 371, 373, 374, 375, 378, 381, 383
Popper 301
Porphyry 415
Poston 13, 102, 108, 113, 143
Prabhananda 15, 271
Pradesh 71
Pribram 432, 433
Prigogine 211
Proclus 285, 415
Ptolemy 285
Purce 178
Pythagoras 284, 285, 287, 290

R

Rabin 292
Radunskaya 198, 201, 205, 232, 438
Ram Dass 14, 27, 31, 41, 42, 276
Rashevsky 123, 142, 229, 246
Rayleigh 164, 165
Renfrew 102
Requardt 297, 304, 314, 323, 349
Ricci 110
Richards 423
Rimington 185, 203
Roentgen 408
Rosch 375
Rosen 123, 142
Rosenberg 184
Roy, P. 14, 233
Roy, S. 9, 15, 46, 295, 297, 304, 306, 313, 314, 315, 317, 323, 325, 327, 349, 405, 411
Ruelle 29, 64, 83, 107, 111, 176, 274

S

Saccas 415
Saraswati 292
Saveur 167
Schaefer 216
Schaffer 180
Schavrien 184

Scholem 292
Schrödinger 265, 351
Schroedinger 408
Schwartz 189, 191, 194
Schwenk 84
Schwinger 304
Scriabin 185, 203
SenSharma 15, 26, 271, 287, 288
Settles 84, 178
Shaivism 287, 290, 431
Shambu 277
Shannon 432
Shaw 56, 164
Shear 119, 292
Sheldrake 9, 14, 21, 23, 227, 228, 230, 232, 233, 241, 245, 261, 290, 291, 319, 320, 375, 408, 413, 422, 427, 438, 442
Shelley 423
Shivaism 50, 375
Sinclair 320
Singh 43, 45, 292
Sinnett 401, 406
Skarda 57
Smale 13, 55, 56, 79, 107, 382
Smith 8, 14, 35, 36, 113, 184, 280, 281, 382, 396
Socrates 298
Soleri 199
Solomon 13
Sorenson 151
Southwell 252, 253
Spinoza 418
Stan 14
Stein 114
Steiner 24, 30, 177, 228, 275
Stewart 108
Strassman 413, 419
Stutten 30, 275
Suger 221
Sunday 57, 143

T

Tabory 396
Tagore 245, 254
Takens 64, 83, 107, 111
Telesio 341
Thierry 222
Thom 13, 29, 55, 56, 63, 71, 81, 83, 86, 90, 92, 99, 107, 109, 142, 143, 176, 178, 227, 228, 233, 274
Thompson, D. 88
Thompson, E. 375
Thompson, J. 304, 408
Thompson, M. 102
Thompson, W. 190, 191, 199, 215, 219
Todd 190
Tomashevich 338
Tomonaga 304
Truesdell 155
Turing 63, 66, 88, 123, 142, 211, 229, 246

U

Ueda 56, 359, 382
Ulam , 305, 114
Uma 280

V

Varela 190, 191, 374, 375
Vasari 220
Vasubandhu 303
Venkatesananda 292
Vidyadhishananda 343
Vinkenoog 13, 184
Vivekananda 349
Volkers 67
von Békésy 84, 89
von Neumann 182, 305, 306

W

Waddington 88, 227
Waley 360
Walker 90, 292, 423

Waller 178, 181, 186
Wasson 51, 395
Weisskopf 304
White 14, 98
Whitehead 110
Whitney 180, 185, 203, 204, 309, 382
Whyte 333
Wigner 106
Wilfred 185, 203
Williams 55
Wolfram 323
Wyman 184

Y

Yorke 56
Yukawa 304, 305

Z

Zeami 361, 364
Zeeman 13, 56, 83, 86, 99, 108, 123, 126, 127, 142, 169, 177
Znarler 109

www.ingramcontent.com/pod-product-compliance
Lightning Source LLC
Chambersburg PA
CBHW050322230426
43663CB00010B/1714